THE MEGA-TRADE METHOD

MICHAEL CHISHOLM
Author

Published by Windsor Books
P.O. Box 280
Brightwaters, N.Y., 11718
Manufactured in the United States of America

TABLE OF CONTENTS

CHAPTER 1

INTRODUCTION

As our subscribers to Mega-Trades and Taurus are well aware, this volume has been a long time in preparation. Actually we began to prepare this book several years ago as the concept of Long-Range trading became more and more important to our overall approach to the commodity markets. The years 1980 and 1981 were tremendously profitable years for our newsletter. We showed substantial profits well in excess of $100,000 for each of these two years in closed trades, trading single contracts of each recommendation. Part of this was due to the "Election Year Phenomenon," but when we researched previous years, we found that the bulk of our profits, especially the large single-trade profits, was due to Long-Range trading.

At that time we became convinced that Long-Range trading was the most profitable approach to trading the commodity markets for a number of reasons. One major reason was that by following the principles of Long-Range trading, we avoided many whipsaw markets and allowed profits to run, and by having a relatively small number of trades each year, which Long-Range trading tends toward, we minimized the amount of commissions as well as substantially reduced the slippage factor.

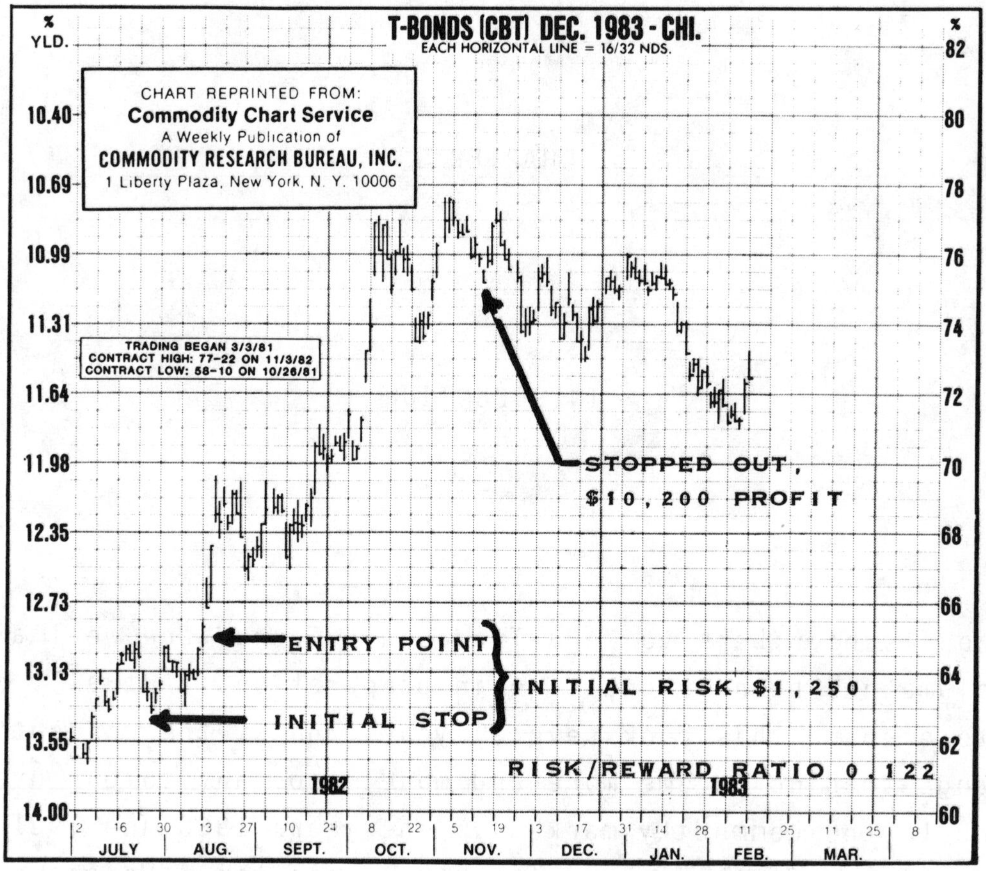

As can be seen from the above graph where the position was held for an extended period of time--the type of trading which most commodity investors do not normally get into--there were substantial profits and there was only one commission for entering and exiting the market. This market also lent itself--as do many Long-Range trades--to pyramiding, and while we have not illustrated above the profitable effects of pyramiding, let us just say at this point that these additional profits were really substantial.

The why of Long-Range trading primarily is to maximize profits, but there are a number of other benefits that come from specializing in Long-Range trading of the commodity markets. One of these benefits is the freedom that Long-Range trading provides the commodity trader in terms of his personal life and the amount of time he must devote to analysis of the markets. Fortunately, with

Long-Range trading, analysis of the market on an "everyday" basis is not always necessary, and this provides the trader with an opportunity to take vacations and the like and be out of contact with the markets for what would normally be considered extended periods of time, without adversely affecting his Long-Range trading positions.

Long-range trading is not always appropriate for all traders for all markets. We believe, however, that all traders will want to utilize some Long-Range trades as part of their overall investment program. And, no matter how berzerk the markets are at any given time, some of the major 32 commodity markets always lend themselves to the principles and practices of Long-Range trading. So the commodity trader is never without at least some Long-Range trading opportunities.

In the following chapters we will attempt to describe in detail and illustrate graphically the principles we have developed--and are still developing--to make Long-Range trading as profitable an investment as possible. These are the principles that we were using unconsciously (i.e., not realizing that we were really engaged in the Long-Range trading) back in 1980, 1981, and earlier and later years. These are the principles that made Mega-Trades the single most profitable newsletter in the country for the year of 1983 in terms of closed out profits and profits per trade.

We have come to look upon Long-Range trading as an exciting adventure, and as with most adventures, it is a growing experience. By that we mean that there will never be any principles which cannot be modified or altered to suit the conditions of the market place. We know that most traders are constantly searching for a "Holy Grail" or a "Perfect System" for commodity trading. Unfortunately, Long-Range trading and the Mega-Trade principles are not the "Perfect System." Nothing is. There never has been and there never will be a flawless, perfect method that never fails.

Commodity trading is an art form in its truest sense. And, as such, it necessitates a certain element of subjectivity as well as the use of judgment and intuition. We do not mean to imply that there is anything mystical about Long-Range trading, only that none of the principles of Long-Range trading is etched in concrete. The principles in this book are guidelines, and while they are extraordinarily sound and practical guidelines, the trader must recognize that that they are guidelines and that he must temper them with his own judgment if he is to be as successful as possible.

This judgment or intuition to which we refer does not imply guessing or throwing darts at a dart board. Rather it is the trader's sound mental integration of all of the principles of Long-Range trading, being able to see their interrelationship with one another in any given market situation, and being able to apply them to the best of his ability.

Long-range trading is not the "Perfect System" any more than any other methodology, if for no other reason than the frequent occurrence in the market place of "Unforeseen Fundamental Occurrences." No matter how soundly a position is based--whether Long-Range or short-term--on technical and fundamental analysis and observations, there is always the possibility that some factor will occur in the world which will affect the position opposite to the direction in which orders have been placed. Every trader is familiar with the negative effect which a sudden embargo, war, strike, disease, government report, or some such other factor frequently does have on an otherwise very sound position. A perfect example of this can be seen in the graph below when what otherwise might have been a very technically and fundamentally sound long position was decimated by President Carter's grain embargo on the Soviet Union.

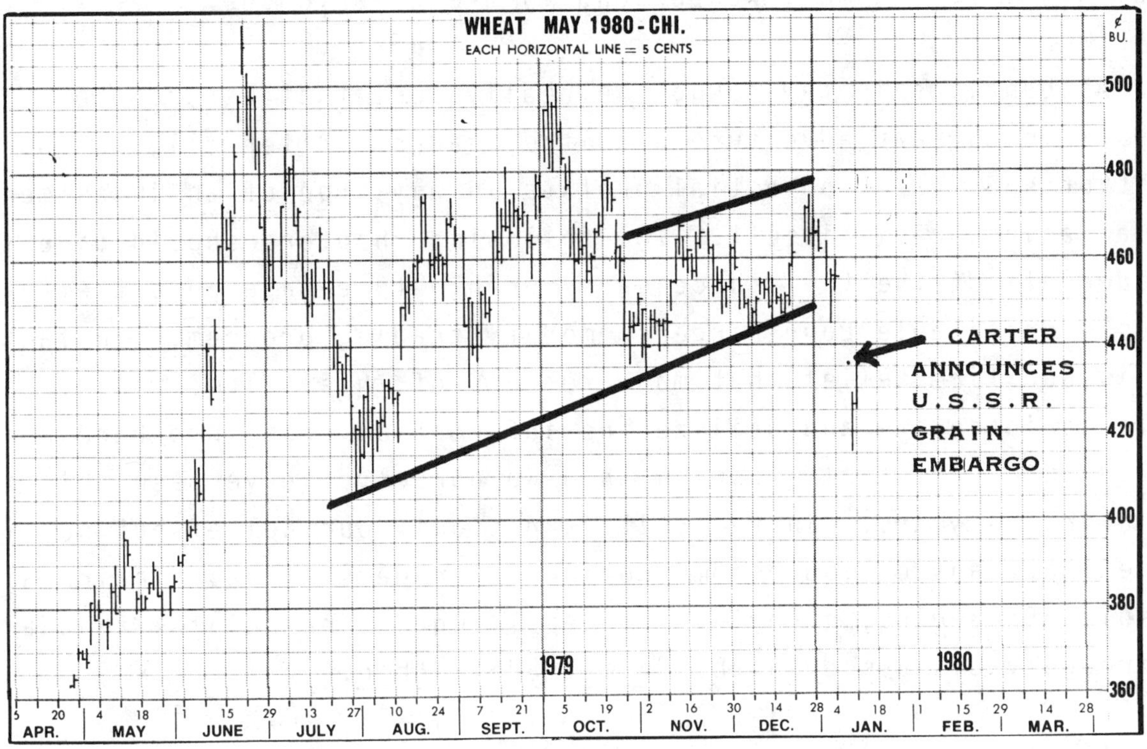

While there is a place in every investor's portfolio for Long-Range trading, and there are always Long-Range trading opportunities in the market place, not every investor will find Long-Range trading to his liking. We will, later on in this volume, examine in more detail the psychological components of Long-Range trading and attempt to resolve any psychological barriers which traders may have against Long-Range trading, especially since Long-Range trading is <u>the</u> most profitable way to trade the commodity markets. In other words, we will attempt to deal with any mistaken beliefs about Long-Range trading, and if the reader still finds Long-Range trading unpalatable despite its profit-making potential, we will make suggestions as to how he or she can deal with these problems.

Throughout this text the pronoun "he" will be used as a convenience to the reader, even though we are well aware that more and more women are becoming actively involved in commodity trading, a development we personally are glad to see.

As banal as it may sound, we really feel that we are about to embark on a great adventure with the reader. After all, the pursuit of such great potential profits in any type of an investment is an adventure in itself. The following chapters should give the reader all of the tools necessary for him to engage in a tremendously profitable Long-Range commodity trading program. In fact, it is our firm belief that many readers of this volume will be able to integrate and utilize the information contained herein in a far more profitable fashion than we ourselves have been able to do over the years. In fact, it is not only our belief but our hope that many of you become commodity traders extraordinaire as a result of reading, studying, and applying the principles that are thoroughly discussed in the Mega-Trade Method.

CHAPTER 2

AN OVERVIEW-PART 1

Unfortunately for all investors as well as commodity traders, there is no sure-fire way to get rich overnight. There are, of course, the lottery winners, the big winners at the casinos and the lucky players at the racetrack who do--through a combination of luck, fate, whatever--get rich overnight. But these certainly are the exceptions to the rule. Many commodity investors enter the market place in order to achieve just this: to get rich overnight. In an effort to dispel these assumptions of instant wealth, we will attempt to convince the reader that the only way he can be certain--or as certain as is humanly possible--of becoming wealthy is to take a slow, patient route.

Given a year or two of trading Big Moves, the commodity trader with at least average intelligence, enormous patience, and the right psychological attitude can definitely make substantial amounts of money trading commodities even if he is not able to reach the "fortune level." With additional time this trader can--over and beyond two years--definitely keep increasing the equity in his account should he choose to do so. Trading single contracts of our _Taurus_ newsletter recommendations from 1976 through 1982 and reinvesting all of the profits from these trades would have netted the trader in excess of $4,000,000 during this six-year year period of time if he had started with only $25,000 in his account. Most of the large profits from these _Taurus_ recommendations during this period of time came from Big Move trading, though today Taurus specializes in short- and intermediate-term trading and Mega-Trades is our newsletter that specializes in the Big Move trades.

What is a Long-Range or Big Move trade? Short-term trades tend to last a period of perhaps a week. Intermediate-term trades last perhaps several weeks to a month. Our definition of Big Move trades are those which last a minimum of one month and more typically anywhere from three months to a year. The following graph illustrates for a single commodity three profitable trades--one of the short-term variety, one intermediate-term, and one Big Move trade which was an actual trade that was made by our Mega-Trades newsletter.

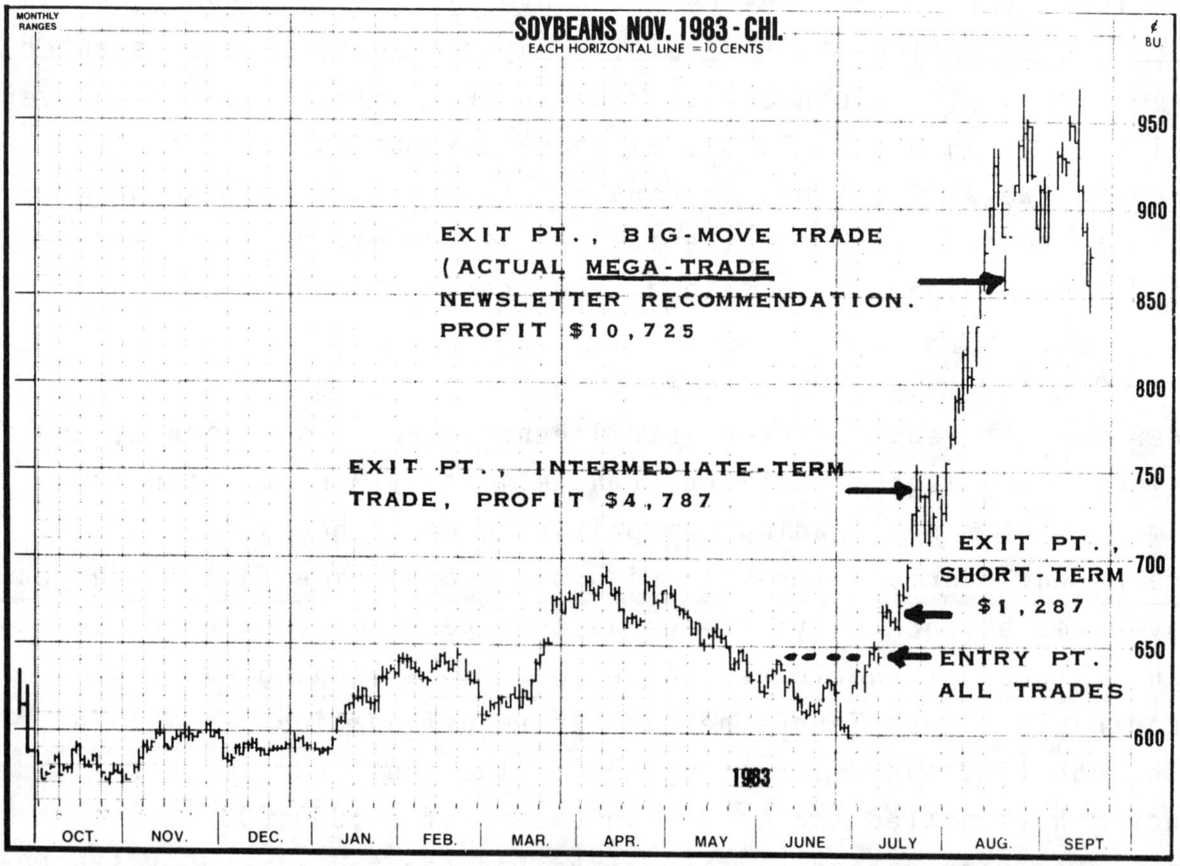

Big Move trading has two major aspects: The "how to do it" and the "how to live with it." The "how to do it" aspect is mainly mechanical in nature and involves selecting the trade's technical and fundamental analysis and all of the other decision-making factors involved in selecting, entering, and exiting Big Move trades. These techniques are the easiest aspect of any type of trading program since, with the exception of the intuitive factor, they can be learned even by high school students given sufficient study, research, practice, and time. The second aspect--the "how to live with it" part of Big Move trading--is just as critical as the trade selection process. It is unfortunate that not all traders have the psychological temperament to engage in Big Move trading. It is a well-known fact that at least 90% of all commodity traders either lose all of their funds or withdraw from the market unsuccessfully within their first 12 months of trading. By and large the bulk of these traders fails in the market place because they are unable to deal with the psychological aspects of trading. We will not concern ourselves at this point with these traders as this subject is thoroughly covered in our other book, GAMES INVESTORS PLAY.

We believe that the reader is most likely one of the 10% of the trading population who has been in the market place either successfully or unsuccessfully for over a year; otherwise he would not have purchased and be reading this book. We will in a later chapter address the subject of the psychological temperament and make-up that is required for Big Move trading. Many successful short- and intermediate-term traders whose psychological make-up is such that they can be and are successful at those types of trading find it difficult to deal with the different approaches necessary for successful Big Move trading.

We have established some arbitrary guidelines as to what, in our view, constitutes successful Big Move trading. Our estimation is that a successful Big Move trader requires 50% of his trades to be profitable. This, of course, is no higher a figure than flipping a coin to make trade selections or throwing darts at a dart board. Fortunately, with Big Move trading--due to the distance of the initial protective stops from the entry point--a success rate of 50% is quite readily achievable if the trader has spent sufficient time analyzing the markets and utilizing the techniques described in this book.

A successful Big Move trade, in our estimation, is one that gives the trader a return of 300% of his original margin or more. In other words, if a trader's successful trades average a 300% return on original margin and the average initial risk is typically 100% of margin, it is simple arithmetic to see how successful a trader can be by year's end if he achieves these results.

For the sake of simplification, let's take Soy Meal as an example. It currently has a margin requirement of $1,000 per trade. Suppose a trader initiated four Soy Meal positions in the course of a year and he risked $1,000 per position and had only a 50% winning trade selection. On his two losing trades, he has lost $2,000. On his two winning trades, assuming that he shows an average return of 300% margin per trade, he has grossed $3,000 per winning trade or a total of $6,000. He has thereby netted $4,000 for the year on his four Soy Meal trades.

This is a handsome return on his investment. While this is a theoretical example, it can be readily seen that by pyramiding, and/or increasing the number of his contracts per position as his equity increases, his equity can grow at a phenomenal rate.

An illustration of this type of risk as compared to the average necessary return on profitable trades is illustrated in the following graph:

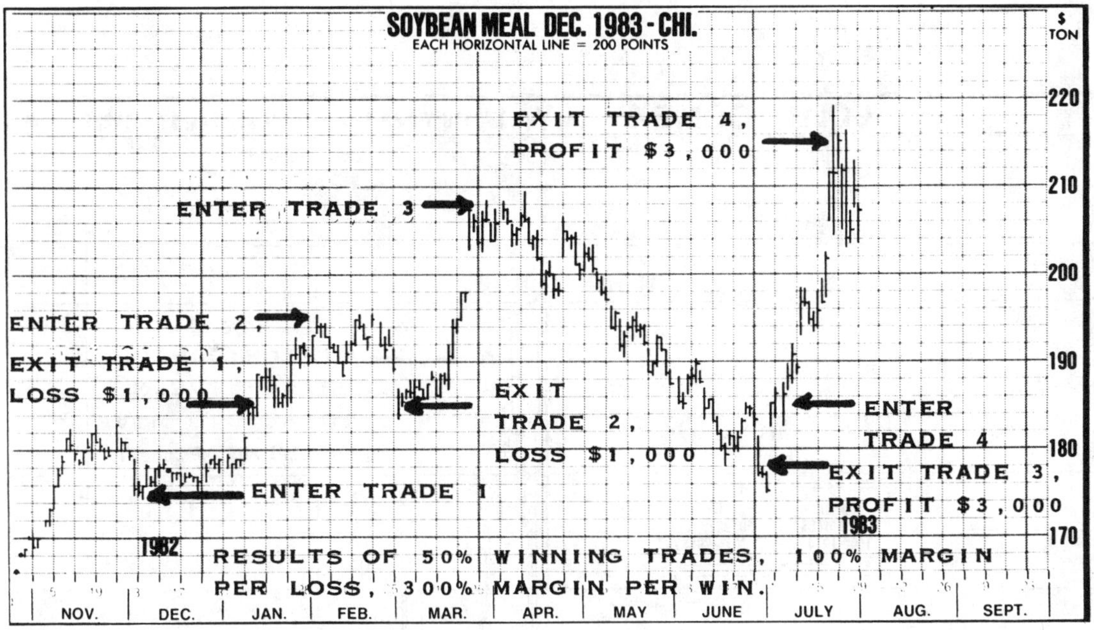

Actually, the selection of potentially very profitable Big Move positions is quite simple. There are basically only two types of markets to consider entering for maximum Big Move trades. As simplistic as this may sound, these two types of markets are: shorting markets which are topping out at historically high levels and going long markets which are at historically low price levels.

The following two graphs will illustrate typical examples of these types of markets from real recommendations we have made in the past:

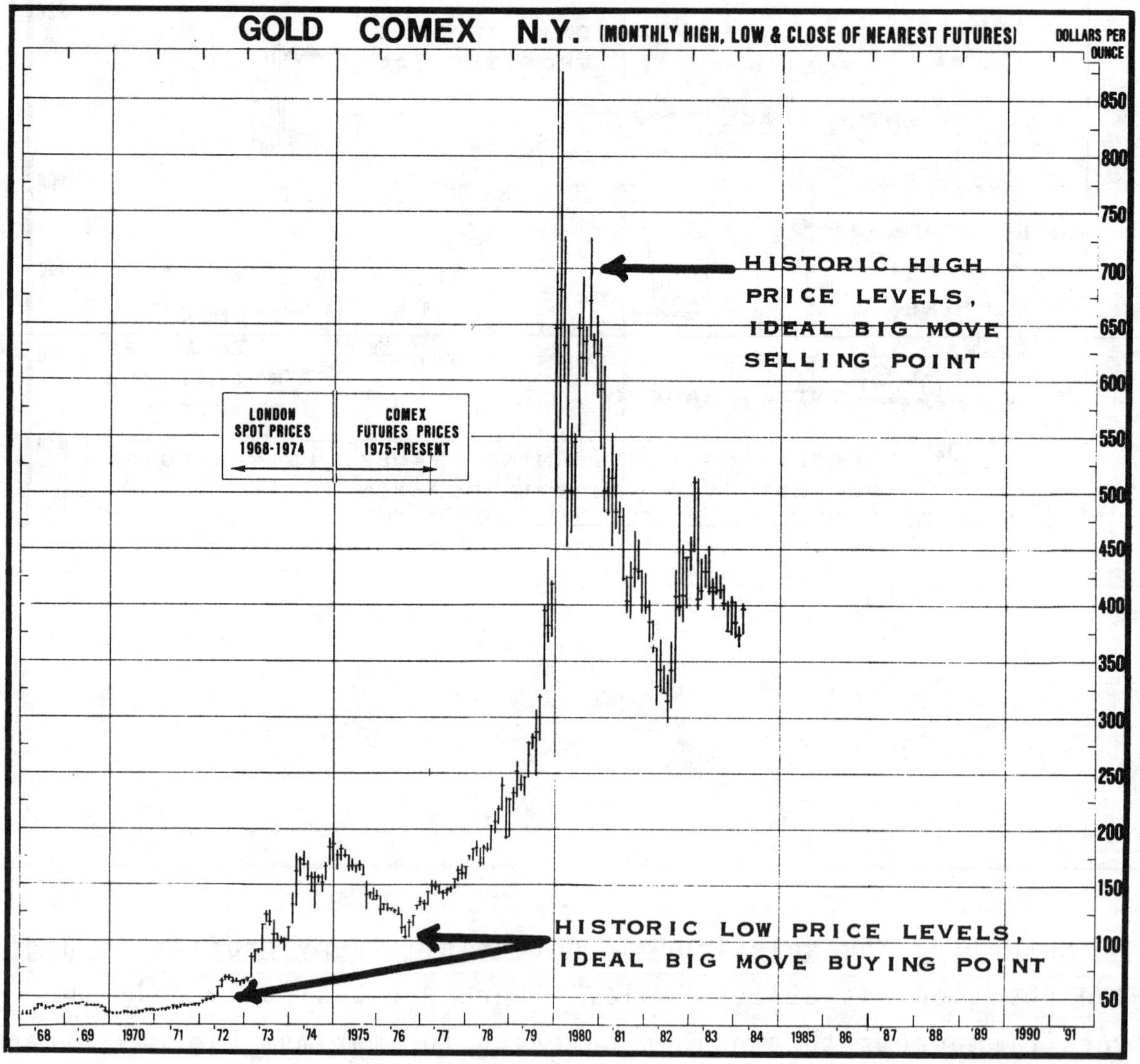

Even though this basic technique of selecting markets for Big Move trades looks like it is extraordinarily simple, and it is, there are many subsidiary techniques that are required in order to make certain a bear market is ready to turn back up or a bull market is ready to top. Just being at historically low or high price levels is not sufficient to guarantee that a market is really ready to turn, for how many times have we seen new historic low or historic high price levels set. Just because sugar, for example, is trading at 4-cents a pound does not mean that it constitutes an ideal Big Move long position. We saw this when a noted commodity advisor last year instructed his clients to buy sugar at 8-cents because it never would drop below 5-cents, the cost of production. When it dropped to 7-cents, he advised his clients to buy more, at 6-cents to buy even more, and at 6-cents he was quoted in his newsletter as saying--and this was perhaps six-to-eight months ago--that he would stake his "professional reputation" on the fact that sugar would never go below 5-cents a pound. As this is being written, sugar is trading for less than 4-cents a pound. We mention this only to illustrate that new historic low and high price levels can be and are frequently set in the market place and that just because a market is trading at those price levels does not make it an ideal candidate for establishment of a Big Move position.

These refinement techniques of knowing when a market genuinely constitutes a good candidate for a Big Move position will be discussed in great detail in the following chapters.* Suffice it to say for now that there are some general guidelines that the reader may want to be pondering as he moves through this book. When looking at extended bear markets and considering establishing a long Big Move position, the most key factor to consider is an extended trading range at these low price levels. The minimum trading range would be a tight pattern of five weeks in duration. As we look at ideal long Big Move positions we will examine this in more detail. We'll look, too, at the other confirmation factors which are required in order to make this potential trade an ideal candidate. For considering short Big Move position where a market is at an historic high price level, the two main indicators that we will consider later are penetration of certain types of trendlines on certain types of charts as indicating a market reversal, and the length of the bull move itself--which must be a minimum of three months--to reach these historic highs. Otherwise, the probabilities of the market's turning and reversing itself downward are extremely low.

For Big Move long positions we will be looking most closely at prices moving out of this compressed trading range we have referred to by an upside breakout through a resistance line drawn immediately above the trading range as illustrated below:

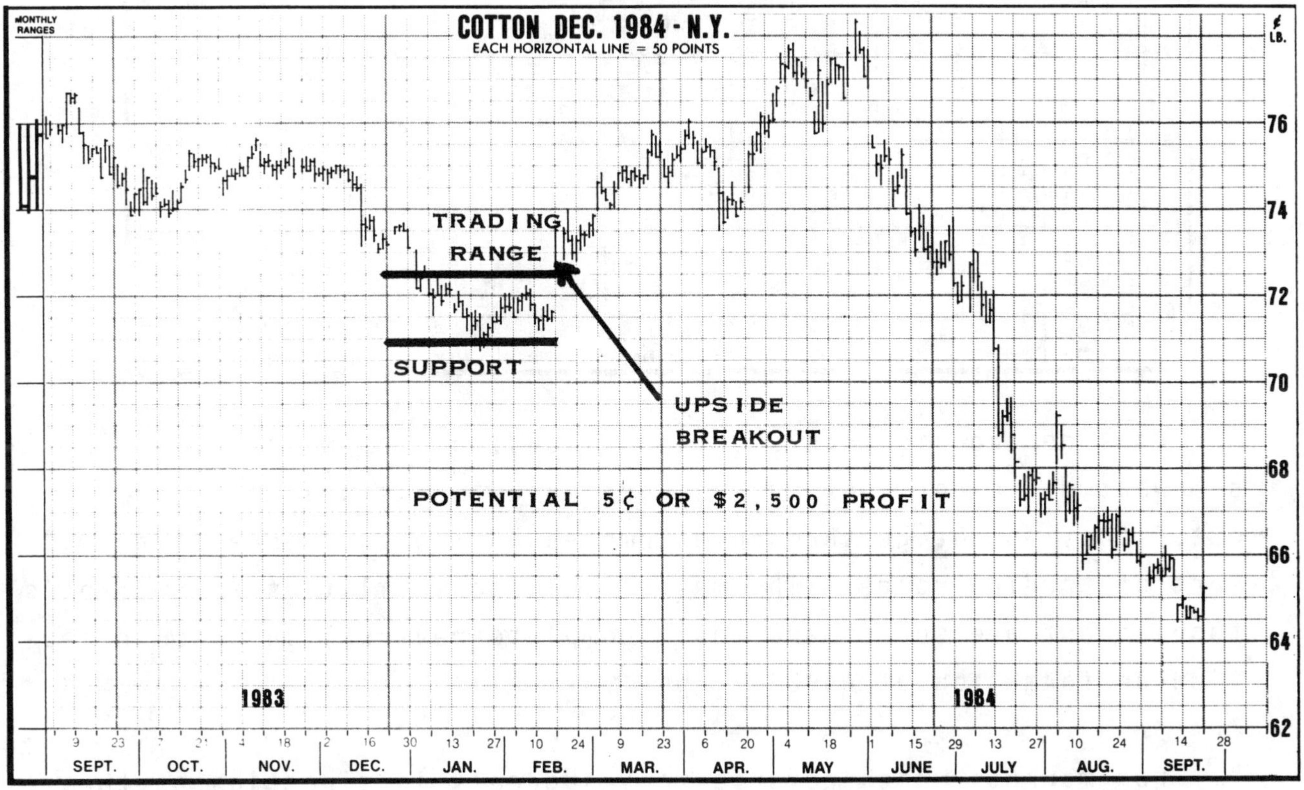

Our safest stop placement is below the horizontal line at the bottom of the compressed trading range, if too much initial risk is not involved. Sometimes even if more than 100% of original margin requirements is involved in the risk by placing our Initial Protective Stop below the horizontal support line, we will consider doing that based upon other factors such as Risk-Reward Analysis. The methodology of doing this is discussed later in this book. An oversimplified example of this is illustrated below:

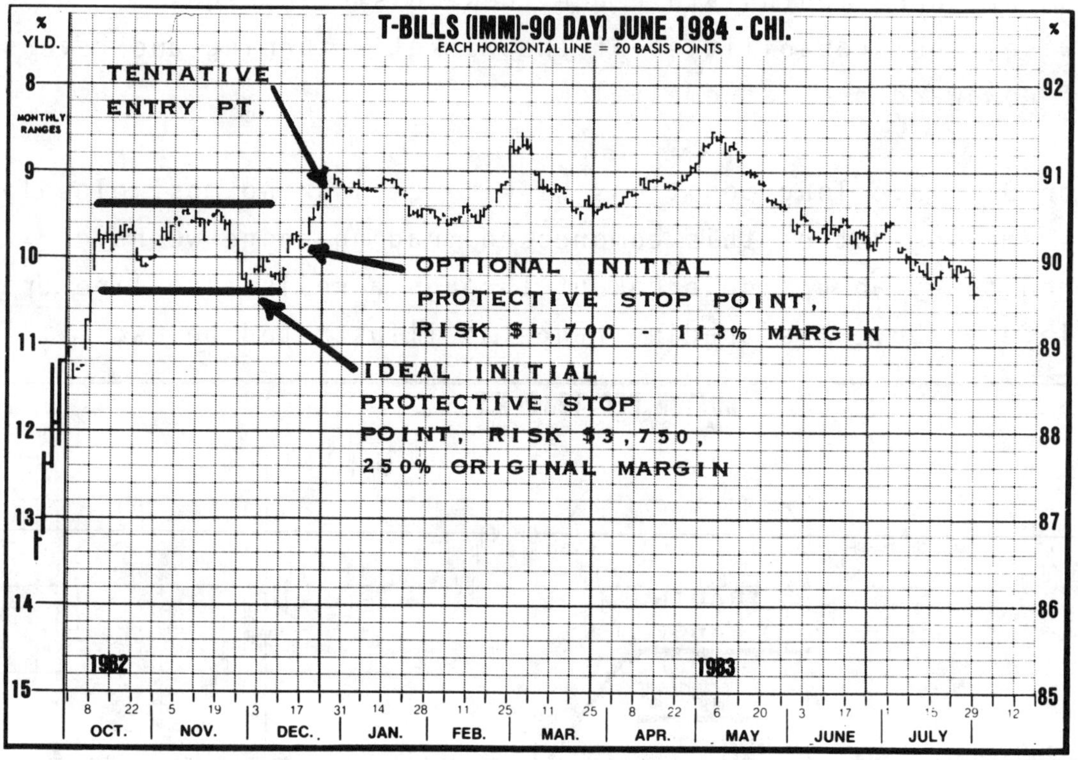

Considering Big Move short positions, our approach will be somewhat different, insofar as when markets historically "top out," they do not go through a compressed trading range or any sort of trading range. The most likely possibilities for market's topping out are sudden and total complete reversal in price direction or formation of double tops.

For markets which reverse very suddenly in direction as they top out, the ideal method of establishing entry points is by penetration of certain types of trendlines, as previously mentioned. In this type of situation, stop placement is above the contract high, if no more than 100% of original margin is involved at risk. If more than 100% of original margin would be involved at risk, then other techniques, which will be discussed later, are used for Initial Protective Stop placement. The following graph gives a simplified example of such a market that reverses very suddenly, showing entry point and Initial Protective Stop placement:

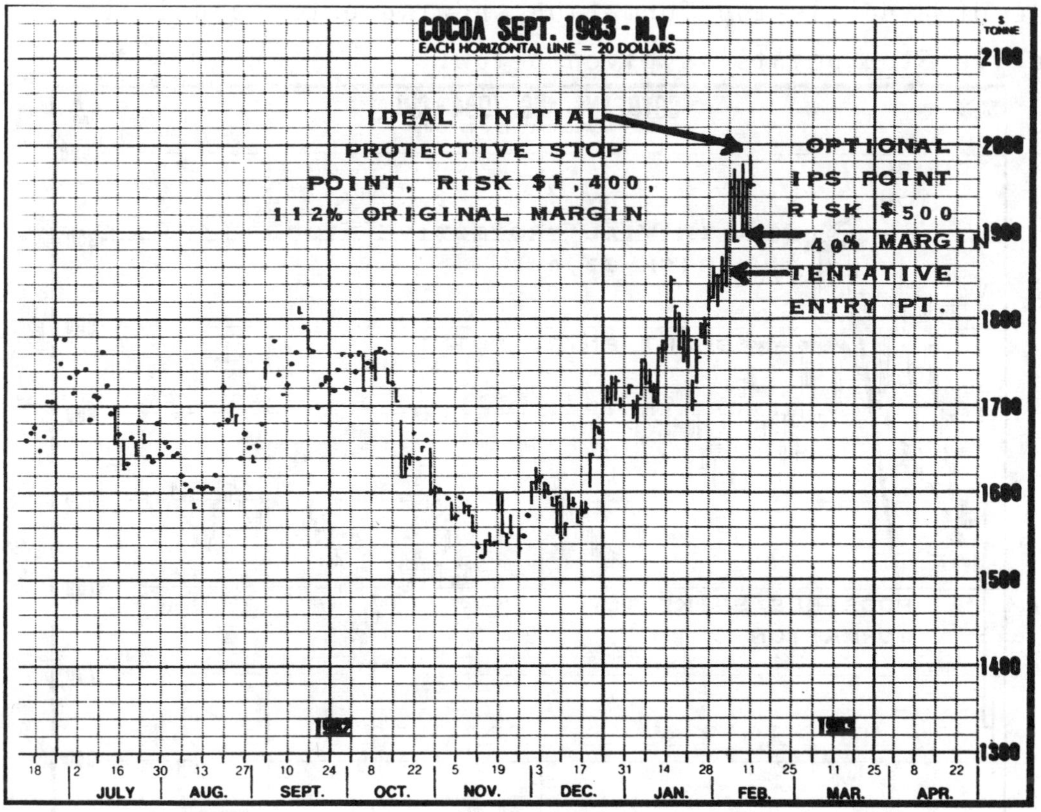

The other type of market at historical highs that is ready to turn is, as mentioned, the double-top market. The entry point for this type of market is established differently, as is the Initial Protective Stop point. Unfortunately, when a market reverses direction at historic high levels, it frequently is very difficult to tell whether it's going to be a "spike" market that reverses completely or a double-top formation. There are techniques which can be used to increase the trader's probability of successfully analyzing which type of top formation will take place. Even without these techniques that we will develop in this book, however, if a trader goes on the assumption that the market is topping in a spike formation, and he is incorrect, he has one losing position. He then can approach the market as being of the double-top formation variety, reestablish his position using different techniques for entry point and Initial Protective Stops, and, most frequently, end up with a very successful trade which more than compensates for his original losing position. An example of a double-top formation showing entry and Initial Protective Stop points is given below:

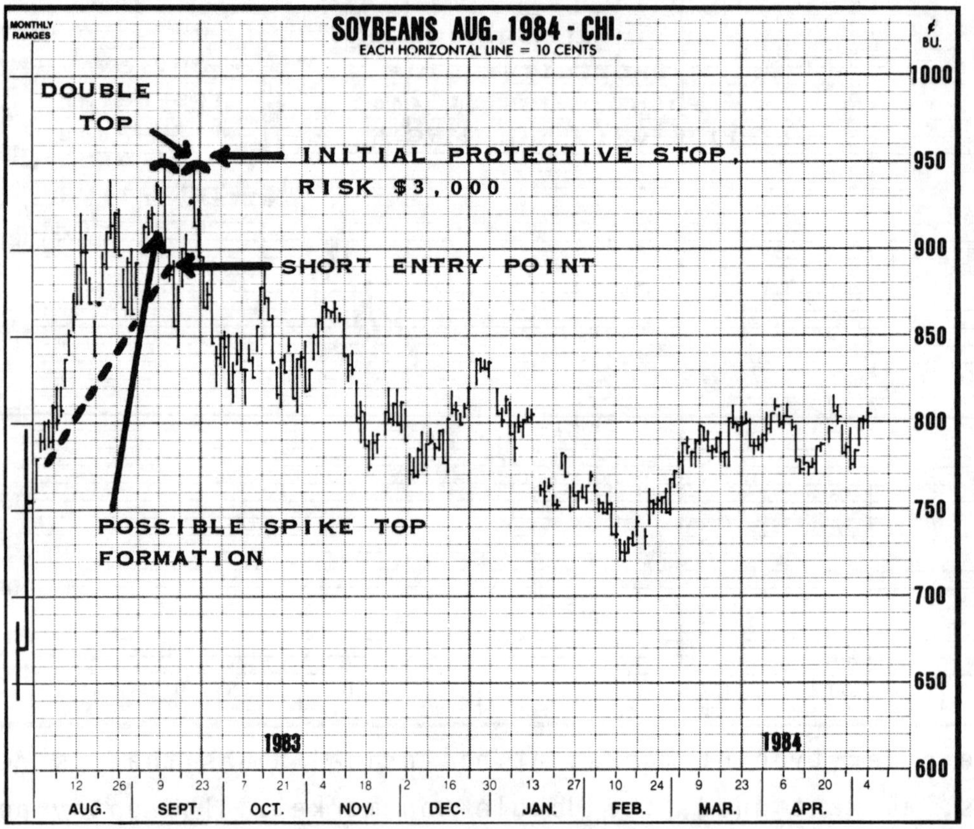

As important as it is to be able to determine ideal Big Move trading candidates, good entry points, and appropriate Initial Protective Stop points, it is equally important to have valid methodology for trailing one's protective stops. There are three major factors which we will consider in Trailing Stop placement. The first is to have our stops sufficiently far away from current price action to prevent our being taken out of the position too soon by a market correction. There are several very valid and useful ways of accomplishing this. The second factor to consider with Trailing Stops is to be able to know when to get them to the break-even point, or your original entry point, as rapidly as possible in order to make your trade a "risk-free" one as soon as possible. This must be done very judiciously in order to eliminate the original risk as rapidly as possible, and yet at the same time it must not be done too rapidly or you will be taken out of an otherwise potentially very profitable position by a market correction. The third factor to consider with Trailing Protective Stops is getting them close enough to the market itself to be taken out of your position automatically when the market has either bottomed or topped, depending on whether your position is a long one or short one. Here, too, fortunately there are several very useful techniques which can be implemented as the market approaches your target level. Here, too, some discretion must be used in order not to be taken out of the market too soon: Just because the market is approaching your target level does not necessarily mean that the market will not continue right through your target level in an explosive fashion. So, you must keep your stops close enough--yet not too close--to current market price as the market price approaches the point at which you think the market will stop.

It was our original thesis years ago that there was no consistently reliable way of establishing price targets. We still believe this to be the case for Short- and Intermediate-Term trading--at least no consistently reliable way of establishing targets for these types of trades. For Big Move trading, however, there do seem to be some moderately reliable ways of establishing target price levels. The reader will notice that we said "levels"--not "level"--as it is still our belief that due to fundamental forces within the market place, it still is impossible to predict with any of degree of accuracy which target levels prices will stop at.

The following graph illustrates on a Long-Range chart a number of such target levels for an anticipated Big Move trade. Prices may move to the first target level, the second, the third, or the fourth, and it has been our experience that as prices reach one target level and that target level is clearly broken, then prices are most likely to continue on to the next target level. So as a rough guideline, we typically move our stops in close as each subsequent price level is approached, backing them off a bit as each subsequent target level is violated.

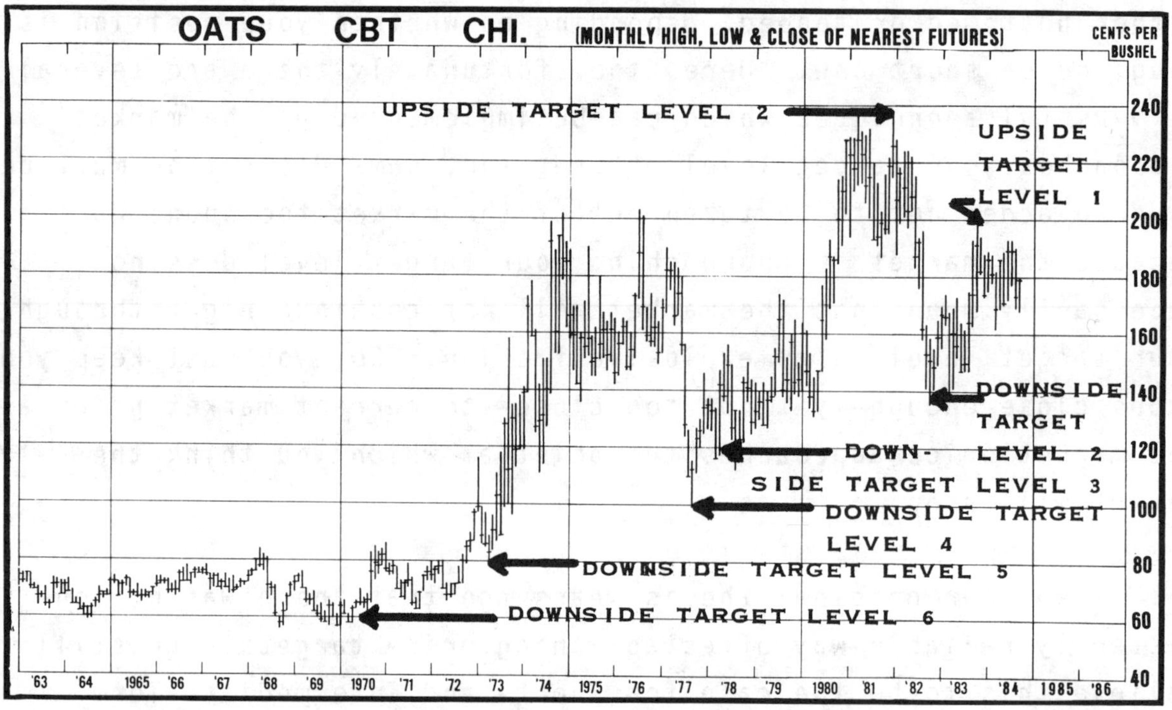

As mentioned earlier in this chapter, just having prices at historic high or low price levels is not enough in and of itself to justify establishing a Big Move position. There are many other factors which should be taken into account by the successful Big Move trader as "Confirmation Signals." We have devoted an entire chapter in this book to each of these confirmation signals in order to thoroughly explain their significance, importance, and utilization by the Big Move trader. At this point we will merely comment briefly on each of these extremely important Confirmation

Signals which must be utilized in order to confirm a trend reversal.

1. Volume and Open Interest. These two indicators are especially important in determining when a Bear move or Bull move is about to terminate and reverse itself. Of all of the Confirmation Signals that we use, these are perhaps the two most important.

2. Bullish Consensus. When combined with other technical indicators, Bullish Consensus is a very potent tool also for confirming when a market is about to reverse itself. It is our belief that used solely by itself, Bullish Consensus is not of great predictive value.

3. Seasonal Patterns. For many commodities Seasonal Patterns can be very reliable in terms of predicting when a move will reverse itself. The key here is the reliability factor of the Seasonal Pattern for a particular commodity for a particular time period. Many commodities have Seasonal Patterns, but they are quite unreliable, either in their entirety or for certain time frames. It is very important for the Big Move trader to utilize Seasonal Patterns as long as he keeps this reliability foremost in his mind.

4. Cycles. When properly understood and applied, cyclical analysis can be of great value to the Big Move trader as long as the correct cycles are utilized and as long as they are corrected for any skewing.

5. Other Miscellaneous Factors. Some of the other factors with great predictive value for establishing when a move is about to reverse itself--when combined with other factors in tandem--are the "Commitment of Traders Figures for Large Speculators," Moving Averages, Relative Strength Curves, Premiums, Fundamentals and

Momentum Oscillators.

Another key element in a Big Move trading program is picking correct contract months to trade. This is relatively simple for the individual investor, while it is much more difficult for newsletter publishers and advisory services. For the individual investor, simple guidelines will be given as to how to determine the correct contract month for long and short Big Move positions, as these are somewhat different. For advisory services, due to the number of traders entering and exiting markets at certain exact points, it is frequently necessary for much closer contract months to be selected, due to their greater liquidity. But this is readily compensated for by constantly rolling over from one contract month to the next, despite the small added commission charges involved in such roll-overs.

An often overlooked element in any trading program, but one which is especially important for the Big Move trader, is the selection of one's broker. There are, unfortuately, very few brokers who are psychologically or financially equipped to deal amiably with a Big Move trading program. An entire section later in this volume will deal with finding, selecting, and working with a broker who can and will deal with a Big Move trading program. Suffice it to say for the time being that this is a very important and frequently overlooked element of a trader's Big Move trading program, and an element which, if not dealt with properly, can totally destroy an otherwise sound Big Move trading program. Fortunately, the area of the broker selection is one that is relatively easy to deal with, given some simple guidelines, and one which should pose no problem for the Big Move trader, assuming that he follows these guidelines thoroughly.

CHAPTER 3

AN OVERVIEW-PART 2

We will attempt in this chapter to complete our broad overview of Big Move trading. Actually, a trader starting with the basic principles discussed in the preceding chapter and in this chapter can use this data as a sufficient foundation to begin a successful program of Big Move trading. But, as we mentioned earlier, there are many refinement techniques to Big Move trading in the areas of Entry Points, Initial Protective Stops, Trailing Stops, Target Selection and the like. Using these refinements will not only assure the Big Move trader of a successful and profitable trading program, but will significantly reduce the amount of stress the trader experiences during the period of time his trades are in the market place.

We will now examine some more of the broad areas which are related to Big Move trading in a general way, and as we did with subject matter in the last chapter, we will reserve a more detailed discussion of all of these factors for later chapters.

As we already explained, the two major criteria for locating Big Move trading opportunities are finding commodities which are trading at historic high or at historic low price levels. There also is one other potential Big Move trading candidate--the commodity which is trading near the mid-range price level.

Commodities trading near the mid-range price level obviously have less profit potential than those trading at extremely high or low price levels, but the rate of success with these commodities is sufficiently high to justify them as potential Big Move trading candidates. This is especially true if the price range between the high and the low has been narrowing as the past year or two have gone by. The following graph illustrates this third type of Big Move candidate:

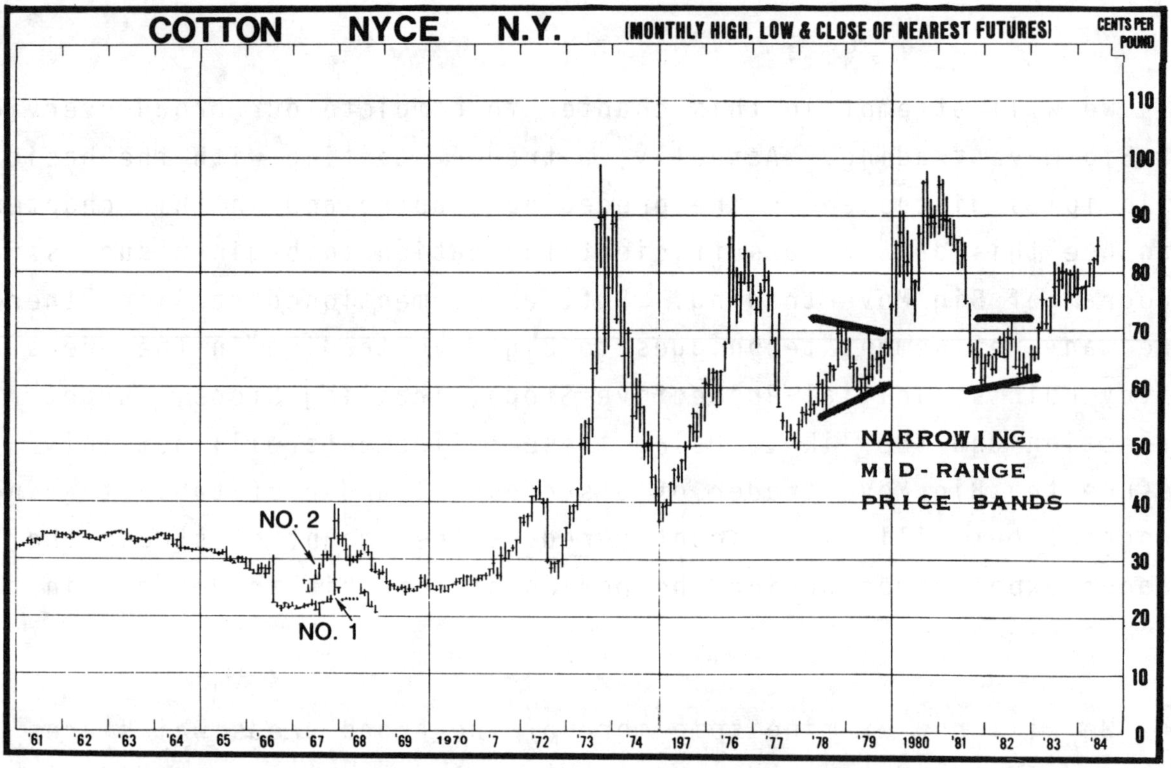

This brings up another topic, and that is the type of charts to use for Big Move trading. Obviously, for determining precise Entry and Exit points and sometimes Protective Stop points, the Big Move trader uses Daily Charts. But to determine high, low and mid-range prices, he must use Weekly and Monthly Charts. In the example just given we prefer a minimum of seven years and preferably 10 years for determining the mid-range price levels, as is the case with the chart above.

Another good guideline for Big Move trading is to eliminate those commodities from consideration which have light Volume and Open Interest. Although we have ourselves on occasion violated this rule, it is definitely most advantagious to trade only those commodities and those contract months with sufficient liquidity to assure reasonable fills. More specific guidelines and rules for determining what constitutes markets that are too lightly traded, or too "thin," will be given later in this volume.

Another factor to be considered is that of diversification. It is very important that a trader not become over-concentrated in any one complex due to the always-present possibilty of UFO's (Unforeseen Fundamental Occurrences).

If all of the metals, for example, are trading at what appear to be historic low levels, the Big Move trader initiates trades in each of the different metals and a UFO should occur in the market place, the trader can be seriously damaged by being so heavily committed to this one particular complex if the particular UFO affects all of the members of that complex. Of course, the other side of the coin is that if there is no UFO and the trader is correct in his analysis, the entire complex will tend to move in tandem and potential profits will be substantially reduced. We believe, however, that this is a risk well worth taking, as opposed to the potential liability of the trader's being seriously hurt by a sudden and unexpected market turn.

It is far better, we believe, to diversify by attempting to have positions in as many different complexes or unrelated commodities at the same time. Some such complexes as Foods and the Fibers and Energy and Woods are so unrelated to one another in typical price movement that each of these can be considered on its own merit. The only exception to this rule is if the overall market place is in a rampant stage of Deflation or Inflation, in which all commodities are moving in the same direction due to economic forces regardless of the fundamentals, at least for a period of time.

In the preceding chapters, we referred to confirmation signals to indicate to the Big Move trader that a market genuinely was getting ready to turn up from historic low levels or down from historic high levels. While the signals we mentioned were the most important ones to use for confirmation of such market turns, there are some others which we would like to mention briefly at this time. The first such signal occurs when there is overwhelming fundamental information which contradicts the other signals and must be taken into account. Such a case existed recently for Orange Juice:

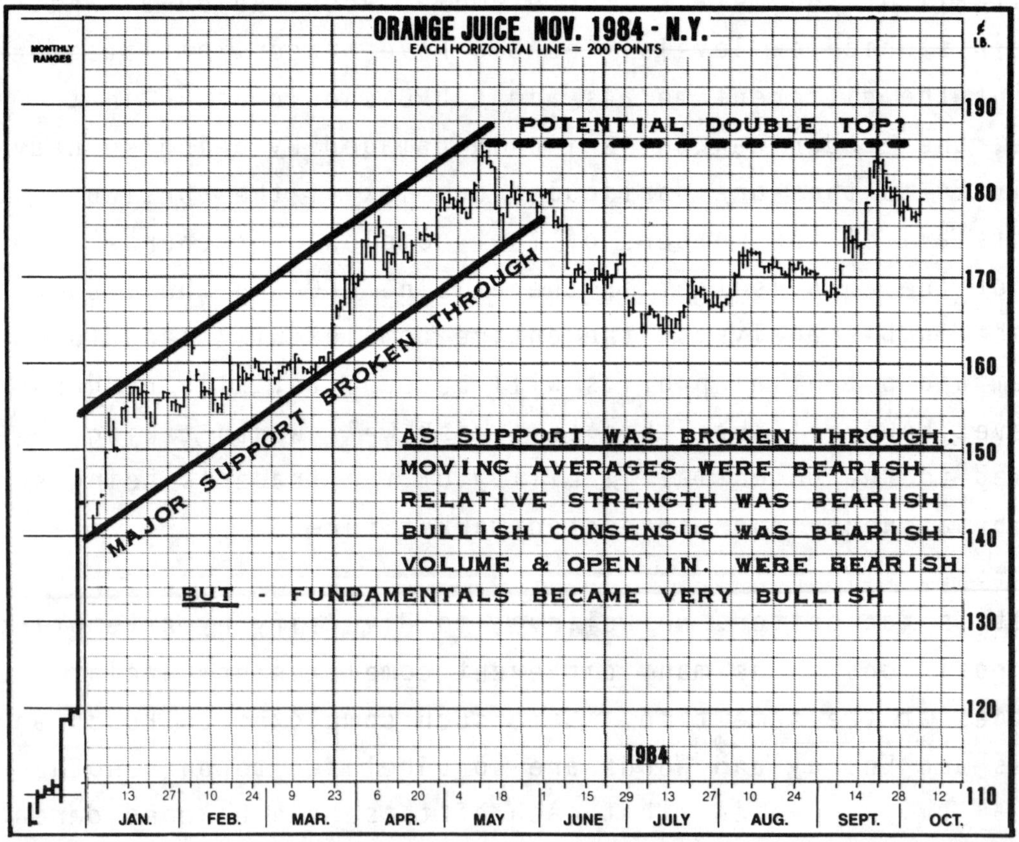

All of the technical information, historic price levels, and confirmation signals indicated that Orange Juice was ready to make a major bear move. After orders for this move had been initiated due to the confirmation signals, a canker was discovered in trees in a major nursery in Florida. This was somewhat analogous to the fruit fly situation of a previous year. Had one not already initiated short Orange Juice positions, this UFO would have been sufficiently overwhelming to stop the astute Big Move trader from proceeding with his short position.

The last confirmation signal to which we wish to refer at this time is that of Positivity-Negitivity, which is often referred to as Bullish-Bearish Divergence. For those readers unfamiliar with this phenomenon, it refers simply to whether the nearby contract months for any particular commodity are selling at a higher or lower price than the more distant contract months. This can be a very useful additional confirmation signal, and we will discuss fully its utilization in a later chapter.

If there were only three points that we could get across to the reader in this entire volume, they would be for him:

1. To select trading candidates from those commodities which are trading at historic high, at historic low, or at historic mid-range price levels.

2. To utilize confirmation signals in order to make certain that the commodities he is examining do in fact have a high probability of changing direction.

3. To use the confirmation signals in <u>combination</u> and to insist that a sufficient number of the confirmation signals do in fact confirm that price direction is going to change and not rely on just one or two of the confirmation signals by themselves. As with all rules, of course, there are sometimes exceptions to this

particular rule. Although these exceptions are exceedingly rare, we will later on discuss what may constitute valid exceptions to this rule.

Since we introduced in this chapter the possibility of a new type of Big Move trading candidate--i.e., that commodity for which prices are trading at the mid-range of their historic price levels for the past seven to 10 years--let us leave the reader with some thoughts to consider before we get into a more detailed discussion at a later point.

Approaching a commodity of this nature obviously has two possibilities--the trader can take either a long or a short position. This emphasizes again the importance of the confirmations signals because these signals typically will indicate in which direction the commodity is going to move from its mid-range trading price--or whether the commodity is going to stay at its mid-range level. An alterative approach to use--although it is not as successful percentage-wise as are the candidates trading at historic high or low price levels--is to utilize an OCO (one order's being filled cancels the other) type of order if the confirmation signals are about evenly split. This type of approach enables the Big Move trader to get into the market move no matter which direction it breaks out in. Typically by using resting buy and resting sell signals for the OCO order, the Big Move trader is not drawn into a false move and enters the position only if a major move up or down begins in earnest. While the profit potential for such a trade is far less than for the first two types of Big Move trade candidates, sometimes few if any of the markets are trading at historic high or low price levels, and this third type of candidate is virtually the only available type of market to trade. Usually we would not recommend trading this type of candidate unless there are few, if any, markets currently near, moving toward, or at historic high or historic low price levels.

One subject frequently brought up is being "whipsawed" by markets which are behaving in an erratic fashion. While such whipsaws are an inevitable part of any trading program, they are substantially minimized by the use of a Big Move trading program. This is due to the fact that the initial dollar risk is typically substantially higher in a Big Move trading program than it would be for either short- or intermediate-term trading. By having his Entry Points sufficiently far away from the current market price and his Initial Protective Stops sufficiently far away from the original Entry Point, the trader substantially reduces the possibility of being whipsawed by unpredictable market action. The possibility is not eliminated, however, as the only way to totally eliminate ever being whipsawed by markets is for the trader to commit to risk much more than 100% of original margin requirements--a rule that we have found best not to violate.

According to our statistical studies, risking much more than 100% of original margin requirements is not cost-effective in that when such trades do turn against the Big Move trader, the losses are substantial enough to significantly reduce overall profits. We have found it far better to adhere as closely as possible to the 100% of original margin requirements for the initial dollar risk for any Big Move position.

The next area that we would like to touch on briefly is the use of commodity advisory newsletters as part of any Big Move trading program. Naturally, as publishers of Taurus and Mega-Trades, we tend to be somewhat prejudiced in this area. Newsletters, however, can serve a useful function for the Big Move trader or they can be very damaging to a Big Move trading program. Newsletters and other commodity advisory services are much like auto mechanics, physicians and therapists in that there are good ones, there are bad ones, and there in-between ones. Even the very best commodity advisory newsletters suffer from periods of time ranging from weeks to even years when their techniques and methodology do not seem to be working satisfactorily in the market place. Even the worst commodity advisory newsletters go through periods of time, usually brief, in which everything seems to be right on target for them. It is difficult, therefore, for the Big Move trader to know exactly which, if any, newsletters to subscribe to and which, if any, recommendations of these newsletters to follow. One of the primary purposes of this volume is to enable the reader to decide upon, initiate, and follow to completion his own trade selections.

Some advisory services, however, can be useful to the Big Move trader primarily in the area of fundamental information of a long-range nature, and we will go into this in great detail in the section of this book on fundamentals.

Many newsletters do not fall into a clear-cut category of commodity advisory newsletters and tend to have more of an orientation towards economics. While these newsletters are very good sources of information, the conclusions which they draw must be viewed very objectively. In any given week, we can review 10 highly respected economic newsletters and see five of them predicting a total collapse of the banking system and complete deflation within the next 12 months and the other five arguing equally cogently that the banking systems will survive and that we will be entering within the next 12 months a period of severe hyperinflation. On top of that we probably can find five other newsletters during this period of time that say we will experience neither inflation or deflation. So the reader must be cautioned to look at the fundamental and economic information presented by any newsletter in an objective fashion and draw his own conclusions, being very careful not to be drawn in to the conclusions which are arrived at by the newsletter publisher.

The use of commodity advisory newsletters with such specific recommendations as those published in Taurus and Mega-Trades can be utilized by the Big Move trader, if the newsletter is one of the successful newsletters going through a good period of trading results or if it is an inferior newsletter going through a good period of trading results, in order to see what their trades are, why they are making these trades (if in fact they do explain why they are initiating certain trades) and if he can utilize this information to assist himself in arriving at his own conclusions. While it seems to be a universal human desire to be "taken care of" and have someone else to do the decision-making for a person, we believe it is very important for every trader to take responsibility for his own trading decisions and trading actions. Even if a Big Move trader follows some newsletters recommendations exactly, he still must take the ultimate responsibility for having decided to enter these particular positions. The most desirable course of action is for every trader to learn how to make his own trading decisions and, as we said, that is the primary purpose of this volume.

Another frequently asked question concerns the amount of money which is required to successfully initiate a Big Move trading program. While this, too, is covered in great detail later in this book, suffice it to say for now that it is possible, though difficult, for a trader to successfully initiate a Big Move trading program with a $10,000 trading account. It is far more ideal for a trader to have a minimum of $25,000 to $30,000 in his trading account, however, as this will enable him to diversify better, not have to trade Mini-Contracts, and increase his overall net equity much more rapidly than he would if he had a smaller account. The ideal account would be in the $40,000-to-$60,000 range, but this is not necessary. In reality, the greatness of a trader's trading account is no excuse for his not initiating a Big

Move trading program since even the smaller $10,000 accounts can succeed if the investor follows the principles in this book and exercizes even more patience than typically is needed in the normal Big Move trading program.

An exciting benefit of Big Move trading is the current status of the tax laws regarding what we consider to be Big Move trading. Insofar that tax laws are constantly changing and may even have changed by the time you are reading this, we suggest that if you are not familiar with the current tax laws, you talk to your accountant or tax attorney about the current status of them. At the time of this writing, however, current tax codes require only the payment of a maximum of 32% income tax on net gains for Big Move trades. For many traders in the upper echelons of the tax brackets, this is definitely quite an incentive to be involved in Big Move trading, and while not as beneficial as a Tax Shelter, the current tax situation is much more advantageous for Big Move trading profits than are the regular income tax tables.

We will conclude our overview of Big Move trading by commenting again on the psychological aspects involved in any successful Big Move trading program. Many traders are unsuccessful at Big Move trading, even though they may be successful at short-term or intra-day trading, because of their desire for excitement, which, in psychological circles, is called "Incident Hunger." This simply means that these individuals--and this probably includes the large majority of the commodity trading population--have a greater than average desire for excitement in their lives. These individuals will find Big Move trading excruciatingly difficult because of the slowness of the moves and the patience required for successful Big Move trading. Fortunately, there are ways to deal with this, if you feel that this may be a problem for you, and we discuss these methods in the later chapter on the psychology of Big Move trading.

A number of your writer's friends have the philosophy that life is "Simple But Not Easy." The same is true of Big Move trading. It is extraordinarily simple to make large profits year-in and year-out by following the principles of Big Move trading. But even publishers of such Big Move trading advisory newsletters as Mega-Trades frequently let psychological issues get in their way in such a fashion that they unconsciously deviate from the proven principles of Big Move trading. This is an area which must be constantly monitored by the Big Move trader (or any other trader, for that matter) in order to make certain that any unprofitable trades are due to circumstances beyond his control or ability to foresee, rather than due to unresolved psychological issues (and we all do have some of them) that the trader may not yet have dealt with successfully. So, as you will find as you go through this volume and either paper trade or trade with real money, successful Big Move trading is "simple but not easy."

The last issue we wish to touch on briefly here--and will discuss more thoroughly later--is what to do with your profits. Strange as this may sound for a manual on how to do Big Move trading, it is an important issue--important from the standpoint that if the successful Big Move trader does not have a plan of how and when to reduce the equity in his account and spend some of his profits, it is a strong indication that he has some psychological issues present which will eventually sabotage his seemingly-successful Big Move tradering program.

With this, we will now move to a very detailed discussion of all of the subjects we have touched one in the preceding two chapters. This will be an exciting adventure for both you and us, and we do hope that you not only enjoy this journey but also find it immensely profitable.

CHAPTER 4

FINDING THE BIG MOVE TRADES

As we mentioned earlier, there are only three types of Big Move trades that we will consider in order to maximize profits. It is true that even after a Big Move trade has started moving--i.e., a market at historic high prices has topped out and has begun moving down--that it is possible to enter such a market at any time on the way down and make profits. But since the market by then will have moved at least a portion of the total distance it will go before reaching a resting point, we want to limit ourselves to entering only those markets which are actually turning in direction at that time and have not already completed a substantial portion of their move. To do otherwise--to enter a market after the move has carried part of its way--does provide some confirmation that the move is in fact a genuine move. But this type of trade then becomes an intermediate-range trade and is not a true Big Move trade.

Many traders may elect to enter these intermediate-range trades, being willing to give up a substantial portion of the Big Move in order to increase the probability of success for the trade in terms of percentage of profitable trades. There is nothing wrong with using this approach as long as the trader realizes that he is not making Big Move trades, but in reality is trading the markets from an intermediate-term standpoint.

The reader may utilize the techniques in this book in order to confirm that a Big Move has begun and instead of having perhaps only a 50% probability of the move's being a profitable and successful one, if the reader trades the market from an intermediate-term standpoint by allowing the Big Move to carry a predetermined amount before entering, he may increase his percentage of profitable trades to as high as 70%. It is a tradeoff of sorts in that he is sacrificing greater profits per trade by trading the markets from an intermediate-range standpoint, while at the same time he is increasing his percentage number of trades which are successful. It is not the purpose of this book to discuss the markets from an intermediate-term standpoint, but we do want to point out that more conservative traders may wish to utilize our methodology from the standpoint of trading the markets only on an intermediate-term basis.

As we said earlier, the three major potential Big Move trading candidates are:

1. Prices trading at historically high levels.

2. Prices trading at historically low levels.

3. Prices trading at an historical mid-point ranges.

The requirements that we have for identifying these types of trading possibilities are such that they point out the necessity of using the proper types of charts not only for identifying the potential Big Move trades, but also for Entry and Exit Points. Monthly and weekly charts are definitely a necessity for initially identifying Big Move trading candidates. Daily charts are necessary for precise Entry, Exit, and Trailing Stop Points; however, weekly and monthly charts must be used in conjunction with daily charts for identifying these three types of points.

The use of these various types of charts will be discussed more thoroughly as we proceed through this book.

It has been our experience that an ideal time frame to use as a reference point to establish exactly what constitutes an historical high or historical low or historical mid-range point ranges from seven to 10 years preceding the current period of time. There are some exceptions to this rule, and we will be looking at them shortly. The following chart illustrates what appears, on a weekly chart, to be an historical high price level:

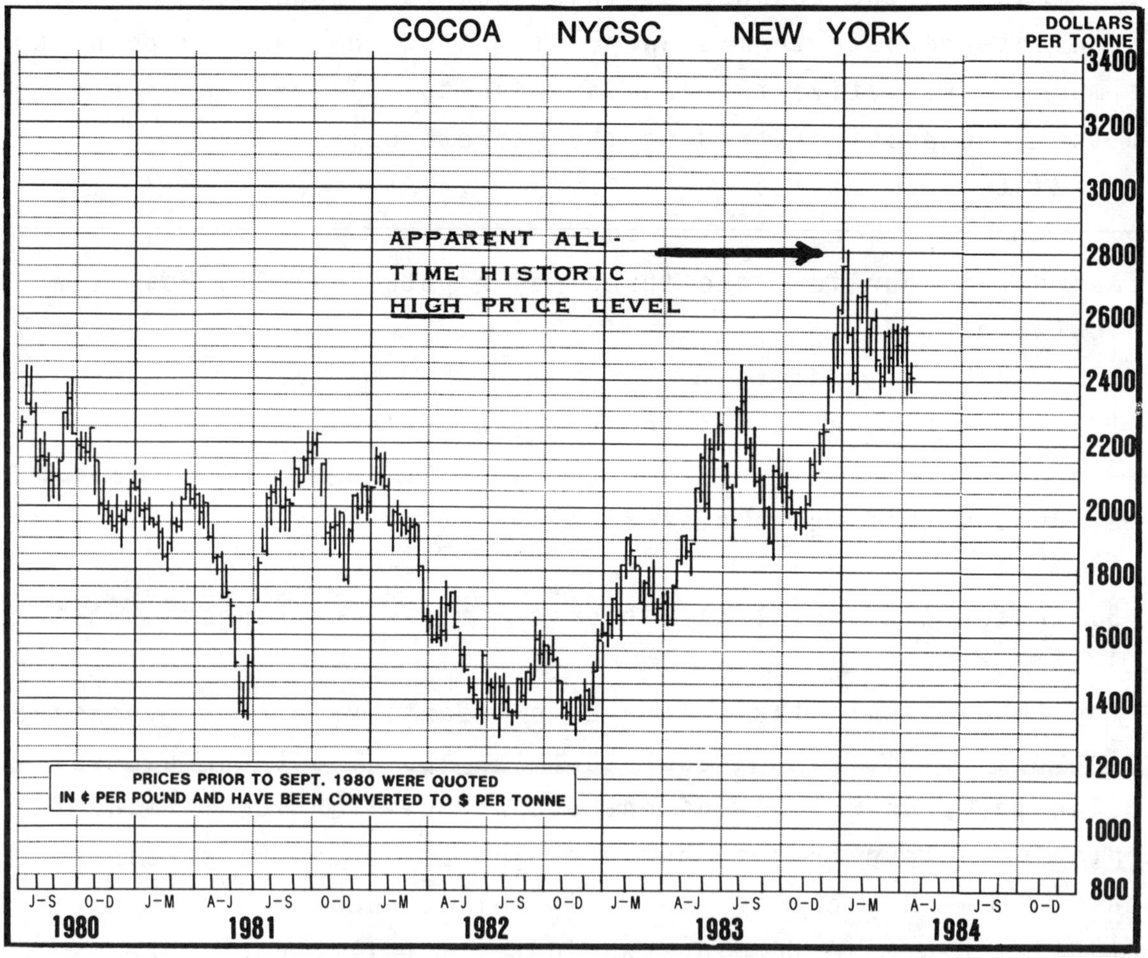

While this appears to be an historical price level, however, it is not, in fact, as can be seen from the following monthly chart:

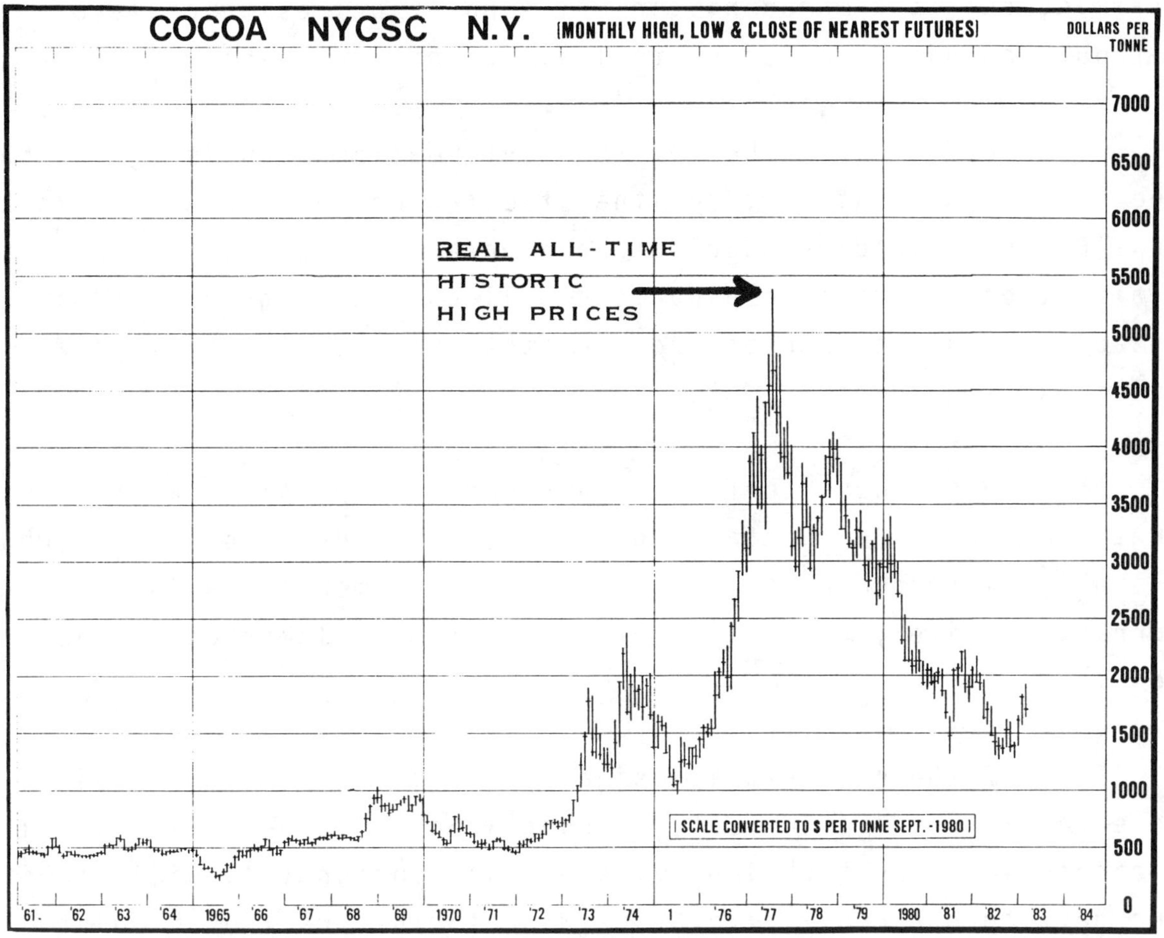

What this suggests to us is that once prices do reach what appears to be an historical price level high or low on the weekly charts, the trader should start examining the commodity very carefully in light of all of the confirmation signals that we have mentioned in the preceding chapters and will discuss later.

Frequently--and this is the exception to the rule--prices will reach what appears to be an historical price level extreme on the weekly charts, when, in fact, on the monthly charts, they do not appear to be that way at all and still be ready for a major Big Move turn in the opposite direction. It is at this time that the trader needs to be watching these confirmation signals closely in order to pick up whether this market is an exception--i.e., is stalling out at a major historical support or resitance level without reaching a major historical extreme in price.

If a sufficient number of the confirmation signals agree that the market is about to turn, then the trader can treat this market as a Big Move trading candidate and enter it accordingly, with the realization that the ensuing move will not be as great, or as profitable, as if the market had, in fact, reached its historical price extreme level.

As many of these confirmation signals as possible must agree that the market is, in fact, going to turn because otherwise what probably is happening is that the market is merely making a correction--i.e., a Bear Market rally or a Bull Market retracement.

Even if the confirmation signals are misleading and indicate the market is, in fact, turning when it is only experiencing a correction, our techniques, as a rule, fortunately will permit our getting our Protective Stops down to the break-even point before the corrective move turns back around again, and, generally, there is little if any money lost during such a trade.

There is little point in illustrating what would be "bad examples" of perspective Big Move trades at high-, low- or mid-range price levels, because the only elements which differentiate "good" Big Move trading candidates and "bad" Big Move trading candidates are the number or the lack thereof of confirmation signals which are calling for a turn in prices.

We do, however, wish to illustrate the major types of ideal potential Big Move trading candidates. First, we will look at those which are at supposedly historic high price levels. The first type of top that we frequently experience is a Spike Top such as:

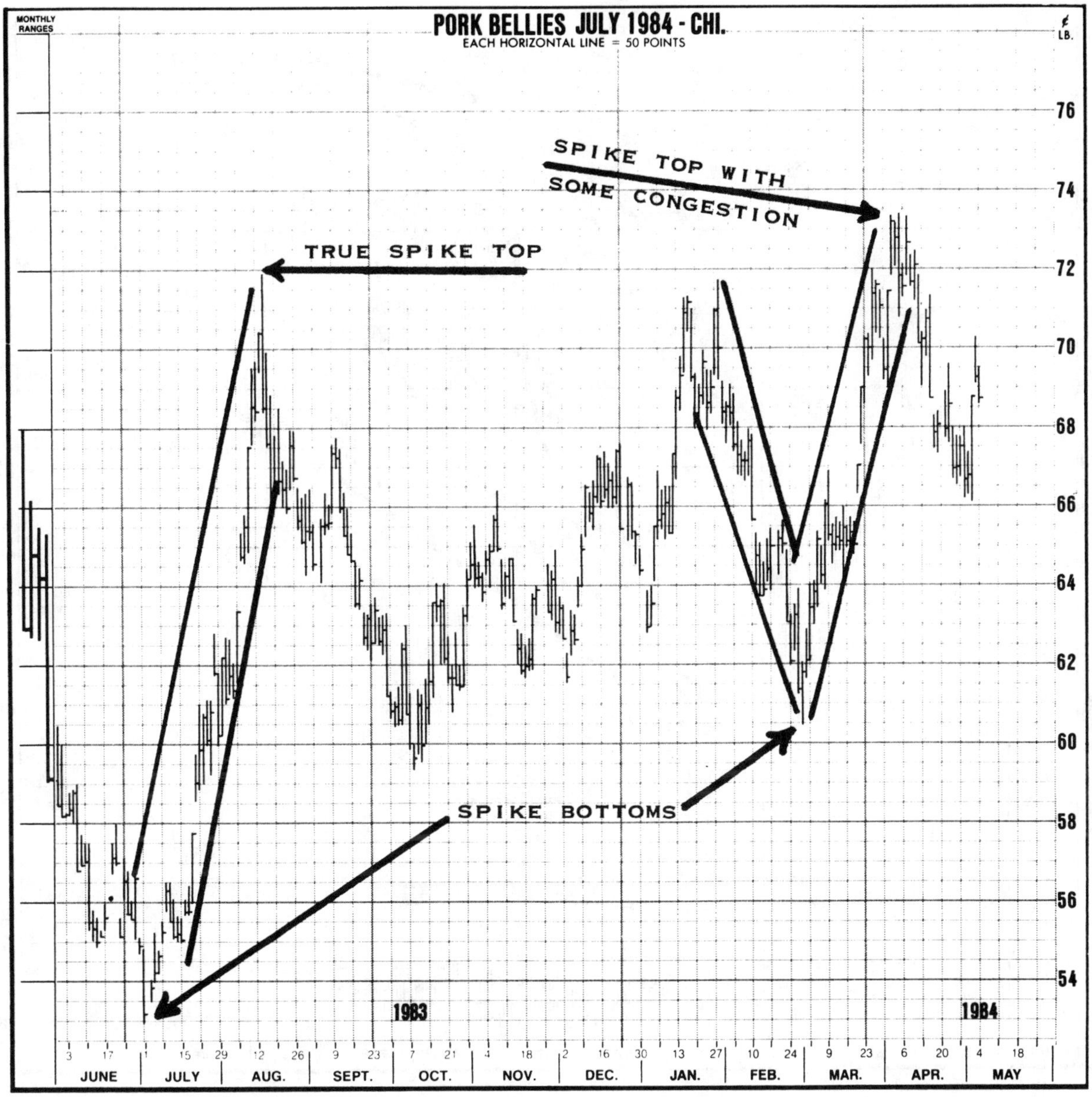

In addition to this type of top, we frequently see a Double Top formation, which we will enter in a different fashion (as we will discuss in the chapter on Entry Points) and trail our stops in a different fashion (as we will discuss in the chapter on Trailing Protective Stops). An example of such a Double Top formation is:

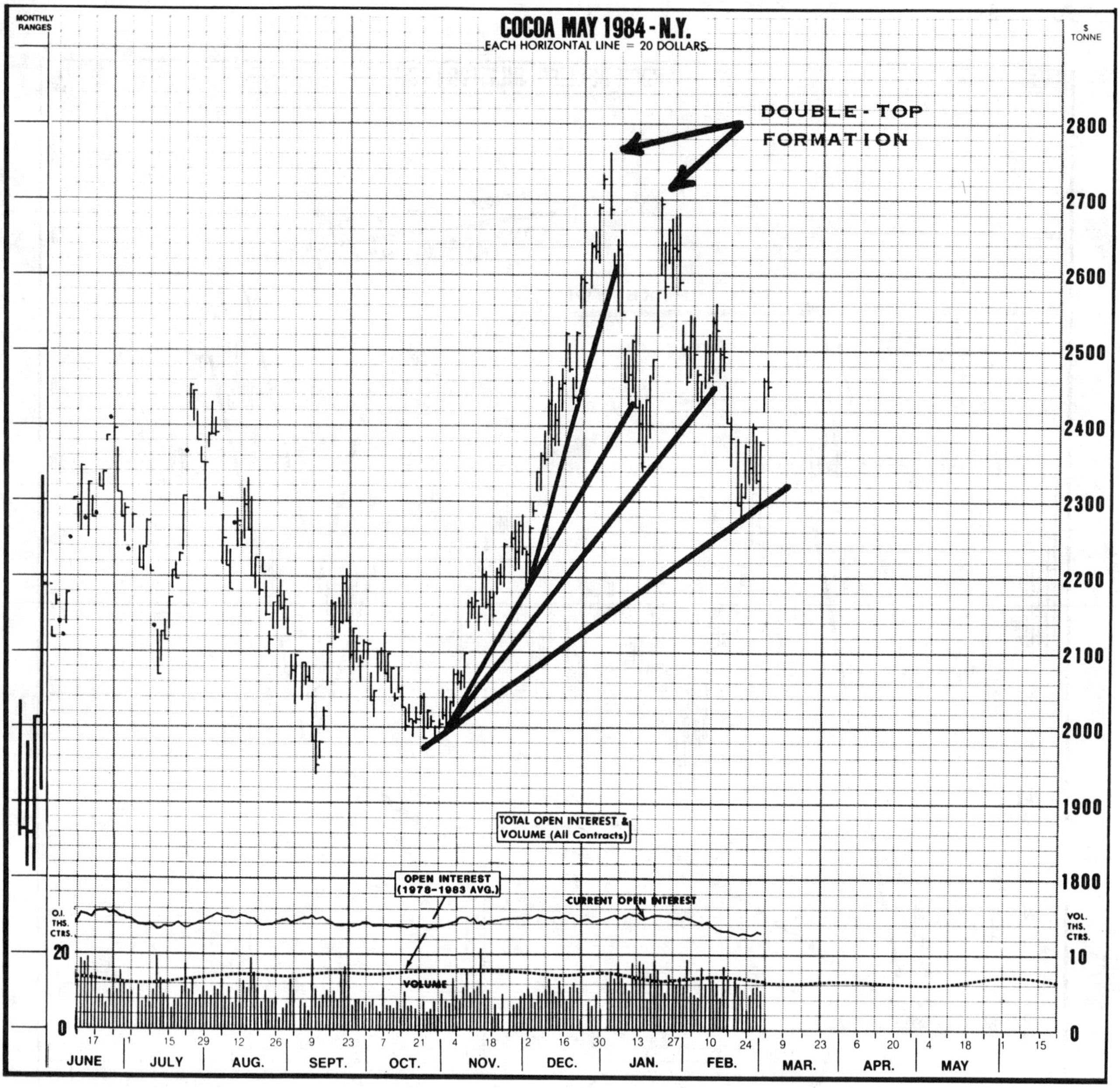

The third major type of top is an infrequently experienced one, but when it does occur, it is an extremely potent sign of a major and sustained down move in prices. This is the Triple Top. Even though the Triple Top is encountered infrequently, when it does occur, the trader may wish to consider doubling up on his initial positions because of the extremely high probability of the move's being successful. An example of such a Triple Top is shown below:

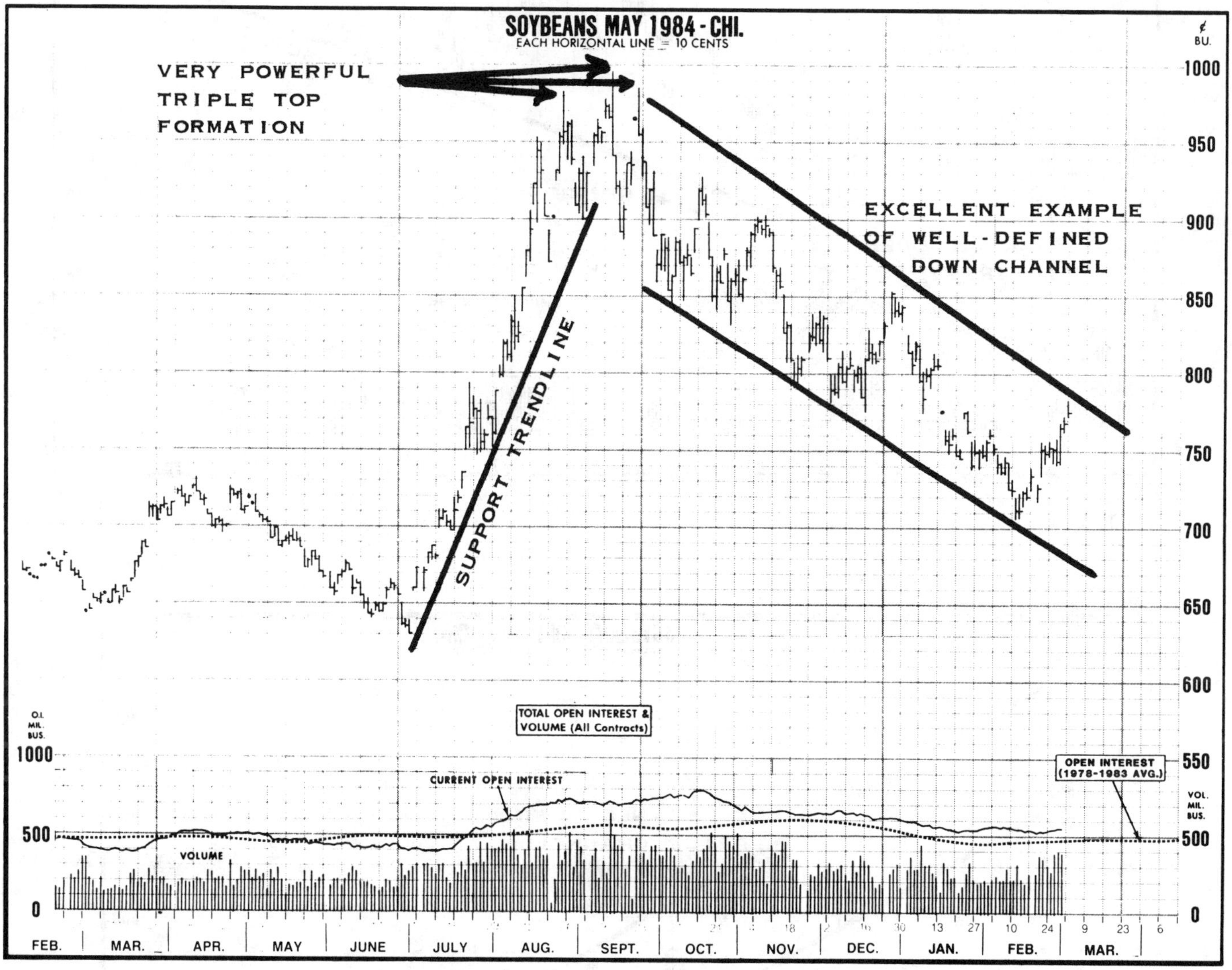

The second major type of Big Move trading candidates is that of prices being at historic low price levels. As with the former candidate, historic high price levels, there are three major types of bottoms. Two of these types are similar to those encountered by markets at historic price levels, such as the Spike Bottom:

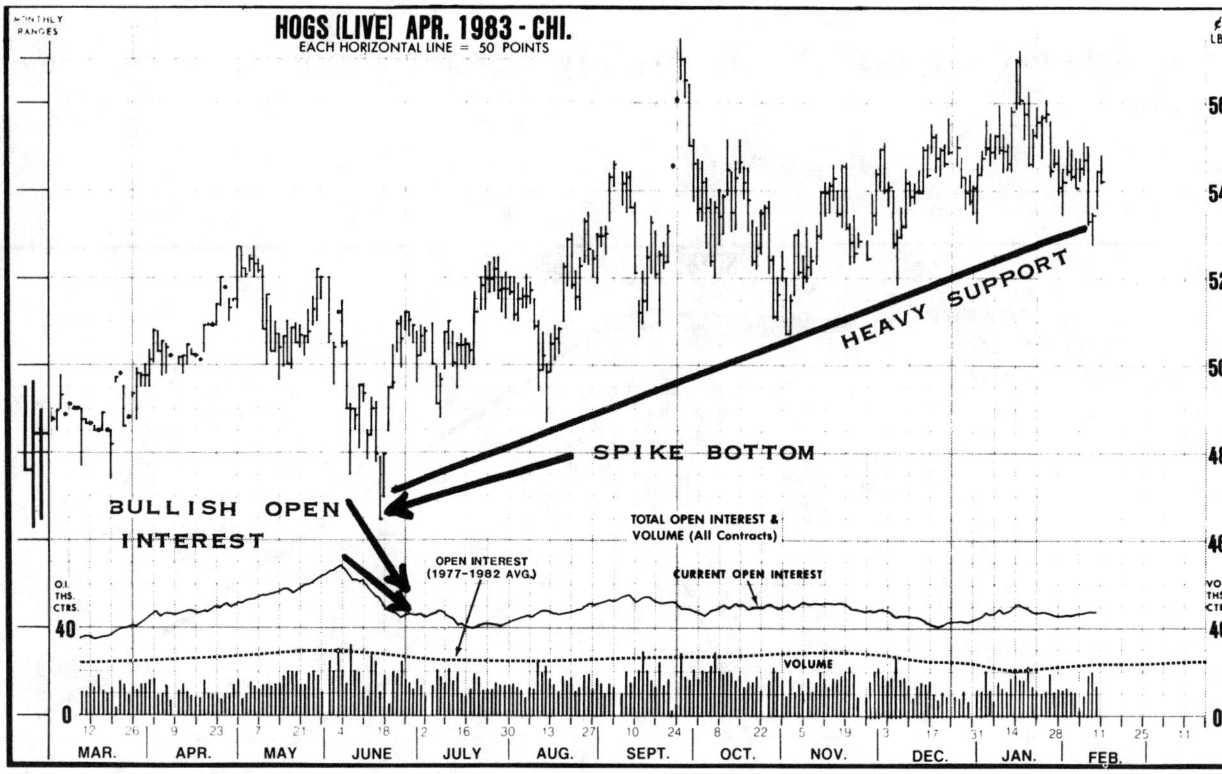

and the Double Bottom:

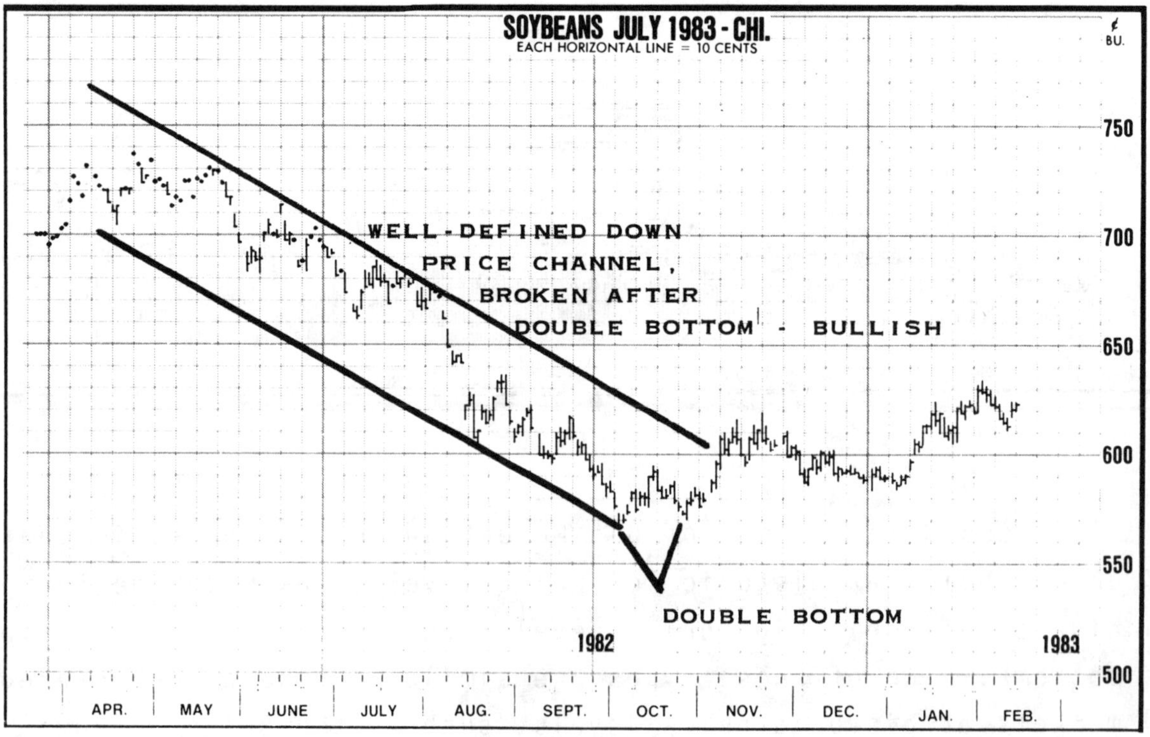

The one difference between historic high and historic low price level "tops" and "bottoms" comes with the Extended Trading Range Bottom. This is one of the most frequently encountered bottoms due to fundamental factors which tend to depress prices and hold them at a low price level once they have reached that point. A tremendous amount of patience is required with this type of bottom formation for the trader to be able to wait for the move to swing upward. Typically, however, when this type of bottom is encountered, the ensuing move upward is well worth the wait. Typically, too, this is an exceptionally easy market to trade from the standpoints of Original Entry Point and Initial Protective Stops. This type of market also has the advantage generally of requiring minimal risk--frequently less than 100% of Original Margin requirements. An example of this type of extended trading range is:

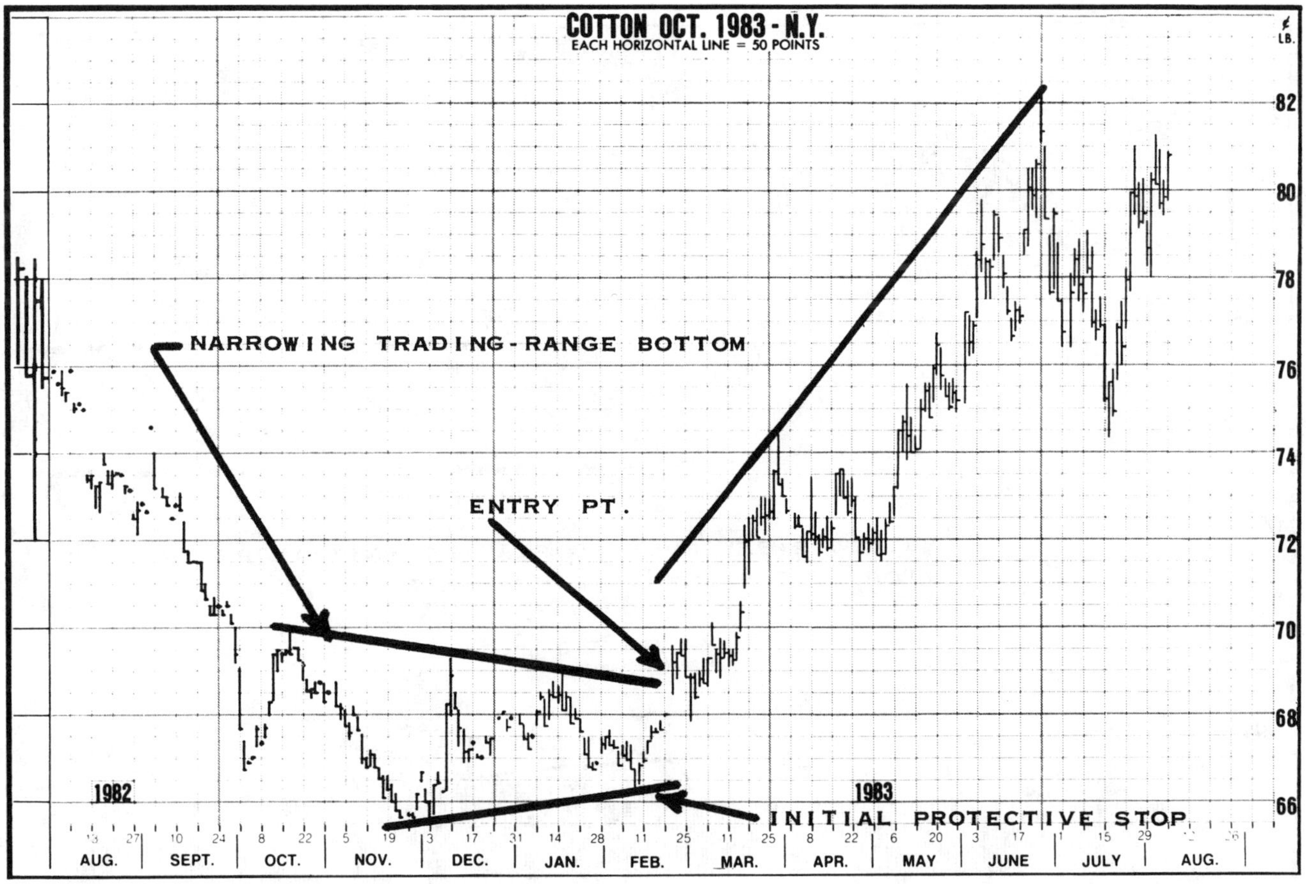

The type of potential Big Move candidate with the least profit potential, the smallest percentage of profitable trades, and, frequently the greatest initial dollar risk is the mid-point trading range candidate. Even though the percentage of winning trades for this type of candidate is the lowest of the three types of candidates, it is still high enough to justify treating it as a Big Move trade. Here, perhaps even more than with the other two types of candidates, the use of confirmation signals is of the utmost importance. Without judiciously using these confirmation signals, the trader will be caught in whipsaw moves and false signals. The most important point to remember about mid-point trading range candidates is to try to locate those in either a narrow or narrowing price range instead of those in a whipsaw pattern or a broad trading range. An example of a mid-point trading range candidate which is not ideal to consider entering because of its unfavorable price action would be:

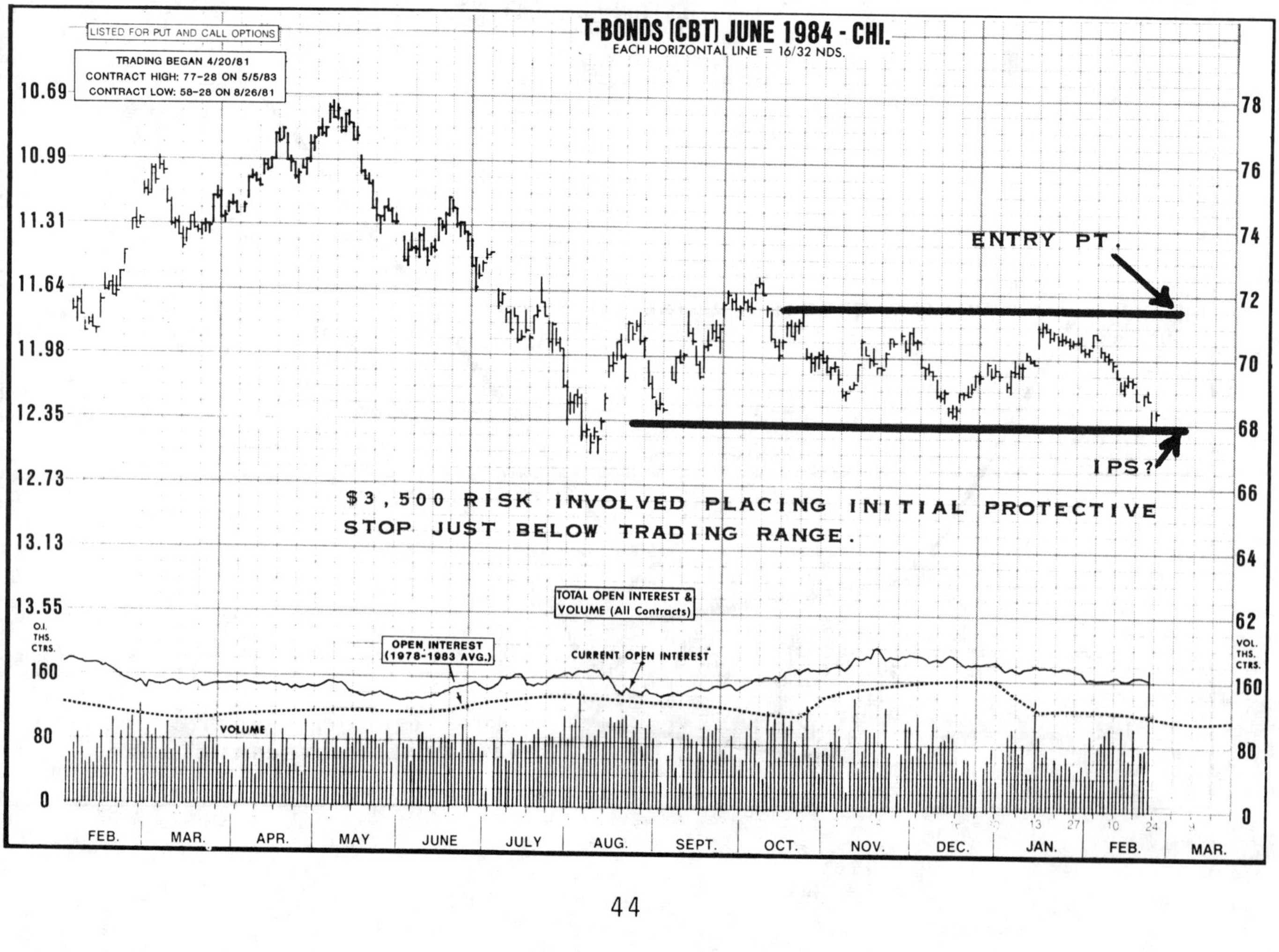

The ideal type of mid-point trading range candidate--one which meets the requirements outlined in the preceding paragraph--instead would show such a recent price pattern as this:

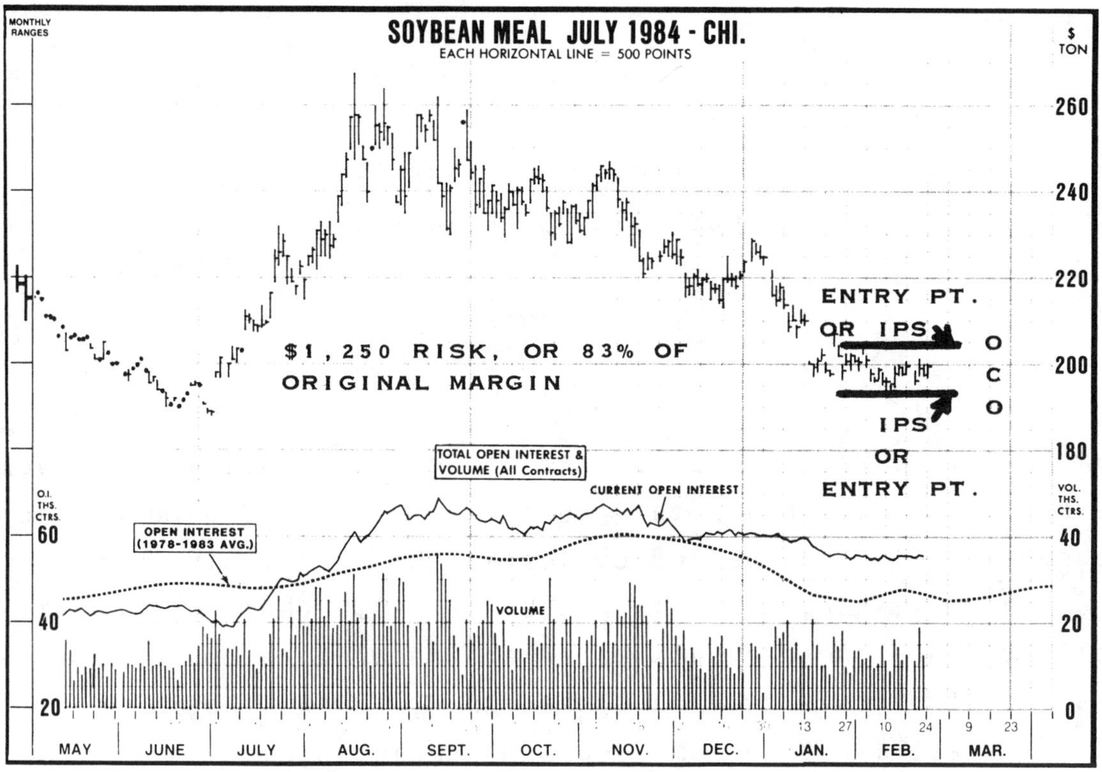

This chapter is meant to give the reader a general idea of what to look for in the charts for potential Big Move trading candidates of the three different types. Once the reader is able to readily identify these types of trading candidates, he is then ready to move on to considering the confirmation signals which must be met before deciding, in fact, to enter a resting buy or a resting sell order. The reader will notice that we do not refer to market orders, but only to resting buy and sell orders because it has been our experience that it is far better to sacrifice a small part of the move in order to get definite confirmation that prices are moving in our direction. We will now proceed in the following chapters to illustrate and define the confirmation signals which are so important to success in a Big Move trading program.

CHAPTER 5

CONFIRMATION SIGNALS-I
CYCLES AND SEASONALS

First, we would like to examine briefly exactly what cycles are before we move on to their utilization in a Big Move trading program. The theory behind cycles is that if events do not occur in a random fashon, but take place with some degree of predictability, then these events occur and recur in a cyclical fashion. As a result of this cyclical phenomenon, so the theory holds, the future is--at least to some degree--predictable.

If this is, in fact, the case--and we believe it is--then cyclical analysis can be a valuable confirmation tool for use by the Big Move trader.

By way of explanation, let us say that the real reason cycles exist in commodities is based upon supply/demand considerations. All cycles which exist in the commodity markets are based upon shortages and oversupplies in the commodity itself--whether it be Corn or the Japanese Yen--and lack of demand or necessity of demand for this particular commodity. The typical cycle pattern for any commodity is that first, a shortage exists; next, producers move in to fill that shortage with an adequate supply; then, producers provide an oversupply of the commodity so they then stop supplying, growing or producing the commodity; and as a result of this, eventually, a shortage exists again.

This is well-illustrated in the following monthly chart for Sugar showing the approximate six-to-seven-year Long-Term Cycle in Sugar which generally is determined by these supply-demand considerations:

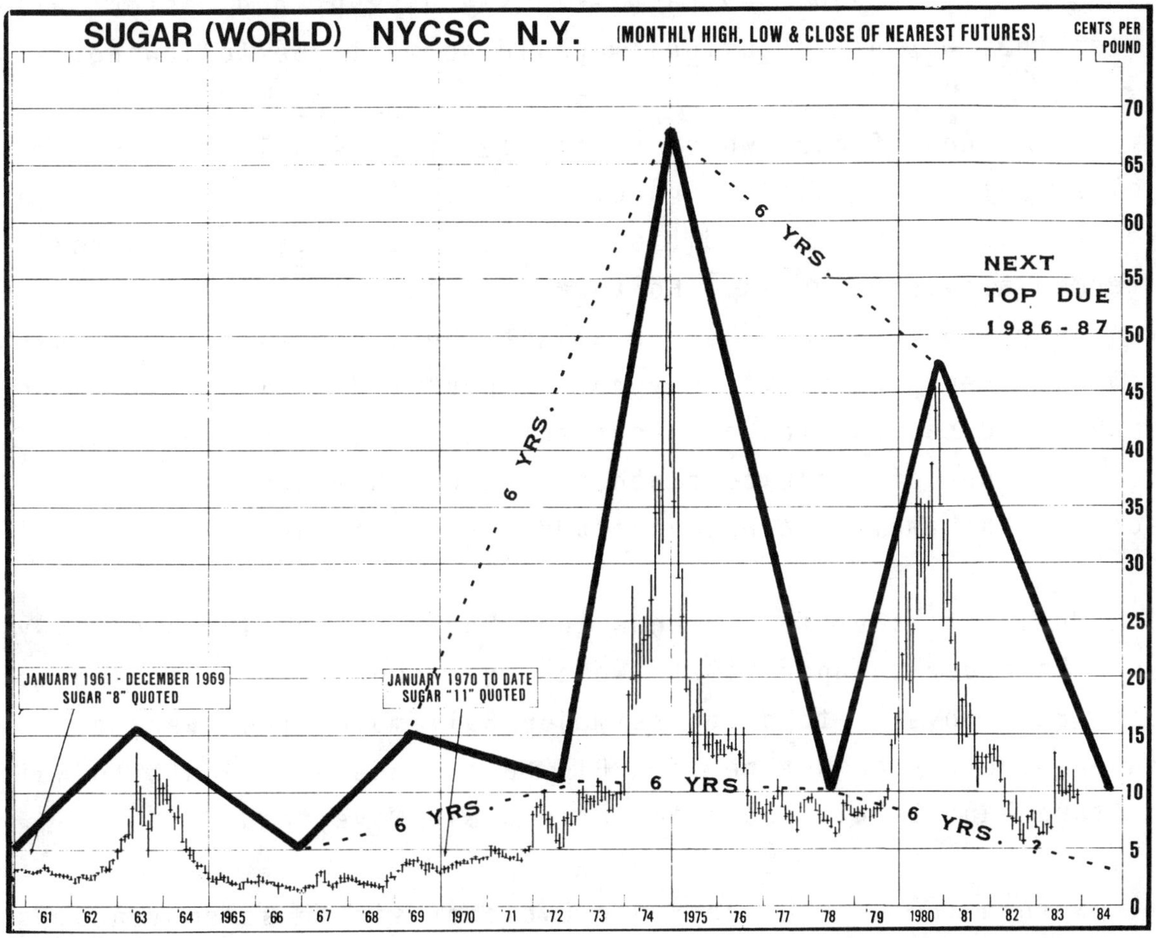

While the ideal methodology for Big Move trading is to trade in the direction in which the Long-Term Cycle is moving--i.e., to trade from only the short side after the Long-Term Cycle has turned down--this is not, unfortunately, a practical way to approach Big Move trading because of the many shorter cycles contained within the Long-Range Cycle.

Long-Range Cycles in particular are subject to distortion, or "skewing," primarily because of two factors. The first factor is our Unforeseen Fundamental Occurrences, or UFO's. Such factors as plant diseases, wars, strikes and embargoes which are unexpected are such UFO's, and while they may be of a cyclical nature in themselves, they are not of the same type of cycle as the Long-Range Cycle and they can seriously disrupt and distort all cycles that any given commodity would normally be following.

The second factor which seriously affects utilization of cycles is the overlapping or combination of all of the different cycles. There are--in addition to the Long-Range Cycles--the Intermediate-Term Cycles, Short-Term Cycles, Intra-Day Cycles and even Intra-Hour Cycles. Since all of these cycles are "marching to a different drummer," they have a push-and-pull effect on one another and can shorten or lengthen the duration of any other cycle because of their combined effect or they can increase or decrease the amplitude or magnitude of any of the given cycles.

While it is useful to know that Sugar has a six-to-seven-year cycle in order to approximate when Sugar should be bottoming its major Bear move or topping its major Bull move, the average trader--whether or not he is a Big Move trader--is loath to wait for three-and-a-half years to enter a Big Move trade.

Within the Long-Range Sugar Cycle of six to seven years, there also is an approximate one-year cycle and also an approximate 60-day cycle. By utilizing the approximate one-year cycle in the same direction as the Long-Range Cycle, the Big Move trader is assured of one potential Big Move trade per year. This is not to say that such a move will occur every year, but the potential for such a move is there, based upon the Intermediate-Term Cycle.

We again show the monthly Sugar chart in order to illustrate this approximate one-year cycle:

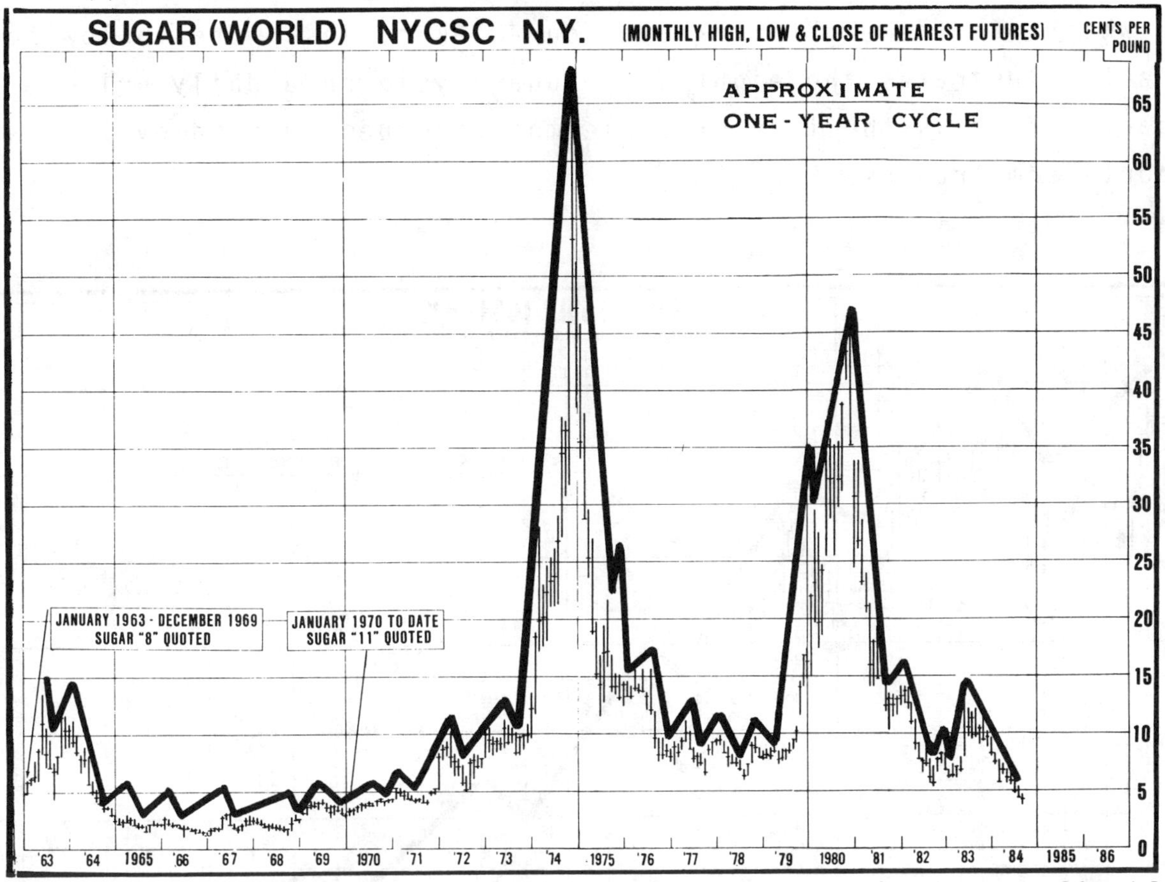

As the reader can see, not every year contained a profitable Big Move trade for the Intermediate-Term Cycle. But a number of years did offer such profitable trading opportunities, especially when the trades were made in the direction of the Long-Term Cycle. By keeping track of the Long-Range Cycles and the Intermediate-Term Cycles on his monthly charts, the trader will have a good idea of approximately when to anticipate being able to enter a Big Move trade in any given commodity.

The use of Long-Range and Intermediate-Term Cycles by themselves, however, is no guarantee of profits in a Big Move trading program. This is due not only to UFO's, but also to the skewing effect of overlapping cycles, including those much longer than six-to-seven-year cycles, such as the 50-year Kondratieff Cycle.

As we mentioned earlier, Sugar has within its Long-Range and Intermediate-Term Cycles a number of other cycles, the most useful of which are the eight-week and four-week cycles. The following chart illustrates the eight-week Sugar cycle on a daily price chart. This is the type of cycle most frequently used by Short-Term traders.

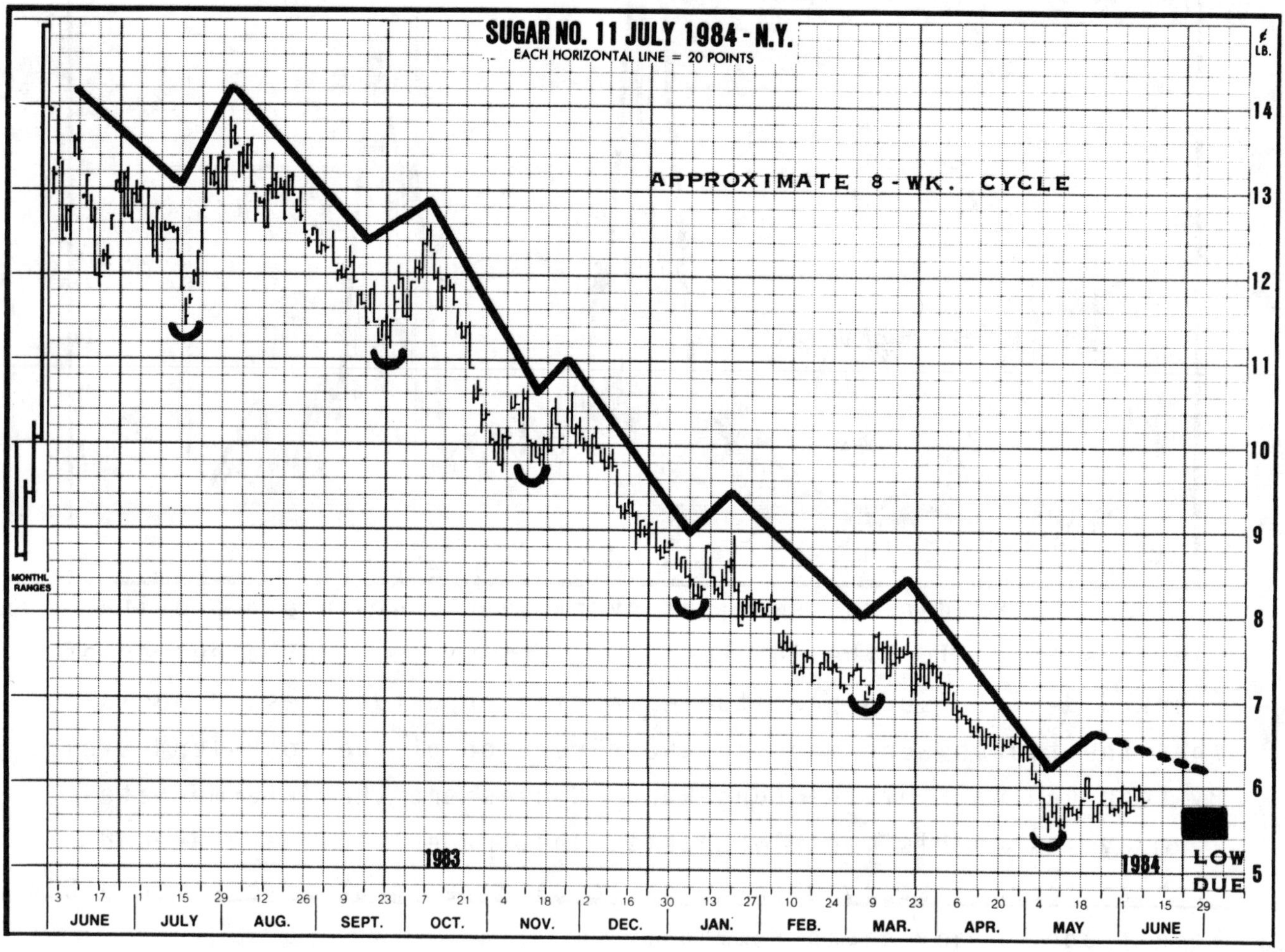

For Big Move trading, this cycle can be used in conjunction with the Long-Range and Intermediate-Term Cycles in order to determine approximate Entry and Exit points for a given Big Move trade. If the reader knows, for example, from his marking up of cycles on his monthly and weekly charts that a Long-Range Cycle is either heading down or due to bottom during given period of time--say within a 60-day period--and the Intermediate-Term Cycle is due to bottom during the same period of time, then he would be looking to establish his long positions, in the case of Sugar, as the eight-week cycle bottoms during this same period of time, placing his Initial Protective Stops a bit below this eight-week cycle low.

Unfortunately, as ideal as this methodology sounds, such an approach by itself typically will lead only to disaster for a Big Move trading program. True, some Big Move trades may be caught only by using such an approach. But due to the factors previously mentioned, there will be many, many times that a Long-Range Cycle is heading in one direction, an Intermediate-Term Cycle is due to top or bottom within a certain period of time, and a Short-Term eight-week or four-week cycle also is due to top or bottom within that same period of time, but the market continues heading in the opposite direction. Only when the other Confirmation Signals--or a sufficient number of them--indicate that the market is about to reverse its direction should such cyclical analysis be relied upon as a further Confirmation Signal.

In Appendix A, at the back of this book, we give the idealized Long-Range Cycles for a number of years into the future. These graphs in Appendix A should be used with the caveat that they are subject to this skewing we have discussed by even Longer-Range Cycles than are illustrated in these charts.

We urge the serious Big Move trader to do his own cyclical analysis on the commodities he is following. While there are a number of advisory services--most of which are excellent--who do this analysis, it is much more beneficial for the Big Move trader to be doing this analysis himself. This is especially so because such analysis of Long-, Intermediate- and Short-Term Cycles takes a relatively small amount of time--especially the Long-Range and Intermediate-Term Cycles.

Such analysis is relatively simple to do, as can be seen in the preceding Sugar charts. The analysis is accomplished simply by marking prominent monthly highs and lows on the monthly charts, the weekly charts and the daily charts. By this simple three-step procedure, the reader will be able--by counting the time distance between highs and lows--to come up with a relatively viable cycle length for Long-Range, Intermediate-Term and Short-Term Cycles for any given commodity.

We particularly urge the reader to do this for Short-Term Cycles because they do show a great proclivity to vary in length (frequency) during any given year. While for one year Sugar may typically have a prominent eight-week Short-Term Cycle--and it generally does--for another year the trader may find that instead of its typical eight-week cycle, it is exhibiting a prominent six-week or 10-week cycle which is much more useful and valid for determining Entry and Exit points for establishing and leaving Big Move trades.

A very useful tool to facilitate such analysis is the Erlich Cycle Finder, which is an accordion-like, heavy-duty plastic tool that makes identifing and marking cycles much easier than attempting to do it by just looking at the charts. The address of the firm which sells this product is in Appendix E at the back of this book. So then, as the reader can see, cyclical analysis and the utilization of such by a Big Move trader is not the obscure technique that many writers would have traders believe. In reality, it is a fairly simple, fast, and easy-to-use approach to Big Move trading, as long as it is used as but one more Confirmation Signal in conjunction with all of the other Big Move methodology.

* * * * *

Seasonal Analysis also is a very useful Big Move confirmation trading tool. Seasonal Analysis--or Seasonal Patterns--is nothing more than examination and utilization of a calendar year cycle. Such Seasonal Patterns or calendar year cycles exist to relatively predictable changes in supply and demand in any given commodity--including some such commodities as Currencies and Financials which would not appear to be subject to supply and demand considerations--during the calandar year. These Seasonal Patterns are one of the most important and reliable cycles of all available to the Big Move trader, when they are behaving as they are <u>supposed</u> to be doing.

As with the other cycles mentioned earlier in this chapter, Seasonal Patterns are subject to skewing due to Unforseen Fundamental Occurrences which take place in the world.

A typical Seasonal Pattern, for Corn, is illustrated below:

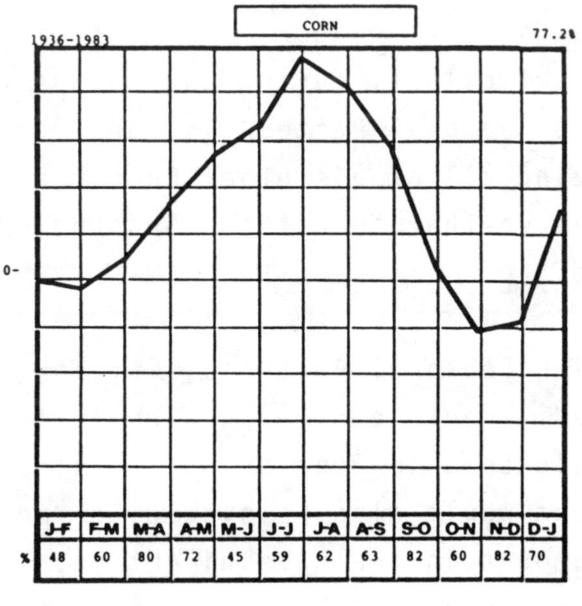

As can be seen, prices tend to peak during the month of

August before the new harvest comes in. As fresh supplies of Corn are available from the new crop, prices then tend to drop through November and then behave irregularly through March, when they start up again as available supplies decrease in availability.

While such Seasonal Patterns are important to all traders--whether they are Big Move traders or Short-Term traders--they are especially important to the former. Typically, the Big Move trader will be looking to establish long positions in either November or March in Corn, especially if the Long-Range Cycle is pointing up and the Intermediate-Term Cycle is either pointing up or due to bottom during these time frames. He will then, of course, utilize his Short-Term Cyclical analysis, in order to determine his exact Entry Point. Conversely, if the Long-Range Cycle is heading down or due to head down and the Intermediate-Term Cycle is due to top or is heading down, the Big Move trader will be looking to establish a short position sometime around August. We say "sometime around" because of the inevitable skewing of Seasonal Patterns.

Ideally, the Big Move trader will be examining the markets very carefully, particularly during the months preceding the period of time the Seasonal Pattern is due to top or bottom, and he will be utilizing all of his other Confirmation Signals in order to determine whether or not the Seasonal Pattern has, in fact, been skewed.

Typically with Seasonal Patterns, if, for example, the seasonal high is skewed a month early--such as in the case of Corn--the seasonal high would come in June or July instead of in August and the seasonal bottom would also be skewed, or moved, an approximately equivalent amount in the same direction. Therefore, in the case of Corn, if the seasonal high occurred during the month of July, then we typically would expect the lows to come in October and February instead of in November and March. By examining and marking the yearly high and low points on his weekly chart, the trader can determine whether or not the Seasonal Pattern has, in fact, been skewed for any particular year.

An important point needs to be made here, and that is that the skewing of a Seasonal Pattern typically does not carry over from one year to the next. By that we mean that if the seasonal high for Corn were in July for this year, there would be no increased probability that the seasonal high would be in July next year. Quite the contrary, in fact. The probabilities are that the seasonal high in that following year would occur during the month of August, when it typically does take place.

Frequently mentioned by writers and analysts of Cyclical Analysis is the reliability or lack thereof of cycles--particularly of Long-Range Cycles, but more frequently of Seasonal Patterns. Long-Range and Intermediate-Term Cycles do tend to exhibit a high degree of reliability--i.e., they tend to repeat themselves, despite being skewed sometimes, with a high degree of regularity (reliability).

The same is not necessarily true of Seasonal Patterns. Some commodities--Coffee, for example, and some of such Currencies as the British Pound, the Japanese Yen and Treasury Bonds--have very low reliability. This simply means that while they may exhibit a Seasonal Pattern of sorts, the percentage number of years during any given decade in which such a pattern exhibits itself is relatively low--probably below 50% of the number of years under examination.

Reliability factors for the different commodities generally are given by cyclical analysts in their works, a number of which are referenced in Appendix E of this book, and while this does not mean that commodities with Seasonal Patterns of low reliability cannot be traded using Seasonal Patterns as a Confirmation Signal, it does mean that such Confirmation Signals must be viewed with a skeptical eye. All commodities have a varying degree of reliability in their Seasonal Patterns for any given month; hence, Corn shows a seasonal reliability of going up in price between March and April of 80%, which means that in 80% of the years studied there was an increase during the months of March and April. But even though the Seasonal Pattern for the month of May-June shows the prices generally increasing, the seasonal reliability for this month is only 45%, meaning that prices did, in fact, increase only 45% of the time during this time frame and actually decreased 55% of the time.

The average Big Move trader will not be totally concerned with percent reliability for any given month since he will be trading from a longer-range standpoint. Since we are utilizing Seasonal Patterns--and, generally, only the high and low points of such Seasonal Patterns--as a Confirmation Signal combined with all of our other Confirmation Signals and Big Move methodology, we can see that the reliability for any given month between the high and low points of the Seasonal Pattern is not too terribly significant, except in the case when a Big Move trader is attempting to fine-tune his Protective Stop placement between the high and low points of the Seasonal Patterns. In such a case, the Big Move trader using these reliability figures obtained from the cyclical analysis reference sources listed in Appendix E might wish to keep his Protective Stops back a bit farther during the May-June time frame since the reliability of the Seasonal Pattern up move is so low during that point in time. We do not believe, however, that this approach is necessary unless the Big Move trader wishes to spend the additional time required to be so very precise in his analysis. Typically, our other methods of Protective Stop placement and movement are more than sufficient to compensate for the very reliability of Seasonal Patterns.

The ideal way to utilize Long-Range and Intermediate-Term Cycles and Seasonal Patterns is to look for those commodities which are exhibiting a good degree of predictability and regularity in following the anticipated Cycles and Seasonal Patterns. If a commodity seems to be completely out of touch with the predicted cycles or its Seasonal Patterns and no obvious skewing is visually apparent, then, generally, this commodity is best avoided since there always are a number of commodities which are very obviously following their anticipated cycles and their Seasonal Patterns to some degree.

In summation, Cycles and Seasonal Patterns are both useful and predictive tools as well as excellent Confirmation Signals. They must be used, however, only in conjunction with the other principles of Big Move trading and the other Confirmation Signals. They should never be used solely by themselves. It is far better for the Big Move trader to determine the cyclical patterns which the different commodities are following on his own and to utilize the already-established Seasonal Patterns as illustrated in the back of this book. Used judiciously, Cycles and Seasonal Patterns can greatly increase the likelihood of success for a Big Move trading program.

CHAPTER 6

CONFIRMATION SIGNALS-II

In the last chapter, we discussed the first two of our nine Confirmation Signals: Cycles and Seasonal Patterns. In this chapter, we shall discuss the next four Confirmation Signals:

Bullish Consensus

Volume

Open Interest

Moving Averages

As with all of the Confirmation Signals we have already discussed and will be discussing in the next chapter also, it is our firm belief that none of the four Confirmations Signals discussed in this chapter can be used solely by itself.

But when these signals are combined with the other Confirmation Signals, then their potency and predictive value increases dramatically.

Bullish Consensus--also frequently called Contrary Opinion--

is a percentage measurement taken from surveying commodity advisory newsletters.

The number that is given as the Bullish Consensus is the percent of those advisors and advisory services that are bullish on any particular market.

Supposedly, when 80% or more are bullish, then the market is overbought and due to reverse itself. On the other hand, when the Bullish Consensus figure drops below 20%, the market supposedly is oversold and ready to turn upward.

The figures of 80% and 20% indicating overbought and oversold conditions are somewhat arbitrary, as some analysts have chosen to use the figures of 75% and 25%, while others utilize 70% and 30%.

The decision as to which figure to use is an individual one, since Bullish Consensus can rarely be used by itself in selecting trades.

Mega-Trades typically uses the 70% - 30% combination, although we are well aware that the predictive value of this Confirmation Signal increases as the percentage figures increase or decrease towards 100% - 0%.

Bullish Consensus data is now available from a number of sources, at least three of which present it in graphical form each week.

The names and addresses of the services which provide this information--both in tabular form as well as in graphical form--are listed in Appendix E at the back of this book.

The following illustration dramatically shows an example of when Bullish Consensus was of no predictive value, since its movement into the extreme range did not forecast an imminent market turn:

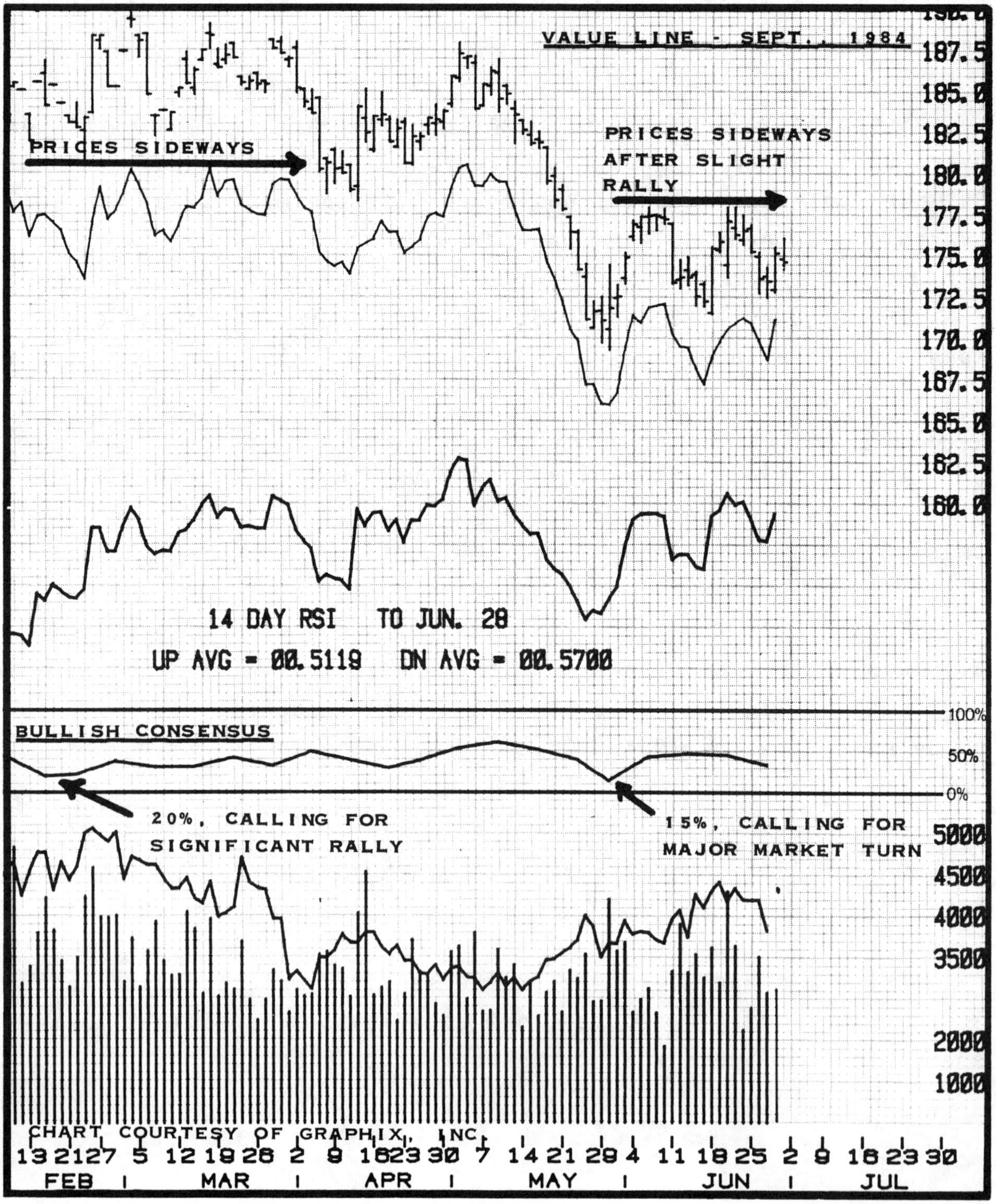

But Bullish Consensus does work very well in many cases when it is combined with our other Confirmation Signals, such as in the following illustration, when a market turn was very correctly forecast by Bullish Consensus:

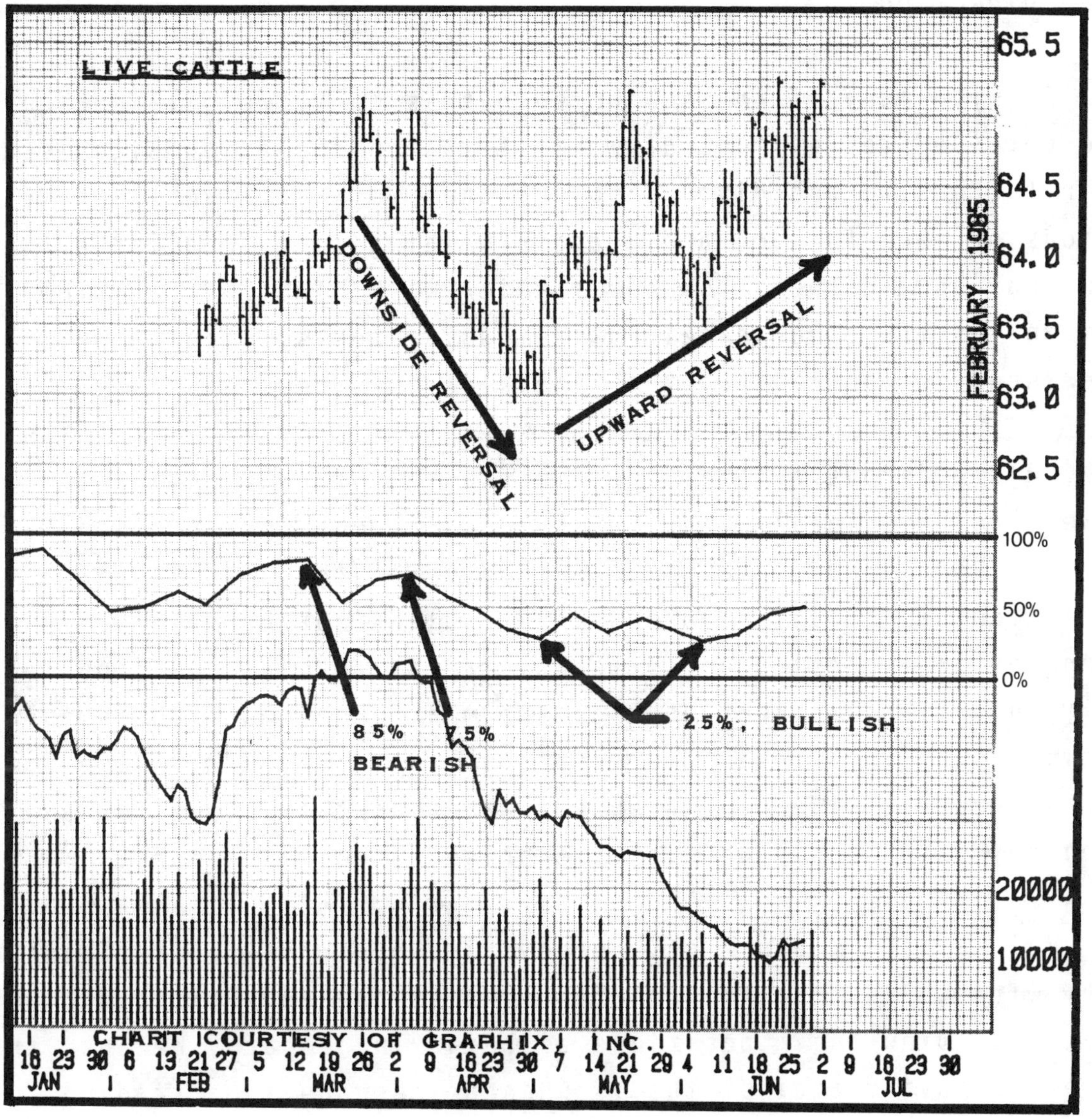

What we want to do, then, when we are utilizing Bullish Consensus is combine it with our other Confirmation Signals, since this particular signal is attempting to identify a turn in market direction. For example, when Bullish Consensus is above 70-80%, if Open Interest increases suddenly and Volume also increases dramatically, this is a key indication that the market is overbought and ready to reverse itself. As the reader will see in the next section on Volume and Open Interest, this is an exception to one of the rules of Volume and Open Interest changes indicating future price direction.

As with many of the subjects in this book, we will not go into detailed definitions of many of the Confirmation Signals and other factors we are discussing. Rather we will give brief definitions of each factor, and readers wishing more detailed definitions may obtain them from our earlier work, THE TAURUS METHOD, or from any of the other excellent commodity texts which we have referenced in Appendix D at the back of this book.

Volume is one of the more important Confirmation Signals. If we were to numerically rank our nine different Confirmation Signals, Volume would be up near the top of the list. Volume is simply the sum total of purchases or sales (not both) for any given day in a particular commodity market. Volume is reported daily in the Wall Street Journal and many other major newspapers. It also is shown by chart services in bar graph form at the bottom of most graphs, lined up in such a way that the Volume for any given day is directly beneath the price action bar chart.

Volume is a measure of urgency: it shows the level of intensity with which traders feel the need to take positions and with which they view their positions as being in jeopardy because the market is moving against them. When prices are in a trading range, Volume normally dries up as traders wait. If prices move out of a trading range and Volume increases dramatically, traders holding positions opposite to the direction in which the market has broken out of its trading range are bailing out and new traders are getting into the market. If prices move out of the trading range and Volume changes only slightly, those traders in the market do not believe the move to be a genuine one and those not already in the market do not want to get in.

The following illustration shows how Volume can be used in this manner:

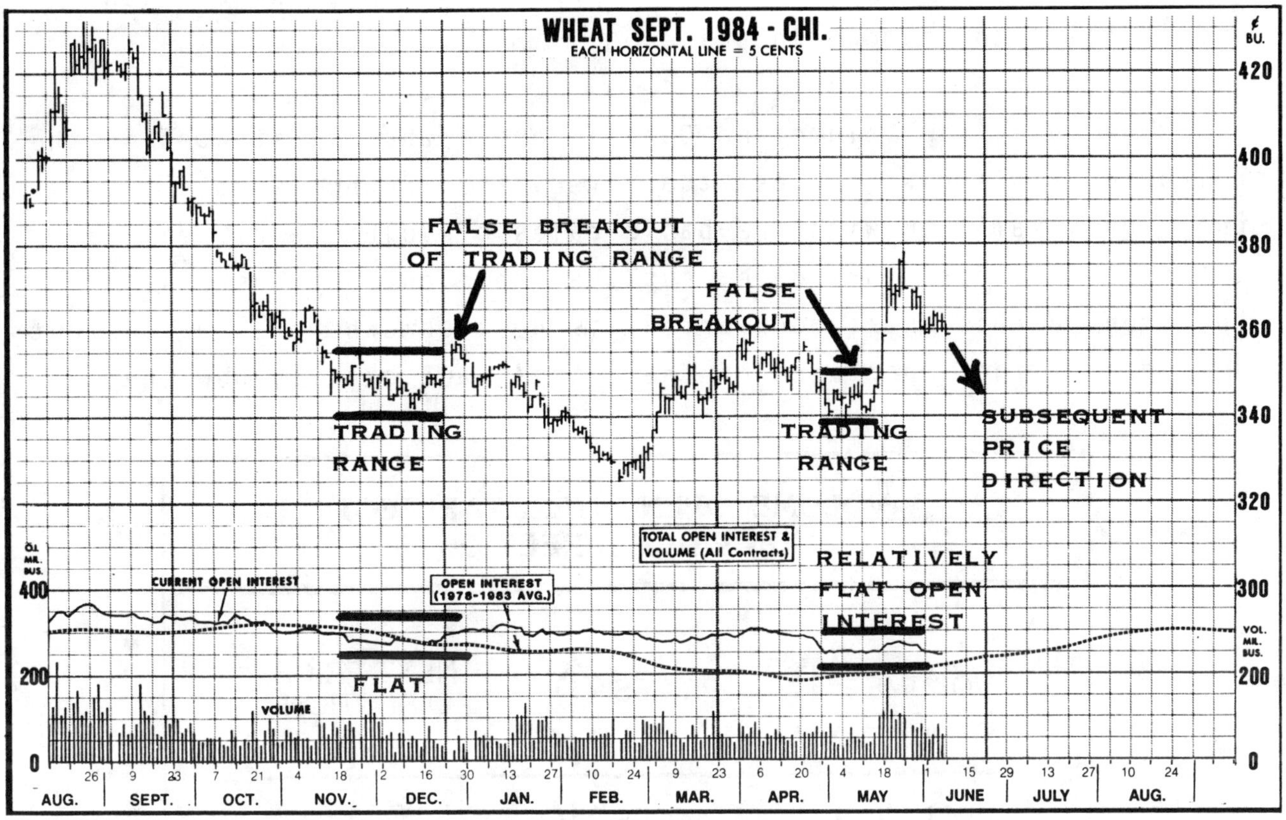

As with all guidelines, however, these rules about Volume when prices are in trading ranges generally cannot be used by themselves alone. Generally, they must be used in combination with other Confirmation Signals.

Two cardinal rules to adhere to with Volume are: Never short a market after a price drop if the Volume dries up, and never buy into a market after a price rise if the Volume dries up.

The two basic rules for Volume are:

1. When Volume increases as prices increase or when Volume decreases when prices decrease, the market is in a BULL position and is going to be moving up.

2. When Volume increases as prices decrease or when Volume decreases as prices increase, the market is in a BEAR position and is going to go down in price.

The rules for Volume and Open Interest are illustrated in the following table. We suggest that every trader who is not thoroughly familiar with the basic rules of Volume and Open Interest duplicate this page, cut the table out and paste it in the front of his chart book or on his desk somewhere as a constant reminder of the importance of these tools and exactly how they work.

VOLUME/OPEN INTEREST EFFECT ON PRICE DIRECTION

				NEXT PRICE DIRECTION
VOLUME	↑	PRICES	↑	↑
"	↓	"	↓	
VOLUME	↑	PRICES	↓	↓
"	↓	"	↑	
OPEN INT	↑	PRICES	↑	↑
"	↓	"	↓	
OPEN INT	↑	PRICES	↓	↓
"	↓	"	↑	

Open Interest is a measure of the overall desirability of any given market. Open Interest is affected by many different variables--such as Margin requirements--and by all of the fundamental factors--such as drought, freezes, embargoes, political developments and the like.

Not previously mentioned in our discussion of Volume is that for Volume and Open Interest, there is a two-day lag in reporting the market information. Newspapers give estimates the following day of the Volume and Open Interest for the previous day's market trading. But these are only estimates, and our research has shown them to be unreliable to the point where they are not only frequently useless, but worse, often misleading. Actual Volume and Open Interest are always reported two days after the particular market action, somewhat reducing the predictive validity of these two indicators. One other point that must be made is that no day trade transactions ever appear in Open Interest figures for that particular day since the positions are opened and closed on the same day.

Another way of looking at Open Interest is that Open Interest is a measurement of the willingness of both Bears and Bulls to hold different positions in the same market. Open Interest is a measurement of the differing opinions between traders about the direction in which prices will move for any given commodity.

When Open Interest is increasing, the increase indicates that the difference of opinion about price direction is increasing among traders. When Open Interest remains relatively constant or flat, new traders are replacing those who get out of the market, or the strong are assimilating the contracts of weaker traders. When Open Interest is decreasing, it is an indication that the willingness of both Bulls and Bears to hold different positions is also decreasing.

The two basic rules of Open Interest--which are illustrated as four different points in the preceding table--are: first, if Open Interest increases as prices increase or if Open Interest decreases as prices decrease, the market is strong and should advance. The second rule is that if Open Interest increases as prices decrease or Open Interest decreases as prices increase, the market is weak and should decline in price. The following illustration shows some of these basic rules in action:

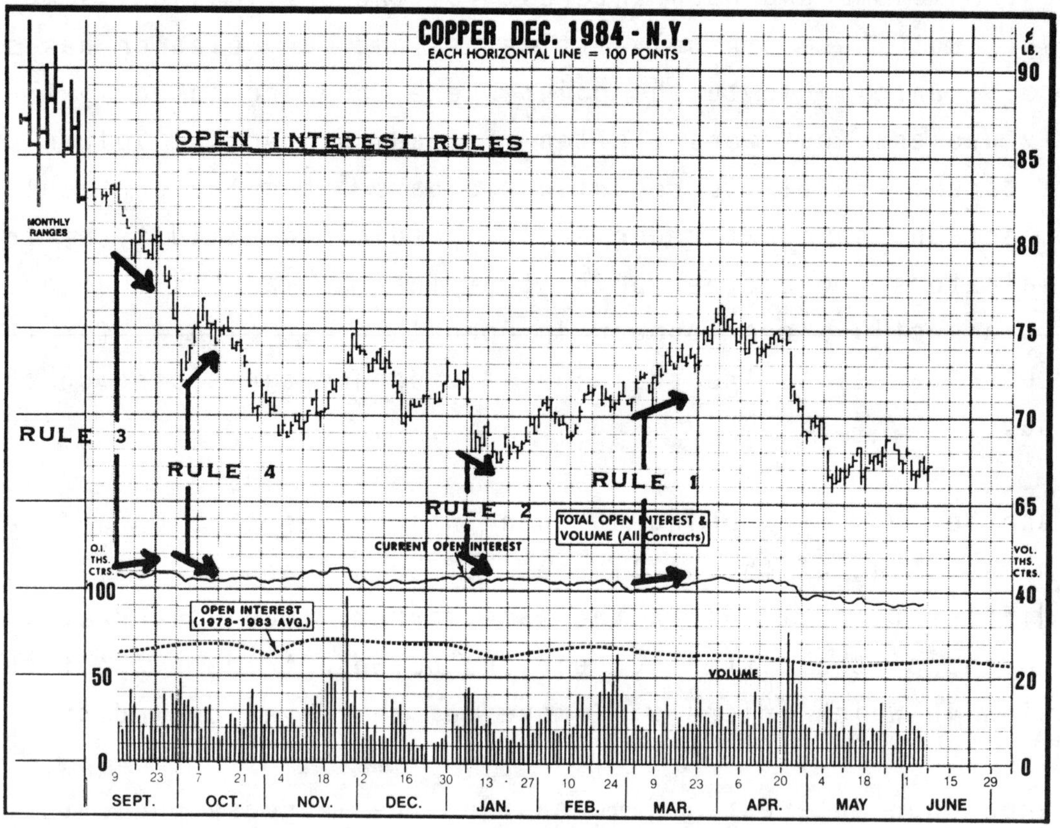

As with all of the Confirmation Signals, Open Interest can never be used by itself. The rules for Volume and Open Interest should be used to validate one another. If they contradict one another, then the best position for the Big Move trader to follow--unless a sufficient number of the other Confirmation Signals all have strong predictive value--is to effect a stand-aside posture.

One good way, for example, for a trader to double-check his

conclusions about what Volume and Open Interest are indicating, is for him to check the status of the Bullish Consensus. Another point that needs to be made is that when Open Interest increases substantially in a lightly-traded, or thin, market, it is a very good indication that something major is afoot in that particular commodity. It also is an excellent idea to avoid whenever possible those commodities which have relatively low Open Interest.

Another useful way to utilize changes in Open Interest is when a particular market is in a trading range. Generally in such a market, if Open Interest increases while prices are in their trading range, the next direction of the market should be down. An illustration of this is:

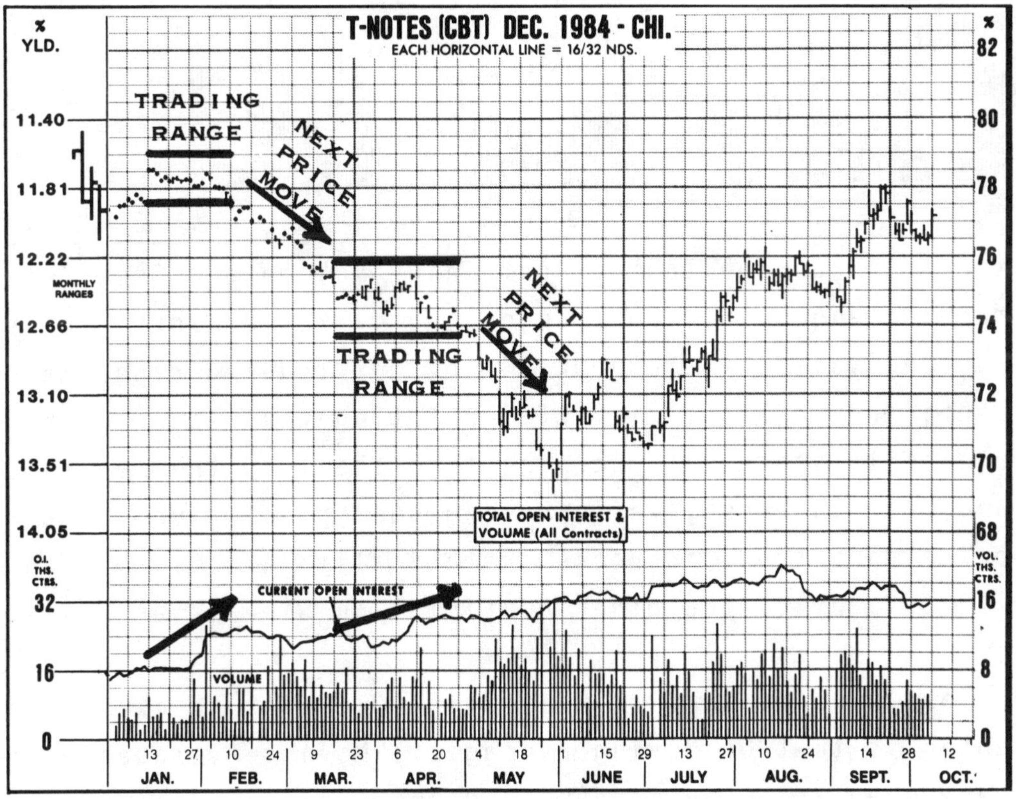

The converse also is true in that when prices are in a trading range, if the Open Interest decreases, the next move of the market generally will be up out of the trading range. This can be seen in the following illustration:

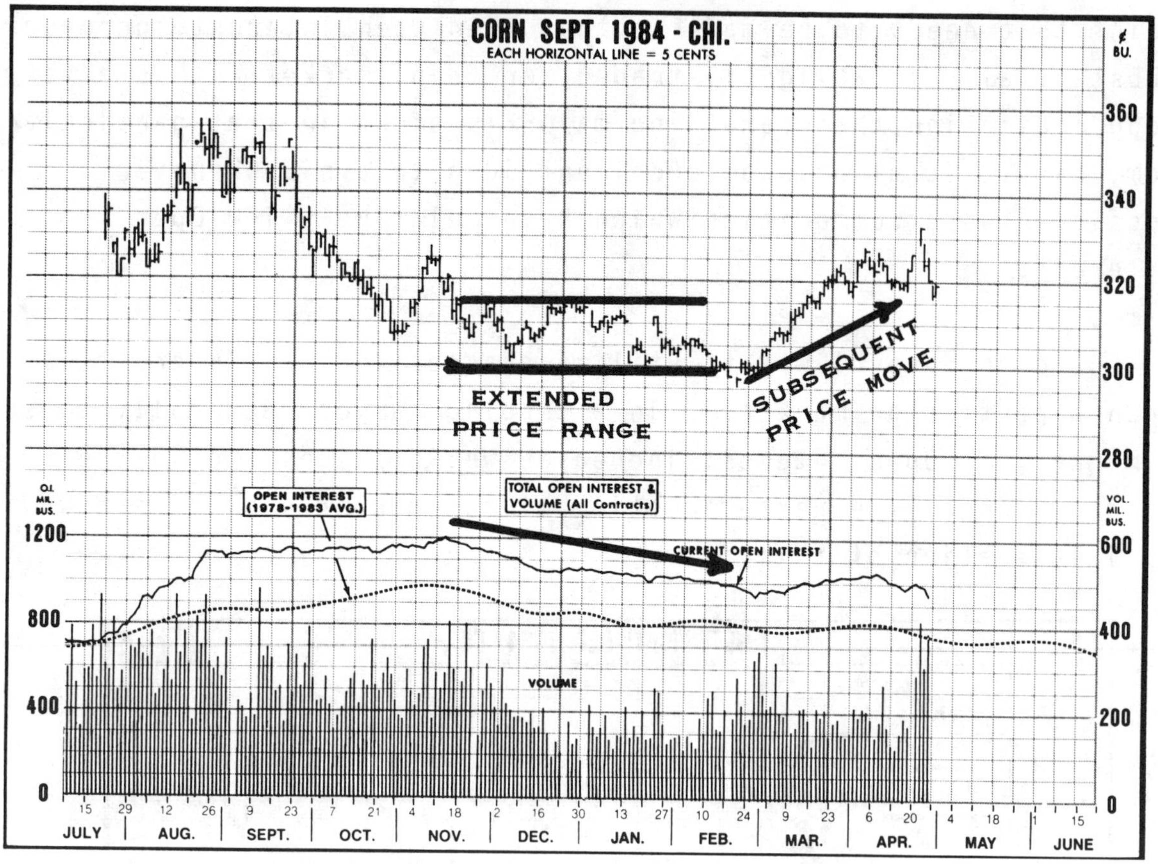

The reader can see that by combining Volume and Open Interest rules, major changes in direction of the market can often be predicted and the validity of breakouts of any trading range market can be confirmed. At the risk of irritating the reader by repitition, we wish to state yet one more time that, by themselves, Volume and Open Interest, while having good predictive value as to future price direction, increase dramatically in potency when combined with as many of the other Confirmation Signals as possible.

The last type of Confirmation Signal we wish to examine in this chapter is that of Moving Averages. Moving Averages have become very popular among traders and professional analysts. This very factor increases their predictive validity by creating a situation resembling a self-fulfilling prophecy. The major reason for the popularity of Moving Averages is their mathematical nature, in that no judgmental factors need be considered. The increasing use of computers by traders and analysts and the way Moving Averages lend themselves to computerization have also increased their popularity.

Moving Averages, quite simply, are made by adding up the closing prices of (X) number of days and then dividing that sum by that number X. Every day, the last price in the series is dropped and the newest closing price added. When these numerical values are plotted on the graph with prices, a very smooth trend can readily be seen. The most popular method of utilizing Moving Averages, especially for Short- and Intermediate-Term trading, is the four-nine-18-day Moving Average. While the four-nine-18-day Moving Average approach is not the optimum for the Big Move trader, it can be used to fine-tune his Entry and Exit Points from Big Move positions.

This approach holds that a buy signal is given when the four-day average is greater that the nine-day average and the nine-day average is greater than the 18-day average. Also, all three averages must be increasing or sloping upwards.

This theory further holds that a sell signal is given when the four-day average is less than the nine-day average and the nine-day average is less than the 18-day average, and all three averages are decreasing or moving downward in slope.

As useful as this may be for fine-tuning Entry and Exit Points--and we urge the reader to utilize this approach for optimization of Entry and Exit (these four-nine-18-day Moving Averages are given by many Chart Services)--we have found for Big Move trading, the predictive value of using 10-40-day Moving Averages is much more accurate in indicating major changes in direction of price. While the use of the 10-40-day Moving Average will result in his getting into moves a bit later--thereby giving up some of his profits, or exiting a move a bit later--also reducing his profits, the conservative trader may find that such a reduction in overall profits is justified because of the greater probability of the trade's being successful by using the 10-40-day Moving Average approach. The basic rules for using the 10-40-day Moving Average approach are: A buy signal is generated when the 10-day average is greater than the 40-day average and both averages are increasing in upward slope of direction. A sell signal is generated when the 10-day average is less than the 40-day average and the slope of both averages is decreasing in direction. The following illustration shows an example of both of these rules for the 10-40-day Moving Average approach:

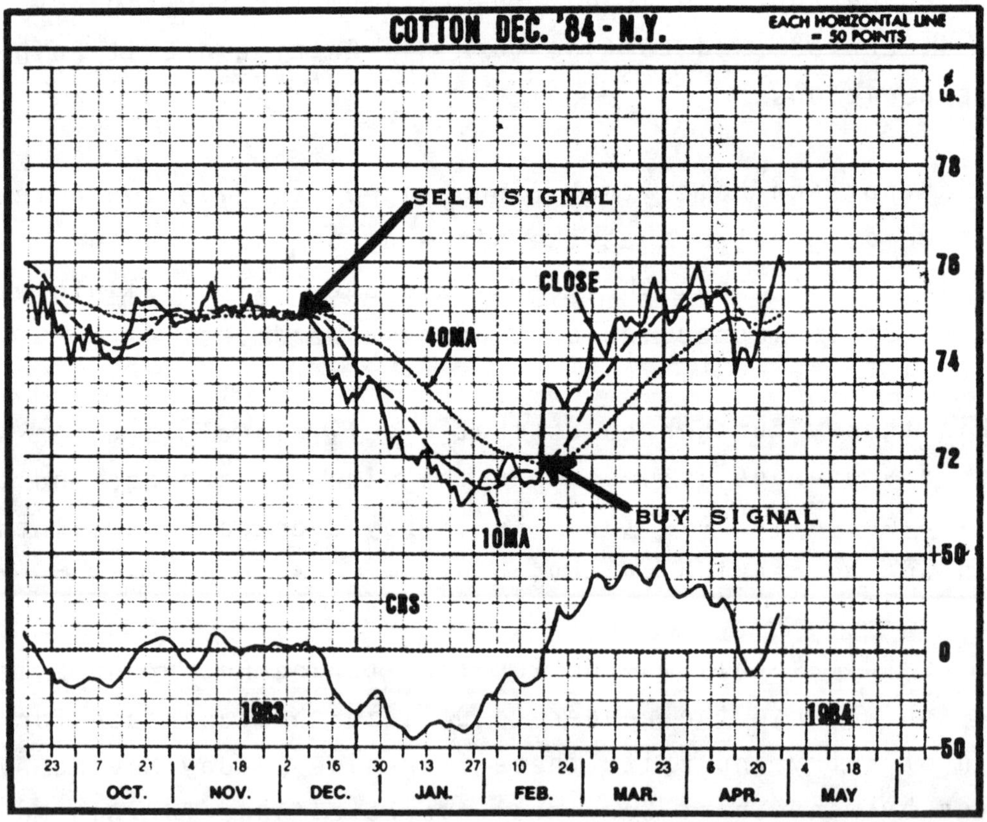

Whether a Big Move trader decides to use the four-nine-18-day Moving Average approach or the 10-40-day Moving Average approach is largely a matter of individual taste. More aggressive traders usually will find the four-nine-18-day Moving Average technique to be more to their liking, although this approach will result in more whipsaws and more frequent losses. More conservative Big Move traders generally will find the 10-40-day Moving Average technique to be more to their liking because even though profits on the average winning trade will be reduced somewhat, their number of losses will decrease and they will enter fewer positions overall.

By now, the reader should be able to see that the Confirmation Signals used to determine whether or not to place a Big Move position appear complex and interrelated. The apparent complexity is not as great as it appears to be at first, however, although the interrelationship of all of these Confirmation Signals is undeniable. Later in this volume, we will explain why these Confirmation Signals are an exercize in simplicity--not complexity--when they are approached and utilized properly by the Big Move trader.

CHAPTER 7

CONFIRMATION SIGNALS-III

In this chapter, we shall be examining the remaining three Confirmation Signals. These three signals have been purposely grouped together because of their relative lack of concreteness and specificity when compared to the previous six Confirmation Signals. This is not to say that the three signals to be discussed in this chapter are not as useful or not as valid in terms of predictive value as the other six Confirmation Signals, but rather that a bit more judgment and care must be used in order to properly evaluate and utilize these particular Confirmation Signals. They are:

1. Premiums

2. Fundamentals

3. Commitments of Traders

Premiums are sometimes referred to as "Premium Spread Analysis," and this type of analysis actually uses technical data as a way of interpreting the underlying fundamental forces in the market place for any given commodity. When more distant contract months for any commodity are selling at a price higher than the nearby months, we refer to these distant months as selling at a "premium" over the nearby months. Some writers refer to this as a

"Bullish Divergence," but we prefer to call this situation "Positivity." An example of this is shown below, as well as its counterpart, "Negativity."

PLATINUM (NYM)–50 troy oz.; $ per troy oz.

Oct	319.00	319.50	318.00	319.00 –	.60	463.00	316.50	492
Dec	325.00	325.00	324.00	322.00 –	.60	337.50	324.00	1
Jan85	328.50	328.50	325.10	327.00 –	.80	447.00	324.00	10,079
Apr	337.50	337.50	334.50	335.80 –	.90	447.50	333.50	3,861
July	343.50	344.50	343.50	344.70 –	.90	449.50	343.50	1,019
Oct	354.00	354.00	354.00	353.70 –	.90	393.00	353.00	376
Jan86	....	....	....	363.20 –	.90	373.50	370.00	13

Est vol 1,043; vol Fri 1,831; open int 15,841, +578.

POSITIVITY

COFFEE (CSCE)–37,500 lbs.; cents per lb.

Dec	134.10	134.40	133.80	134.38 +	.05	154.50	116.40	5,085
Mar85	133.15	133.75	133.00	133.63 +	.16	153.50	123.50	3,276
May	132.25	133.00	132.25	132.97 +	.32	152.00	122.01	1,229
July	131.60	132.20	131.60	132.04 +	.24	149.20	121.00	659
Sept	130.50	130.50	130.50	130.88 +	.38	147.50	127.00	460
Dec	129.90	130.00	129.60	129.63 +	.13	141.00	129.25	133
Mar86	....	....	....	128.63 –	.37	130.50	130.50	1

Est vol 856; vol Fri 1,194; open int 10,843, –22.

NEGATIVITY

Negativity, shown in the right example, has the near month selling at a premium--i.e., at higher price--than the more distant months. We refer to this as situation as Negativity.

When the more distant months are selling at a premium over the nearby months--in other words, they are exhibiting Positivity--it means that the large commercial traders, who generally have an excellent or at least above-average feel for the ultimate direction of the market, have concluded that there will be, for whatever fundamental reasons, a shortage of that particular commodity in the more distant future. As a result of this conclusion on their part, they are indicating to us that there is an excellent likelihood of an ensuing Bull market in the future. While this in and of itself does not indicate the time window for the beginning of a Bull market, the Big Move trader is well advised to consider entering long positions only when such Positivity is in evidence.

The converse is also true in that most major Bear markets are preceded by some exhibition of Negativity--i.e., the nearby months are selling at higher prices than the more distant months. This means that the large commercial traders believe that while they have an immediate need for the commodity in question and are willing to pay a premium price for the nearby or spot contract months, they have concluded that, for whatever fundamental reasons, prices for the given commodity are going to be lower in the future. Again, while this does not indicate exactly when a Bull market is going to turn and head down, the Big Move trader is well advised here, too, not to enter short positions in a Bull market unless such Negativity in the price spread is apparent <u>or</u> the other Confirmation Signals are so strong that a particular market may be an exception to these premium analysis rules.

Our analysis and research has indicated that more than 70% of all major market turns--whether ensuing Bull markets or Bear markets--have been preceded by this type of Positivity or Negativity. As with all the other Confirmation Signals, premium analysis is but one weapon in your arsenal of predictive signals.

Our approach in Big Move trading to using Fundamental Analysis will be somewhat different than most typical approaches to this subject matter. Conventional Fundamental Analysis concentrates on such supply-demand figures as the actual supply and demand statistics, comparison of present prices to past prices under similar conditions, domestic government programs, general deflationary and inflationary tendencies, international commodity agreements and price cartels, labor union considerations, political considerations and the like. We will be more interested in a very broad approach to utilizing Fundamental Analysis as a part of our Big Move trading program.

Instead of comparing supply and demand statistics to determine whether there will be a shortage or a surplus of a commodity and then positioning ourselves appropriately in the markets, we will instead concentrate on some of the other areas of Fundamental Analysis mentioned above. The type of factors that we will be considering are what we define in our earlier book, <u>THE TAURUS METHOD</u>, as "Sudden Fundamental Changes."

While we definitely believe that detailed Fundamental Analysis of supply-demand figures and study of all of the other factors that go into an exacting and rigorous Fundamental Analysis are the optimum way of utilizing fundamentals in Big Move trading, we also realize that the average Big Move trader has neither the time nor the resources available to him to actually perform this type of Fundamental Analysis. Hence we will instead concentrate on approaching Fundamental Analysis for a Big Move trading program in the light of these Sudden Fundamental Changes. Let us point out, however, if the reader does have the time and resources available to him to actually do that very precise type of Fundamental Analysis, then by all means he should do so since this will improve his overall Big Move trading program results to at least a noticeable degree.

We have found the best sources for information on these Sudden Fundamental Changes to be the ones listed in Appendix E of this book--one of which is available on a daily basis and the other of which is available on a weekly basis.

The Big Move trader must be careful to differentiate between Sudden Fundamental Changes which are truly significant to a Big Move trading program and those Sudden Fundamental Changes which would be more appropriate to a Short- or Intermediate-Term trading program. For example, it frequently will be mentioned in one of these sources of fundamental information that a particular market will be either up or down on a given day or during a given week due to an anticipated period of dry weather or wet weather, or to daily or weekly slaughterings, or to some such other reason. While this kind of fundamental information may very well indicate the trend of the market over the next few days or even a couple of weeks, for our overall purposes of catching Big Moves, this is not the type of Sudden Fundamental Change information we are looking for. We must point out, however, that these short-term Sudden Fundamental Changes can be useful in determining Stop Placement and Entry and Exit Points because they give a good indication of the short-term direction of the market.

What we are looking for instead in our Big Move program as a Confirmation Signal is a Sudden Fundamental Change which will have a Long-Term effect on the market. Examples of these types of changes would include such items as grain embargoes, unexpected and apparently protracted strikes, an unexpected war, the intensification of a drought situation and sudden flooding. Perhaps the best recent example would be the canker disease affecting orange trees in Florida.

Since the average Big Move trader will not be utilizing precise and detailed supply-demand statistics as a Confirmation Signal and instead will be using these Sudden Fundamental Changes, this particular Confirmation Signal will not always be present one way or the other. As an example of how the Big Move trader might utilize a Sudden Fundamental Change situation as a Confirmation Signal for the establishment of a long position, let us say that our analysis of the Copper market indicates that it may very well be bottoming due to the fact that many of the other Confirmation Signals appear to indicate an upward turn in prices. We would consider a Bullish Confirmation Signal as a Sudden Fundamental Change if, for example, there were a bill pending to restrict imports of Copper into this country and the news media was indicating that Congress would most likely pass the bill. This would be a Sudden Fundamental Change of a very Bullish nature; a confirmation of this, which would be sudden, would be the actual passage of the bill and the signing of it into law.

An example of a Sudden Fundamental Change of a Bearish nature would be if Copper were trading at relatively high historic price levels and a number of our other Confirmation Signals indicated that the Bull market were getting ready to turn and then, in the fundamental arena, the United Auto Workers announced their intention to strike one or more of the major automotive manufactures, or a government report came out indicating a significant slowdown in the economy or in construction, or if the government suddenly announced a program to permit increased importation of Copper from foreign countries. Any of these types of Sudden Fundamental Changes would be another strong Confirmation Signal to establish short postions for a Big Move downward in prices.

A salient point needs to be made here, and that is that there are certain times when it is important to completely disregard Sudden Fundamental Changes. When any particular commodity is trading at historically high or low price levels, and, in the case of high price levels, a Sudden Fundamental Change occurs that is of a Bullish nature, this Sudden Fundamental Change should be ignored completely and not taken as an indication that short positions should not be established. Conversely, when the market is trading at historically low price levels and a Sudden Fundamental Change of a Bearish nature is announced, the Big Move trader should not let this deter him from establishing long positions. These apparent contradictions are due to the fact that, typically, when markets are at historically high or low price levels, such Sudden Fundamental Changes have little, if any, bearing on these markets' continuing on their present price course. Nor do these situations imply that any particular market is about to reverse its price direction. Instead, these types of Sudden Fundamental Changes in the apparent direction of the historic high or low price levels are, in effect, totally neutral, based upon our experience.

The last of our nine Confirmation Signals is the Commitments of Traders factor. This tool gives us the holdings of large and small traders and whether they are long or short and the change from the preceding month. This information is made available as of the last day of every calendar month of the year, and it is published by at least two of our recommended sources of information listed in Appendix E. The illustration below shows one such table from one of these sources:

COMMITMENTS OF TRADERS—LARGE HEDGERS, SPECULATORS AND SMALL TRADERS
Open Interest Positions Shown in Percent (Rounded) as of January 31, 1984

	LARGE HEDGERS				LARGE SPECULATORS				SMALL TRADERS			
MARKETS	Long	Short	Net	Δ	Long	Short	Net	Δ	Long	Short	Net	Δ
Cattle (Live)	22	32	-10	+11	6	6	0	-12	67	57	+10	+2
Cocoa	62	62	0	+20	12	23	-11	-18	23	13	+10	-3
Coffee	44	60	-16	-13	13	7	+6	+6	40	30	+10	+7
Copper	38	72	-34	+3	9	15	-6	-3	51	12	+39	-1
Corn	57	49	+8	+7	2	6	-4	-3	39	43	-4	-4
Cotton	46	49	-3	+6	6	9	-3	+3	44	38	+6	-10
Crude Oil (N.Y.)	78	66	+12	+4	3	5	-2	+4	16	25	-9	-8
Gold (Comex)	62	58	+4	0	4	7	-3	+4	24	26	-2	-4
Heating Oil #2	54	49	+5	+1	13	10	+3	+3	29	37	-8	-4
Hogs	11	18	-7	-4	14	16	-2	-12	66	58	+8	+14
Leaded Gas (N.Y.)	69	76	-7	+4	5	6	-1	-6	23	16	+7	+1
Lumber	18	16	+2	+4	7	20	-13	-3	71	60	+11	0
Oats	15	67	-52	-5	1	3	-2	-1	85	30	+55	+7
Orange Juice	38	44	-6	+44	14	9	+5	-7	45	44	+1	-37
Platinum	29	70	-41	-5	21	7	+14	+5	49	22	+27	0
Pork Bellies	6	17	-11	-2	22	18	+4	+9	52	45	+7	-6
Silver (Comex)	34	50	-16	+4	8	8	0	+2	45	29	+16	-6
Soybeans	37	49	-12	+6	4	4	0	-8	49	37	+12	+2
Soybean Meal	47	59	-12	+12	4	6	-2	-11	42	29	+13	-2
Soybean Oil	50	60	-10	+12	6	4	+2	-9	38	29	+9	-2
Sugar "11"	47	75	-28	0	14	8	+6	-2	37	15	+22	+3
Wheat (CHI)	28	44	-16	-18	8	13	-5	-14	58	38	+20	-4
Wheat (K.C.)	68	52	+16	-3	6	4	+2	0	25	42	-17	+5
Wheat (Minn)	48	56	-8	+16	*	*	-5	-6	52	44	+8	-11
Ginnie Maes	56	64	-8	-11	11	7	+4	+10	21	17	+4	+1
T-Bills (90 Days)	37	66	-29	-2	26	4	+22	+3	27	19	+8	+1
T-Bonds	46	61	-15	-4	9	4	+5	-1	31	21	+10	+4
NYSE Composite	11	26	-15	+4	20	23	-3	-5	62	43	+19	+2
S&P 500	28	39	-11	-4	25	30	-5	-4	45	29	+16	+9
Value Line	2	6	-4	+1	7	29	-22	-20	85	59	+26	+19
British Pound	42	40	+2	-15	22	28	-6	+19	36	32	+4	-4
Deutsche Mark	17	46	-29	-3	21	20	+1	+8	59	32	+27	-6
Japanese Yen	19	61	-42	+35	29	20	+9	-19	51	17	+34	-15
Swiss Franc	20	38	-18	+27	14	31	-17	-14	57	20	+37	-11

As a rule of thumb, the Big Move trader can assume that the large traders are more frequently correct in their positions than the small traders, especially from a Long-Range standpoint. Since it is a well-validated fact that more than 90% of all traders lose money in the commodity markets and since the bulk of the trading public is composed of small traders, it is not only fair, but also accurate, to assume that the small traders are wrong much more frequently than they are right, while the large traders, who most likely comprise no more that 10% of the overall trading public, are right much more frequently than they are wrong about future market direction.

Using the Commitments of Traders for Short-Term trading is virtually useless, especially since these figures are reported only once a month. So, for our purposes, we will use only the middle column of the Commitments of Traders table as illustrated--the columns for Large Speculators. These columns not only show the relative proportion of how many large speculators are long as compared to how many are short and the difference between the two, but also provide a Delta figure indicating the change from the preceding month.

The important things to look for here are: If the Net column and Delta figure column are both negative and our other signals are indicating that a Bull market or a trading-range market is about to turn down, then these negative figures in the Net and Delta figure columns are indicative of a further Confirmation Signal that, in fact, we are correct in establishing Big Move short positions. On the other hand, if the Net and Delta figure columns are both positive and our other Confirmation Signals indicate to us that a Bear market or a trading-range market is about to turn up, then this data from the large speculators' positioning in the Commitments of Traders figures gives us one more validation that we are most likely correct in establishing our Big Move long positions.

We have seen some data from subscribers to our newsletters to indicate that it may be possible to trade a Big Move trading program solely on the basis of using the approach just outlined from the Commitments of Traders data. While we have not had sufficient time to determine whether this, in fact, is possible or not, and while our approach is to utilize the Commitments of Traders figures in conjunction with our other Confirmation Signals, this feedback from our subscribers serves to illustrate the importance of this Confirmation Signal to the trader as part of his approach to his Big Move trading program.

* * * * *

This completes our examination of Confirmation Signals, and while to some it may appear that our approach has been of a cursory nature, let us emphasis that this is in keeping with our overall philosophy of trying to make our Big Move trading program analysis as simple as possible, while at the same time keeping it as valid as possible. While there will always be exceptions to every rule, a good approach for a trader to use in his Big Move trading program is to insist that as many Confirmation Signals as possible be positive and in the direction in which he is considering establishing his Big Move positions. A good rule of thumb would be to require that a minimum of four or five--depending upon the fundamental situation--Confirmation Signals actually confirm that a change in trend is, in fact, getting ready to take place. By locating commodities which are trading at historic high, historic low or at mid-range price levels and then by utilizing these Confirmation Signals to validate that a change in direction is, in fact, imminent, the Big Move trader has a potent set of tools at his fingertips with which to approach the markets. And it is a set of tools which does not require an exorbitant amount of time to utilize.

We will now proceed to examine in the next chapter exactly how the Big Move trader determines his Entry Point for each position, his Initial Protective Stops and his Trailing Stops.

CHAPTER 8

ENTRY POINTS AND STOPS

One of the most important parts of any trading program--whether a Big Move trading program or one of a shorter-term variety--is knowing where to enter the market. The reader may think at this point that by following the Confirmation Signals discussed in the preceding three chapters and by having a sufficient number of these signals indicating a change in the market direction, he can then enter the market for a profitable Big Move trade. This is, to some degree, true. When a majority--or at least four of the nine Confirmation Signals--indicate an imminent change in market direction, a trader can almost leap into the market right away. But to precipitously get into any market in this manner may very well increase the trader's risk and/or decrease his potential profits sufficiently to necessitate his utilization of more exact market entry methods.

While there are many techniques to determine market Entry Points--a large number of which were listed and discussed in THE TAURUS METHOD--in our desire to keep our Big Move trading program approach as simple as possible, we will list and examine only those methods which are the simplest to use, while at the same time being the most effective. We realize that many sophisticated traders will opt instead to use their own entry methodology, whether it be a weighted moving average method, an optimized point and figure technique, or whatever else they feel most comfortable with. The three market entry techniques, however, that we are about to discuss are, in our estimation, as reliable as those methods which require infinitely more time and patience.

We hope the reader does not feel cheated by the simplicity of these entry techniques, since it would be very simple for us to use instead a very complicated mathematical formula of some sort that, while it might seem very impressive, would not add anything to the reader's Big Move trading program and would instead cost him an inordinate amount of time to use.

There is a trade-off of sorts between these three different ways of entering market positions for Big Move trades. Each one of these techniques involves differing amounts of risk and differing probabilities of the trade's being successful--i.e., having the trend actually reverse in major direction. The method with the least amount of initial risk--assuming that the Big Move trader uses our techniques for placing Initial Protective Stops--at the same time has the lowest probability of indicating a valid turn in market direction. The technique which has the highest probability of indicating a complete major market reversal at the same time entails the greatest amount of risk between the trader's Entry Point and his Initial Protective Stop. Many readers may choose to use the method of selecting their Entry Points which is a compromise between the two extremes; this will give them the median amount of risk and probability of success.

In our attempt to keep our approach to Big Move trading as simple as possible, we could have chosen to have gone only with this compromise method, but due to the differing personalities of traders, we felt it best to give all three approaches to market entry. This, in itself, is our own compromise between going with one technique or describing well over a dozen different other market entry techniques.

First, we will discuss this median technique. It should be noted at this point, however, that all three techniques are based upon our original premises that the commodity under study is either at historical high, historical low or mid-range price levels and that at least four or five of the Confirmation Signals are calling for a turn in market direction. Without market price levels meeting one of these three requirements and also without a sufficient number of favorable Confirmation Signals, the market should not even be under consideration in the first place as a potential Big Move trade.

The median technique consists of entering positions when the approximate four-week cyclic low (in the case of markets which appear to be topping out) or approximate four-week cycle high (in the case of markets which appear to be bottoming out) is violated. We say approximate four-week cycle high or low because this is the approximation of the short-term cycle and, when it is violated, this connotes a fairly reliable probability of a change in major market direction.

Earlier in this text when we were discussing cycles, we urged the reader to keep track of cycles on his own charts rather than use published cyclical data for Short- and Intermediate-Term Cycles, due to their fluctuation from quarter to quarter and year to year. What last year may have been a short-term seven-week cycle in Cattle may this year be a four- or five-week short-term cycle in Cattle. So it is important for the Big Move trader to keep track of what the approximate Short-Term Cycle is for each commodity which he has under evaluation.

The following graph shows an example for instituting both a Long-Range Bull position and a Long-Range Bear position utilizing the Short-Term Cyclical Technique:

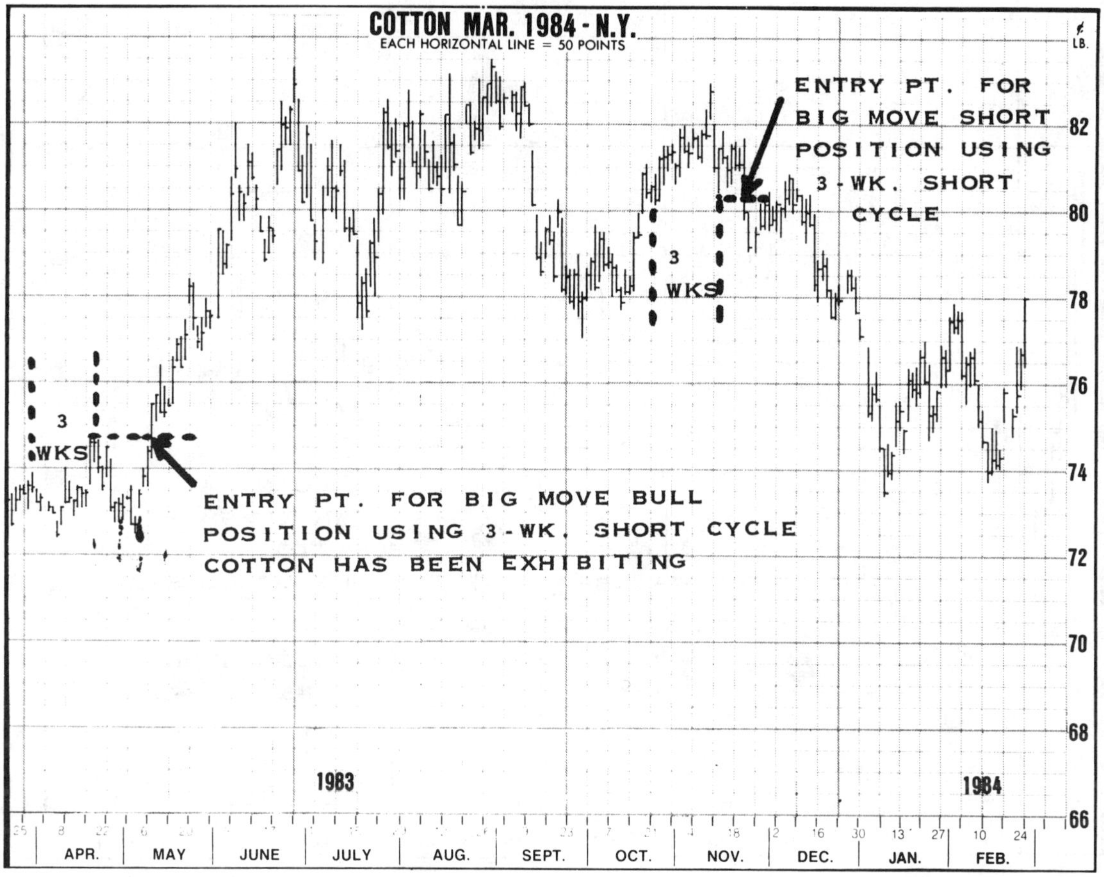

The next method consists of entering the market when there is a violation of an eight-week cyclical high or low--in effect, the "next back" short-term cyclical high or low. When this high or low is violated, the probabilities increase tremendously that the major trend of the market has, in fact, reversed.

But, as can be seen in the following example, using the same chart as for the previous method, substantial profits are lost and initial risk is greatly increased by using this technique, even though the probability of success, percentage-wise, is vastly increased:

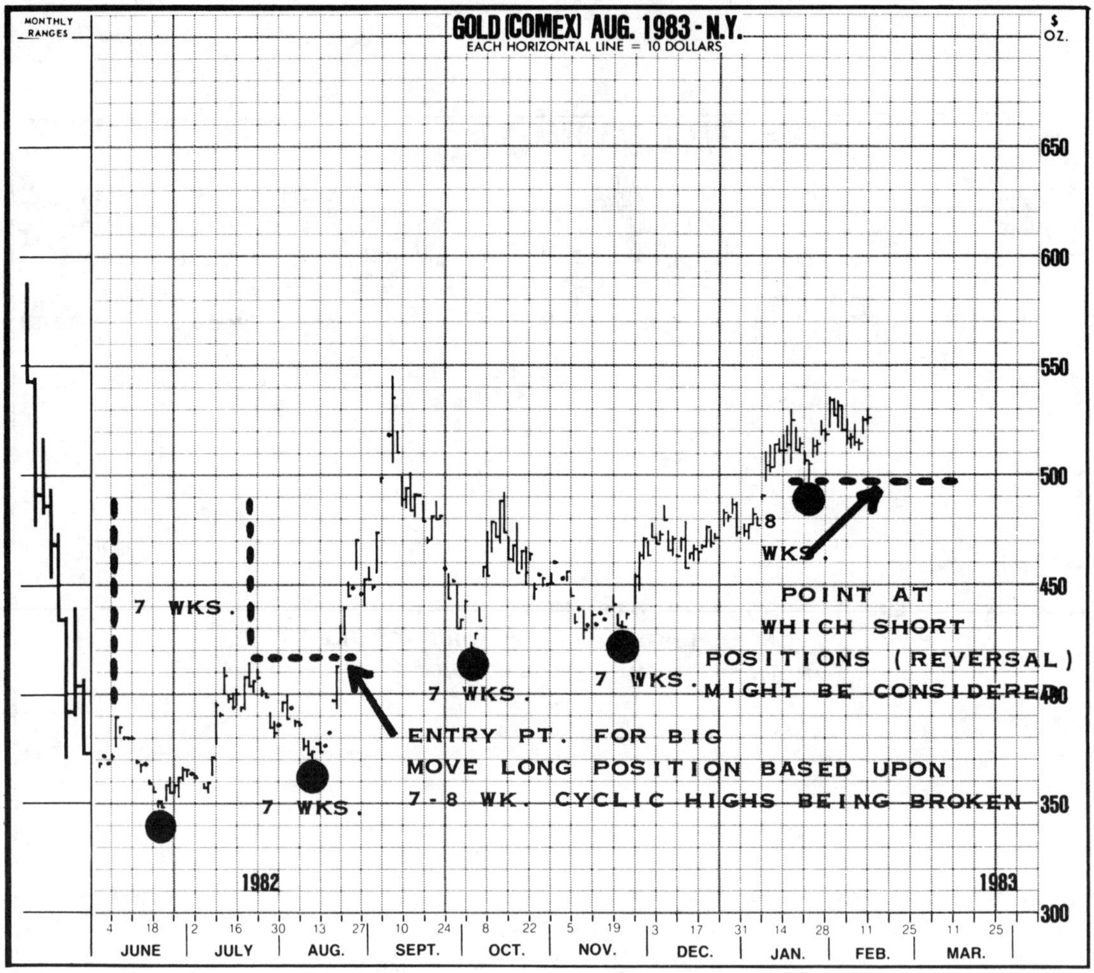

The method with the least amount of dollar risk but also the lowest probability of success--although the probability, generally, is high enough to justify considering using this technique--is the Short-Term Trendline Method. In this technique, the Short-Term Cycle lows (in the case of a rising market) or the Short-Term Cycle highs (in the case of a falling market) are connected by a trendline. Where this trendline would be broken is considered to be the Entry Point for the position. Generally, in a Bull market the trendlines will be of an ever-increasing slope as the market explodes upwards, while in a market which is bottoming, this technique is far less useful since most market bottoms do not occur in a spike fashion as is frequently the case with Bull markets when they are topping out. The reader, of course, can speculate on using an eight-week trendline, which merely serves to illustrate that there are an infinite number of possibilities for developing market entry techniques.

Again, we have limited ourselves to the three techniques which seem to work best, although this last technique does not work particularly well when a market is bottoming. An example of this technique is shown in the following graph:

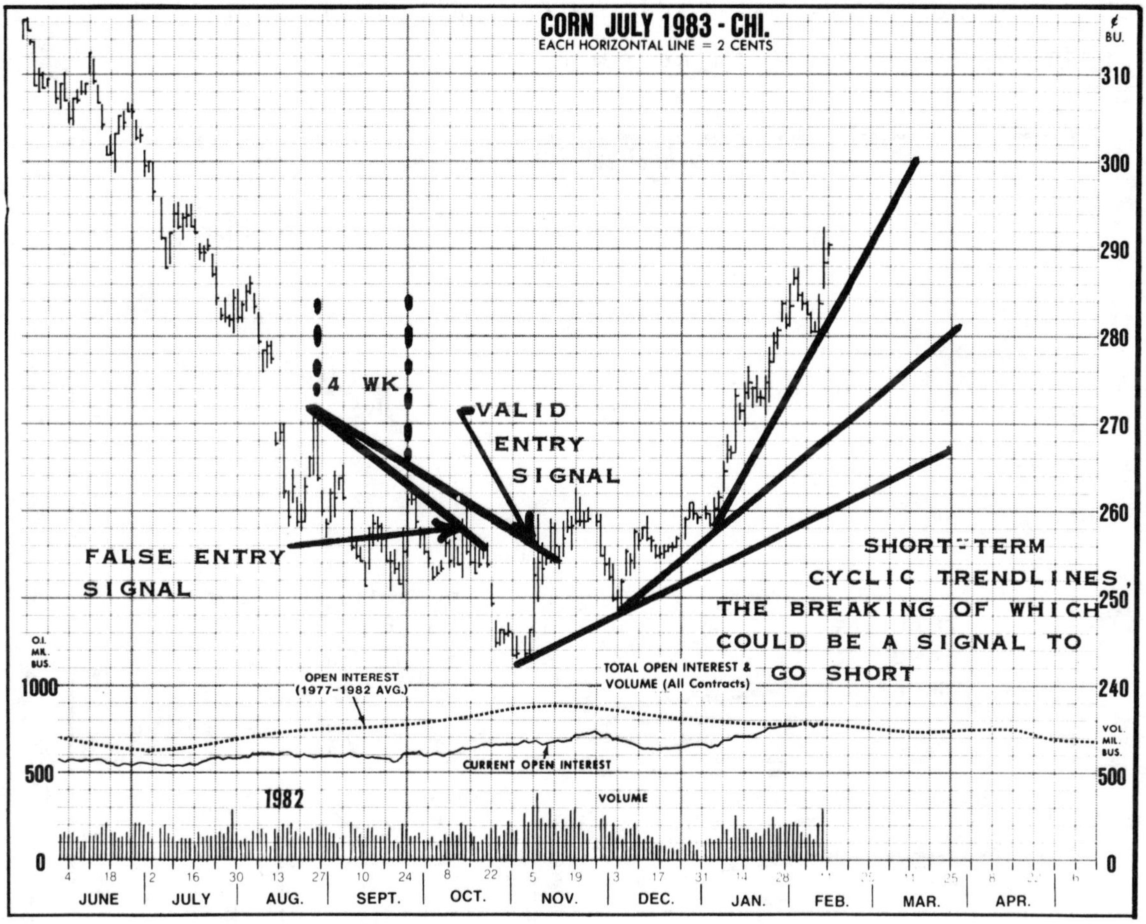

There is one other market entry technique which, typically, will rarely be used when a market is topping out. Generally, this technique is most advantageous when a market is trading at a mid-range price level or is bottoming. This is what we refer to as the Trading Range Method, in which the Entry Point is placed just beyond the extremes of the trading range itself. A trading range, by definition, is a relatively compressed, lateral price motion. Here, perhaps more than anywhere else, the use of our Confirmation Signals is of utmost importance, because trading range patterns frequently are violated briefly by false signals, only to turn and reverse themselves then and break out of the trading range in the opposite direction. An example of such a Trading Range Entry Point is given below. Generally, we have found that for Big Move trades, a minimum of five weeks--and preferably at least eight weeks--of such sideways trading range action is required to constitute a genuine trading range formation:

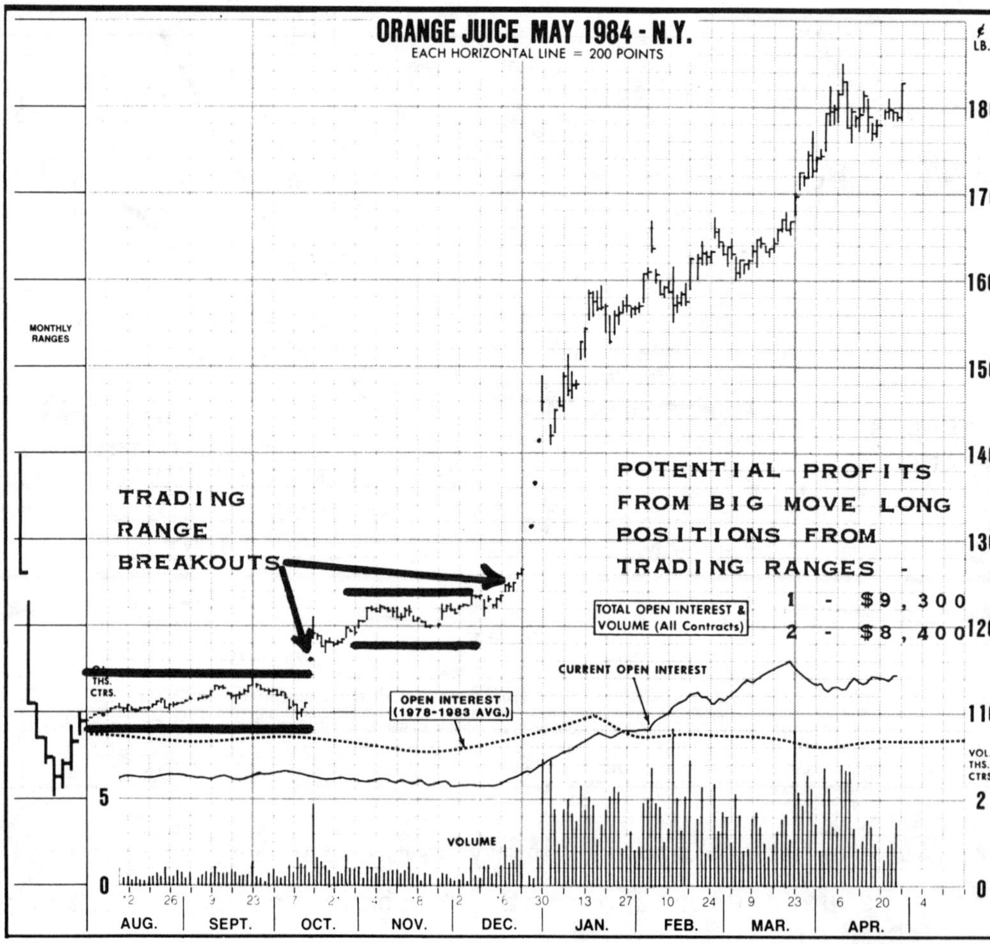

We could provide illustrations showing false signals for all three types of Entry Points, but due to space considerations in this volume, we will leave it to the reader to look at his own charts and see how frequently these false signals do appear. These false signals can be avoided to a great degree by properly utilizing our Confirmation Signals, as we have been discussing.

We now move from Entry Points to placement of Initial Protective Stops.

As with initial Entry Points, the placement of Initial Protective Stops varies in the amount of dollar risk and probability of success. A general rule is: The greater the amount of initial dollar risk required, the higher the probability that the Initial Protective Stop will be placed at a point which will not be violated by corrective market action.

As with original Entry Points, there are three basic techniques for establishing Initial Protective Stops. While the technique involving the greatest amount of dollar risk does offer the greatest probability of success, it may not suit the tastes of all Big Move traders; hence, we will examine all three of these techniques. Also, as with original Entry Points, these are only three of literally dozens of methods of establishing Initial Protective Stops. But these are the simplest, most useful and most highly reliable methods that we have found to be the most advantageous in a Big Move trading program.

The safest--yet most risky dollar-wise--method is to place the Initial Protective Stop beyond the end point of the move--i.e., if a market appears to be topping out, place the Initial Protective Stop just a tick beyond the highest point which prices have reached in the move; and if a market appears to be bottoming out, place the Initial Protective Stop just a tick below the lowest point which the market has reached.

An example of this is given in the following graph:

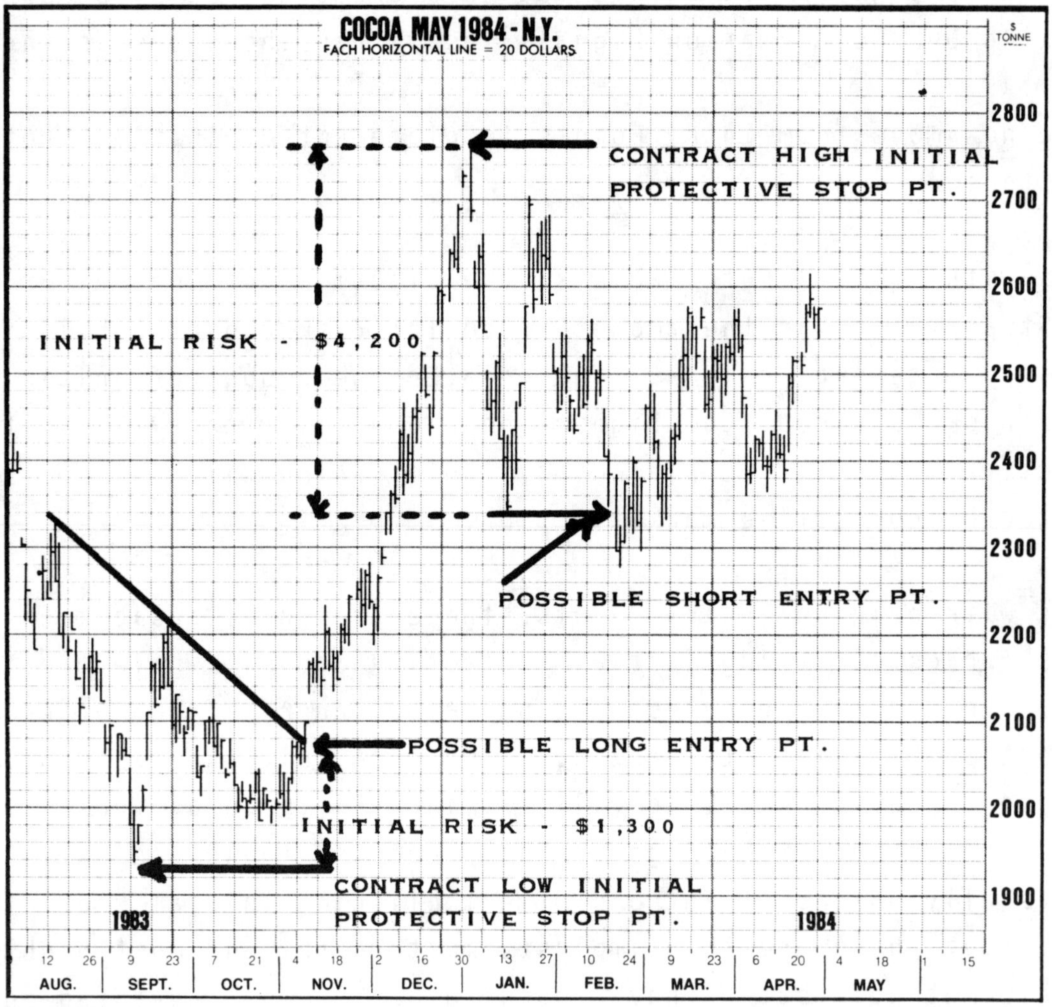

The second method--which involves the least initial dollar risk, but also stands the greatest probability of being stopped out due to a whipsaw or a corrective market price action--is to place the Initial Protective Stops a tick beyond a trendline drawn connecting the short-term (or approximate four-week) cyclical highs or lows.

An example of this is given in the following illustration, using the same graph as for the previous method:

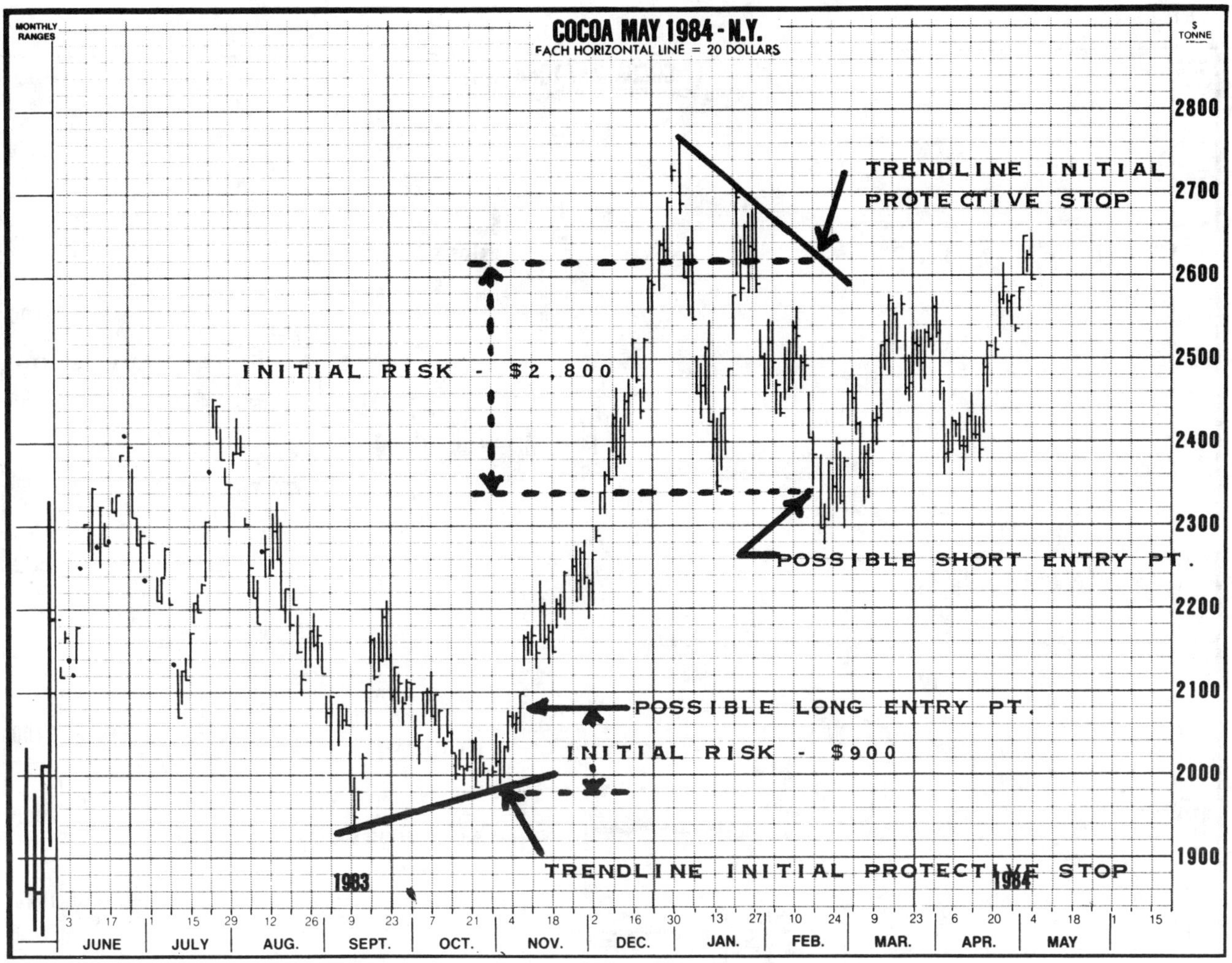

The last method of Initial Protective Stop placement we will consider is again a "compromise" method. It involves placing the Initial Protective Stops a tick beyond the most nearby short-term or <u>very</u> short-term (possibly one or two weeks) cyclical low or high.

Again, we will use the same graph we did for the previous examples in order to illustrate this technique and to show the differing amount of initial dollar risk. All three Initial

Protective Stops would have been successful in this illustration, but the relative probability of the trendline method typically is the least successful, although the illustration does not show this.

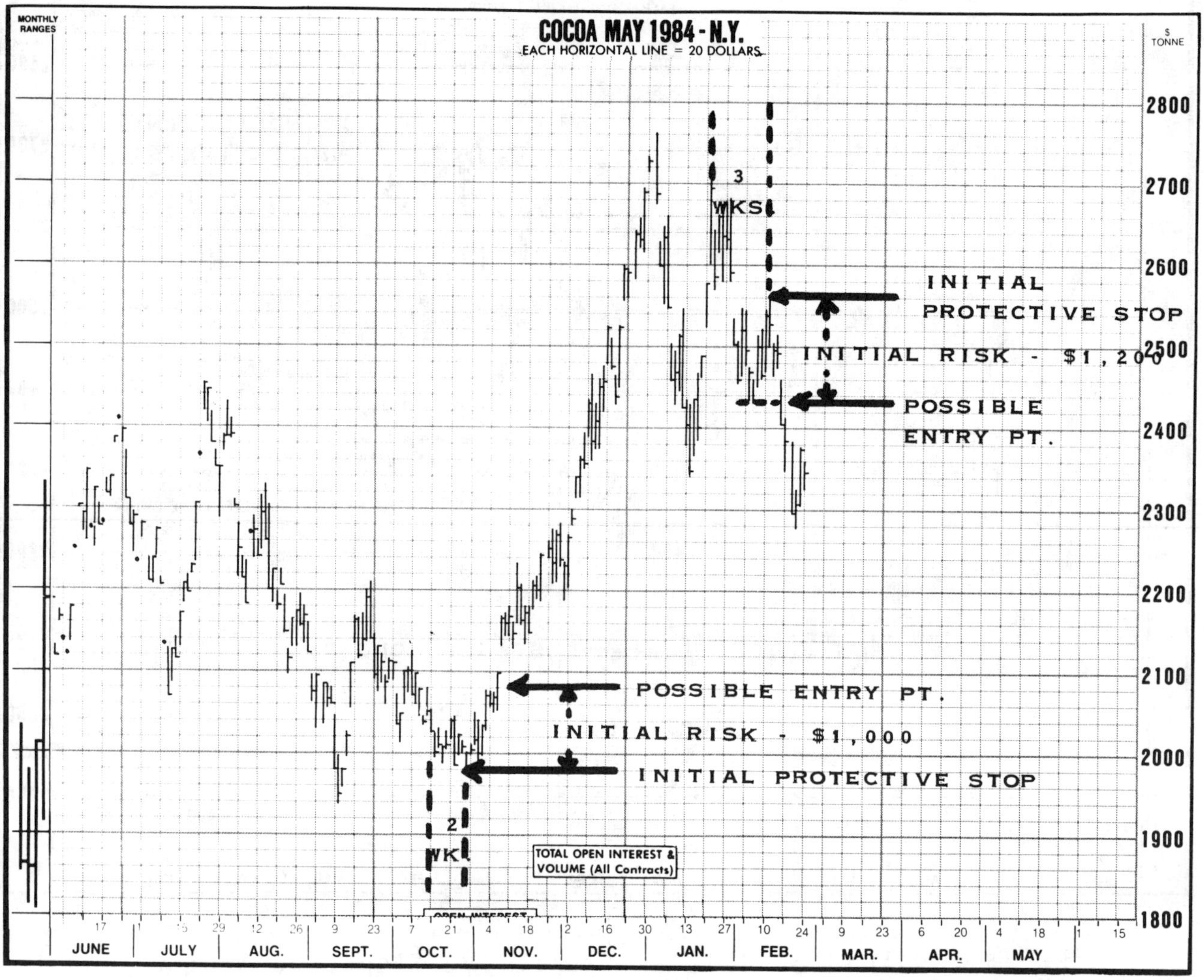

We will proceed now to examining how the Big Move trader might best trail, or move, his stops after achieving entry and after prices have moved sufficiently far enough that it appears his Initial Protective Stop can safely be moved in the direction of the price move. His aim is to move his stops initially to a break-even point and then to start locking in profits. The next chapter on targets will illustrate how Trailing Stops are moved in more closely as it appears the particular price move is reaching its climax.

As with Original Entry Points and Initial Protective Stops, there are literally dozens of techniques which a trader can use to trail his Protective Stops. We have found, however, that it is best to select and stay with one particular method--whether it be the method as we will discuss in the upcoming paragraphs and illustrations or the trader's own favorite method of trailing stops. The reason for this is for the trader to develop some sort of consistency in his Trailing Stop placement instead of switching from one technique to another. By staying with one method of Trailing Stops, the trader will gain a kind of "averaging-out" which takes place over a period of time, providing him with substantially greater profits in the long run.

Statistically, we have found that it is most advantageous for a trader to move his stops as close as possible to the break-even point (the Original Entry Point) as soon as possible once a new short-term (approximate four-week) cyclical low or high point is established.

Once prices have moved beyond a trader's Original Entry Point, the market has had a correction and a new short-term cyclical low (in the case of his having a long position) or high (in the case of his having a short position) has been established, then the trader should move his stops at least to the break-even point or to a tick beyond the short-term cyclical low or high.

An illustration will help the reader to understand this procedure:

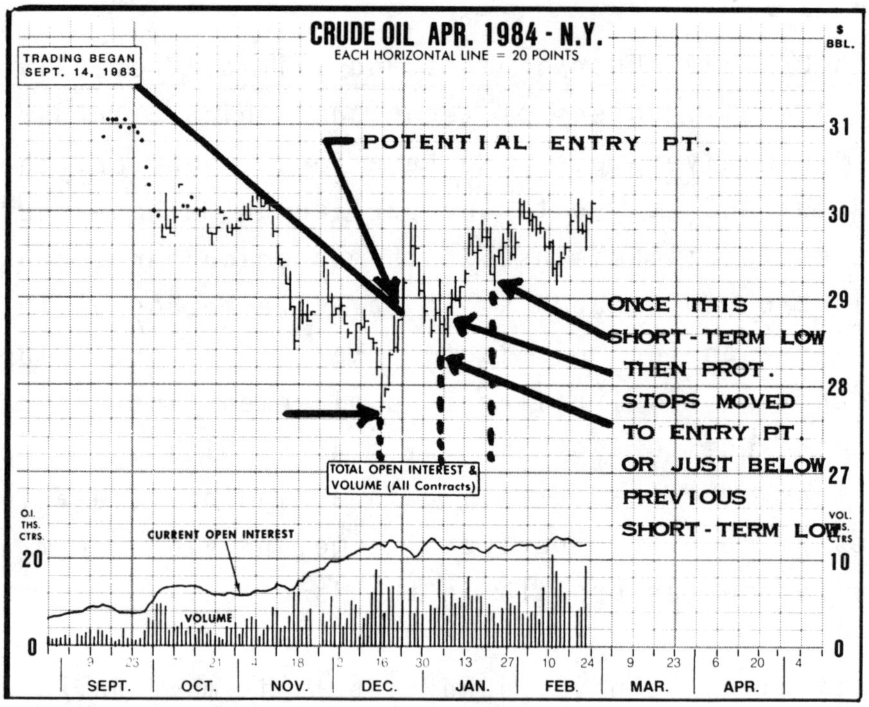

While it is true that sometimes a market correction may carry prices back to this break-even point and stop the position out, statistically this happens infrequently enough that it is judicious for the trader to eliminate his initial dollar risk by getting his stops to this break-even point by using the procedure just outlined.

After the trader has moved his stops to this break-even point, he has two major techniques for subsequently trailing his stops until the general Target Area is approached.

As with the techniques for Original Entry Point and Initial Protective Stop placement, these two techniques for trailing stops after the break-even point has been reached vary in the amount of profits they lock in relative to the amount of risk the trader exposes himself to by a potential market correction's taking him out of his position. We will discuss both techniques--although we prefer one over the other and we will point out which one--again because we realize that different traders have different philosophies and personalities and will prefer one technique over the other.

The first technique for trailing stops, after the break-even point has been reached, is the one which we prefer. It involves moving stops a tick beyond the approximate eight-week cyclical low or high points throughout the duration of the price move. It could be argued that the short-term (approximate four-week) cyclical high and low points could be used, but we have found by experience that these points are violated frequently enough to justify using the approximate eight-week high and low points for trailing our Protective Stops. The following illustration shows this technique:

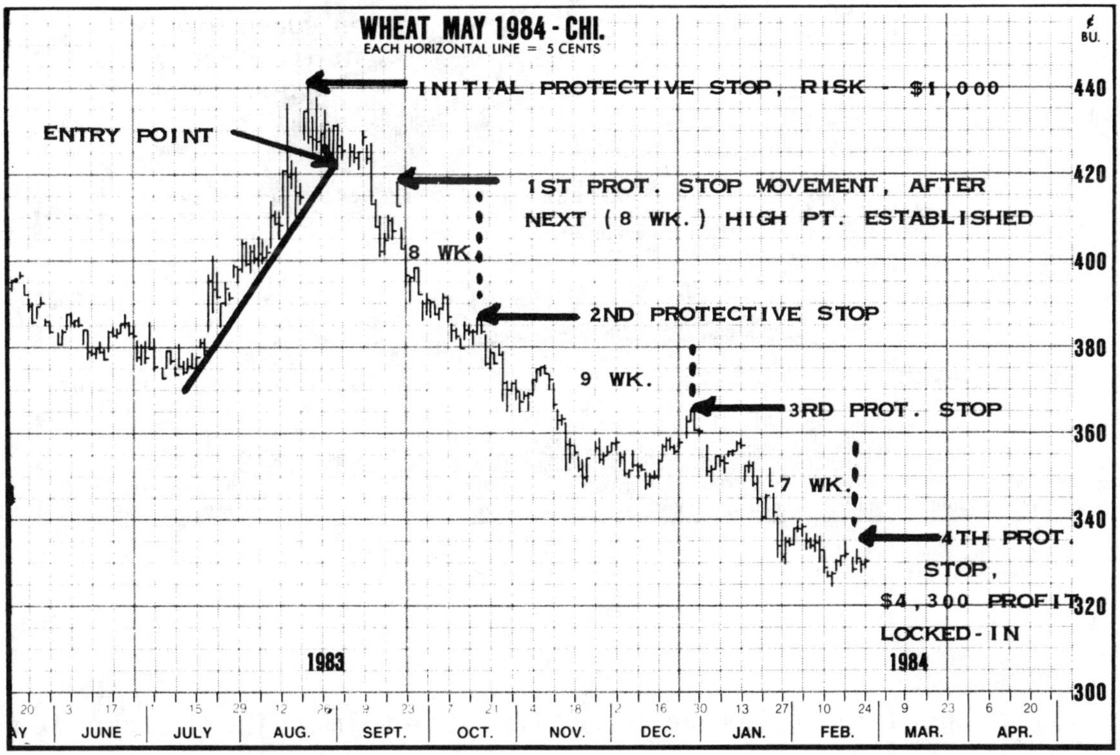

The other technique for trailing stops involves keeping them just beyond the trendline. The trendline can be constructed by using either the approximate four-week or approximate eight-week cyclical low or high points, and if we were compelled to use a trendline technique for trailing our stops, we would construct the trendline along the approximate eight-week cyclical high or low points, rather than use a trendline connecting the approximate four-week cyclical high or low points.

An example of the technique of using the trendline approach is shown below:

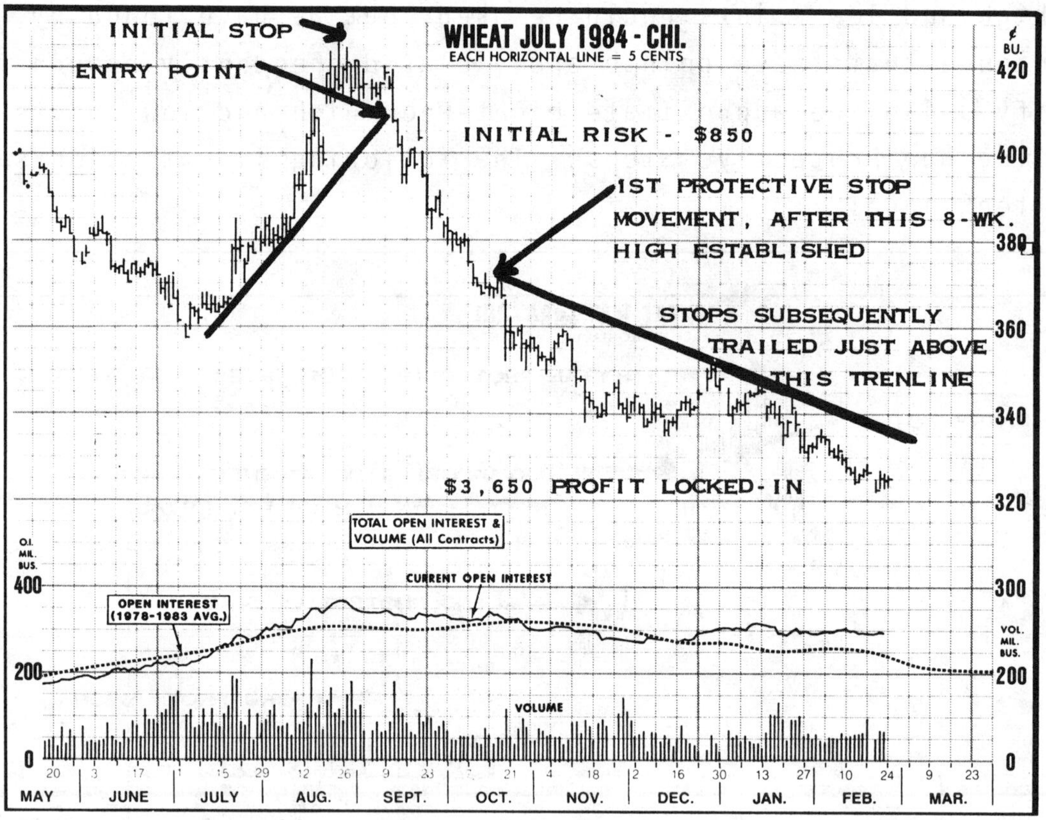

* * * * *

While the techniques we have discussed in this chapter for establishing Original Entry Points, Initial Protective Stop Points and Trailing Stop Points may seem somewhat simplistic to the reader, it has been our experience that in these areas--as well as in most areas of commodity trading--overcomplicating trading methodology does not necessarily, and generally does not, improve trading performance results. We urge the reader to keep an open mind and not reject this methodology because of its apparent simplicity.

The techniques discussed in this chapter work--and they work extremely well--when they are followed as described, requiring only a minimum amount of judgment on the part of the trader.

CHAPTER 9

TARGET SELECTION

The general philosophy behind Target Selection is for the Big Move trader to be able to determine several factors before he even establishes himself in a Big Move position. One such factor concerns the time frame. The time frame factor will indicate to the Big Move trader approximately how long he can expect to have his money tied up in a particular trade or how long it will be before he will need to pay extremely close attention to the position. Equally important is Risk-Reward analysis, whereby when he has an idea of the Target Area to which prices have a high probability of moving, the Big Move trader can determine whether or not the potential profit between his potential Original Entry Point and the Target Area is sufficiently great to justify his initial dollar risk. Also by having at least an approximate idea of the amount of profit potential, based upon the estimated Target Area, the Big Move Trader may choose--if the profit potential is sufficiently large--to utilize a more conservative (higher initial dollar risk) Initial Protective Stop point. Conversely, if the Target Area indicates that the potential profit is of a relatively lesser amount, then the Big Move trader will most likely go with such an Initial Protective Stop technique--as discussed in the preceding chapter--as a trendline technique to reduce his initial dollar risk, thereby improving his Risk-Reward Ratio.

Probably no area of commodity analysis is more difficult than establishing Target Areas. Over the past decades, we have examined literally dozens of Target Area selection techniques, attempting to find either the optimum method or some combination of methods which would work most efficaciously or to find different methods which would work best for different markets or in different market situations. Unfortunately, we have been able to find no better methods than the ones we outline in this chapter, which are, however, in keeping with our philosophy of keeping our approach to Big Move trading as simple as possible.

The techniques we will outline appear to be very simple, and they are. As with our other methodology, however, the reader should keep foremost in his mind that overcomplicating methodology in any area of commodity analysis does not necessarily improve a trader's results. Generally, such overcomplication not only reduces a trader's year-end profits, but also exerts excessive stress upon the trader and gives him the proclivity to alter his methodology as time goes by instead of keeping it standardized with a simple approach.

Our basic premise in establishing Target Areas in a Big Move trading program is: While prices will not always do so, they have the greatest probability of at least approaching significant historical resistance and support levels as seen on weekly or monthly charts. While these historical support and resistance areas are frequently penetrated and the move extends beyond these points, these Target Areas provide enough of a guideline that Protective Stops can be moved in more closely as these levels are approached and broken through. So if, in fact, new historical highs or lows are set beyond the significant historical support and resistance levels, the Big Move trader frequently can stay in these moves until new historical highs or lows are established and the market reverses itself, stopping him out with substantial profits.

We frequently are asked why we do not just take our profits when prices reach these Target Areas instead of trailing our stops insofar as prices often bounce off these historical levels and stop our moves out with profits less--sometimes substantially less--than they would be if we had closed our positions out when these levels were reached.

Going over such moves for the past two decades has shown us that these historical support and resistance levels are broken through frequently enough--thereby giving such Big Move trades substantially larger profits--to justify our not just taking our profits when these historic support and resistance levels are reached. It may appear to the reader to be a trade-off, and at times this is true.

The reader may choose to take his profits instead of continuing to trail his stops as these historic price levels are reached. Sometimes by using this method, he will show greater profits than he would if he simply trailed his stops in the hope that these historic levels will be breached. These levels are penetrated frequently enough, however, in our view, to justify using the Trailing Stop techniques we outline. When a market moves to the next historical support or resistance level or establishes new all-time highs or all-time lows, the additional profits from such moves more than make up for whatever profits may be lost by trailing stops when markets do, in fact, bounce off the first historical supply or resistance level.

Therefore, we prefer to mark our long-term charts up in such a way as to reflect the different significant historical support and resistance levels, designating them as Target Levels 1, 2, 3, etc., rather than going with one single Target Level. We typically designate these on our long-term charts as: TL1, TL2, TL3, etc., as in the following illustration:

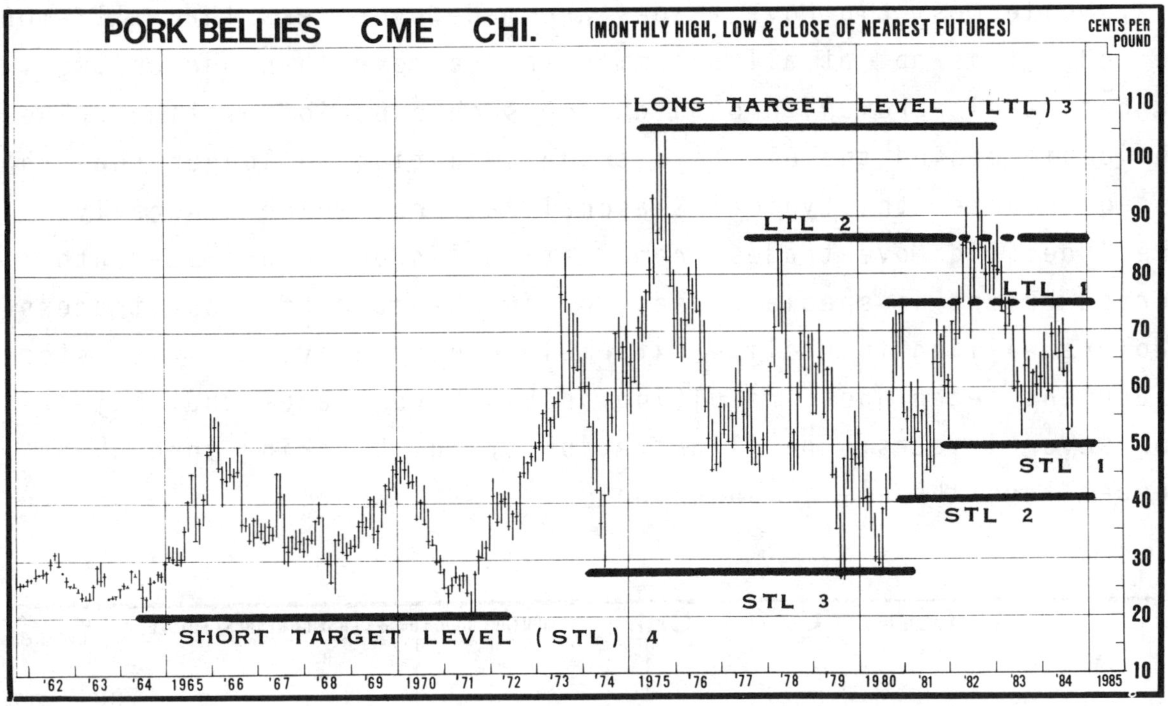

As can be seen in the preceding illustration, there are, in fact, a number of historical support and resistance Target Levels above and below current market price. The reader also should remember that due to fundamentals, the most extreme of these levels--whether a historic high or an historic low--may, in fact, be violated and new all-time historic highs or lows may be established.

We have found the best indicator of whether or not a particular market will break through any given Target Level to be our nine Confirmation Signals. If a particular market has been moving in our direction with five or more of our Confirmation Signals favorable to our position and these Confirmation Signals remain essentially unchanged (or only change marginally) as any of the Target Levels are approached, then the likelihood that the price move will break through that Target Level and proceed to the next

Target Level is very high.

While most Big Move trades are made over less than a 12-month period, it is not at all uncommon to see more than one or two Target Levels broken through during such a period of time. The rationale behind the Big Move trade's lasting no longer than this is, of course, the typical Seasonal Pattern, which generally precludes Big Move trades from lasting longer than a 12-month period except in special cases, or in the case of those traders who are willing to utilize extremely conservative and wide stop placement techniques, resulting in Big Move trades that may last for several years. An illustration of the breaking through of these Target Levels is shown below:

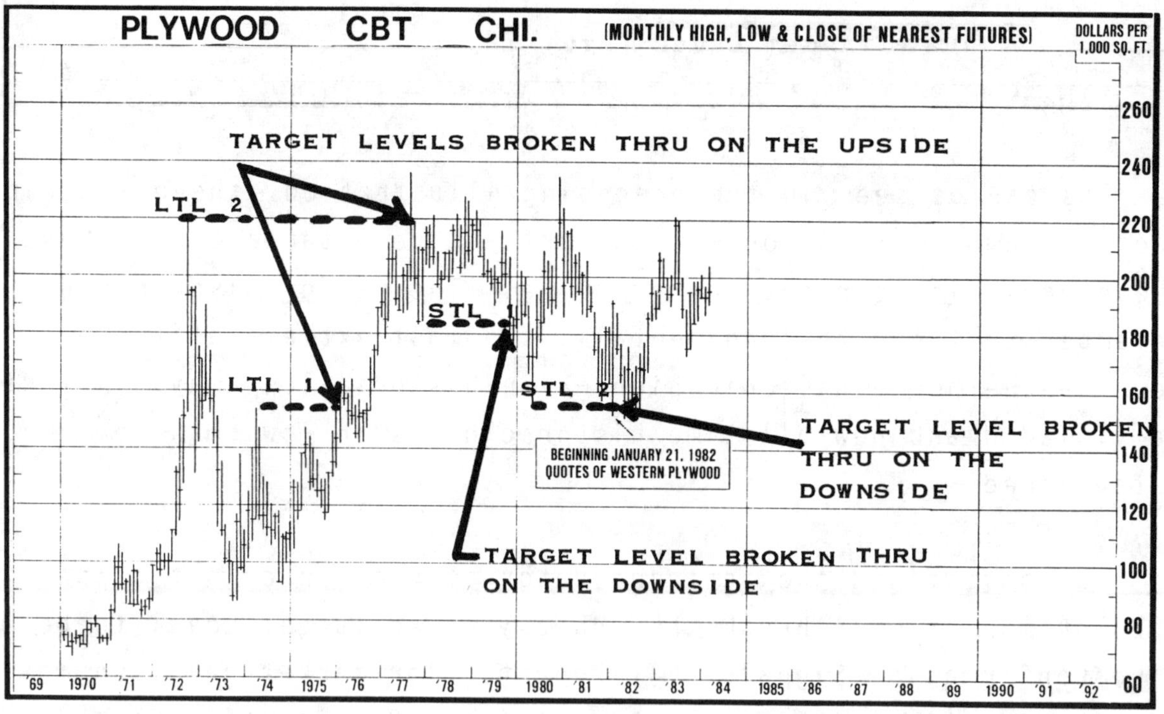

We suggest that the reader take his own weekly and monthly charts for the commodities which he follows and go through them, marking up the resistance and support Target Levels as we have done in the previous illustration, as a guide for his own future positions.

The reader will recall our earlier discussion in this book of Long-Range Cycles, and our best estimation of them is given in Appendix B at the end of this book. These Long-Range Cycles can be very useful in determining also when Target Levels will be broken through and/or new historic highs or lows established. One difficulty here is that what we refer to as Long-Range Cycles are, in reality, relatively short when compared to even longer-range cycles which affect what we call Long-Range Cycles. Hence, each Long-Range Cycle topping does not necessarily mean new historic highs, nor each Long-Range Cycle bottoming mean historic lows, as the reader probably knows. As a Long-Range Cycle is nearing its peak, however, the likelihood that Target Levels will be broken through dramatically increases, as can be seen from the following illustration:

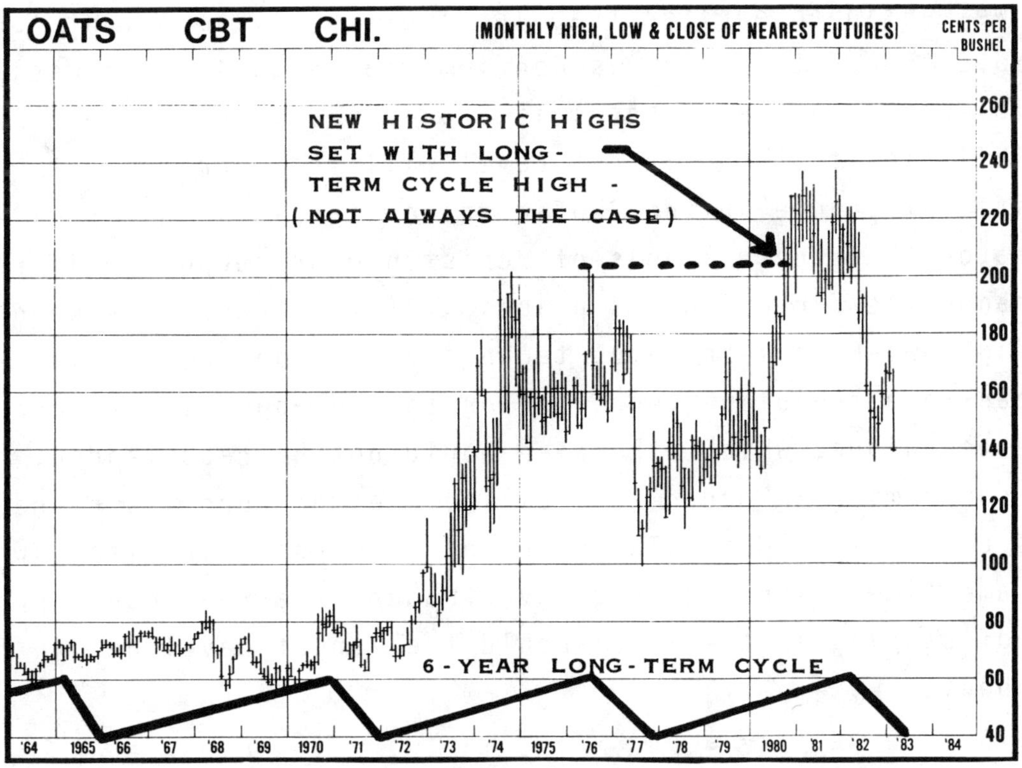

The other case in which Target Levels can be rapidly sliced through during either a Bear or a Bull move occurs when the Seasonal Pattern crests or bottoms, assuming that the commodity in question is following relatively closely its typical Seasonal Pattern. When a Seasonal Pattern is skewed or not behaving as it typically does (as shown in our Seasonal Pattern graphs in Appendix A at the end of this book), then the Target Levels are more likely to stall out the price move at the first Target Level. In such a case where the Seasonal Patterns are atypical, the Big Move trader may very well elect not to continue to trail his stops, but instead to either take his profits as the Target Level is approached or hit or move his stops in extremely close to the current market action to lock in as much profit as possible, realizing that even though the Seasonal Patterns are not performing as expected, there is always the possibility that fundamentals will propell prices through the one Target Level to the next Target Level.

We mentioned earlier that it is extremely important for the Big Move trader to watch his Confirmation Signals as closely as possible as each Target Level is approached in order to detect any possibilities that the Target Level will stall prices out. Significant change in the Confirmation Signals is an excellent indicator that these levels of resistance or support will retard or change the directions of prices. If the trader has been using the eight-week Trailing Stop technique, perhaps he should switch instead to a trendline technique or to the approximate four-week cycle technique, which otherwise would not be recommended. This is a compromise in order to lock in some more profits by having stops closer should the Target Level stop price movement, while at the same time assure the Big Move trader of a reasonable probability of staying in the move should the Target Level be, in fact, breached.

If a trader is fortunate enough to be in on a Big Move which is establishing new historic high prices or new historic low prices (historic low prices as shown on the monthly chart), then we would suggest that the trader go to whatever increasingly steep trendline as new historic price levels are achieved--such as very short trendlines connecting very short-term cyclic lows or highs--as shown in the following illustration:

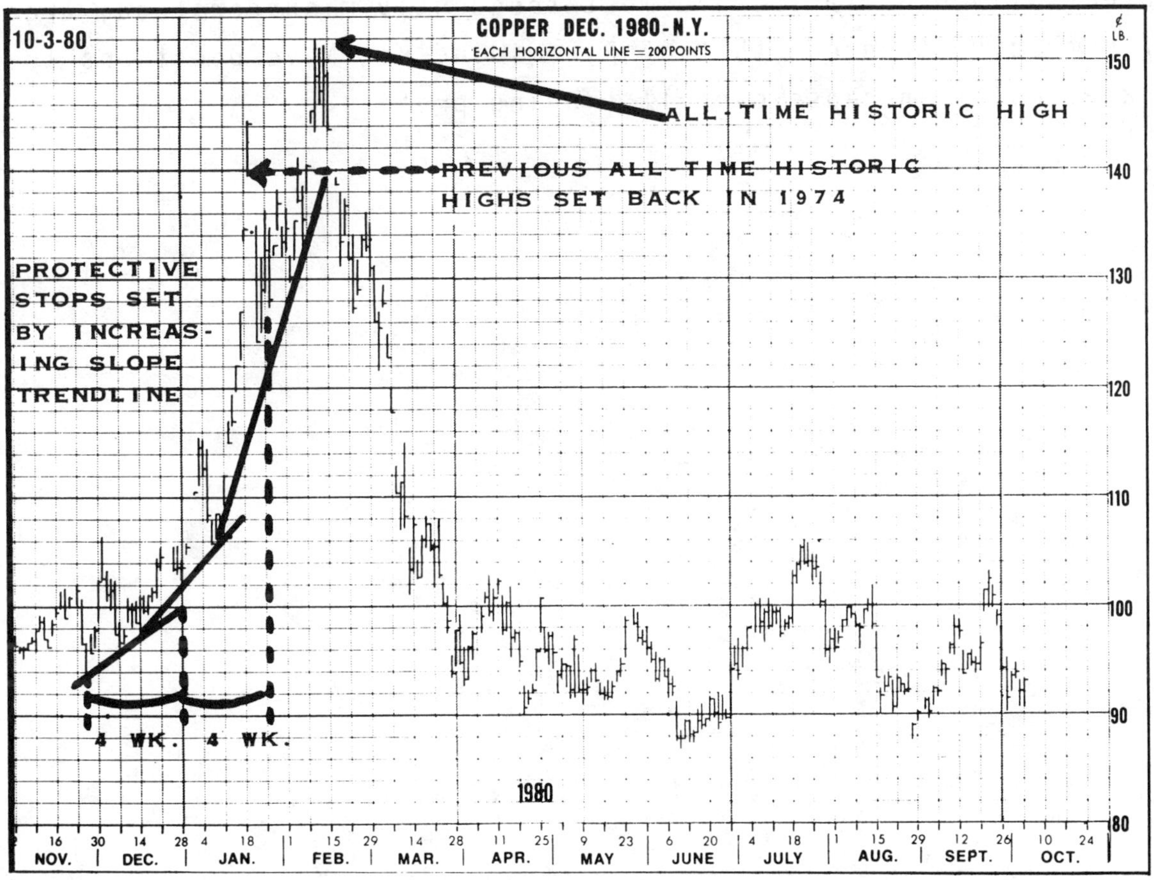

While Target Level selection may be considered one of the more imprecise areas of commodity analysis, the guidelines given in this chapter have worked sufficiently well over the past two decades to ensure a relatively high degree of success in exiting positions.

At this point now, we have discussed how to identify potential Big Move trading candidates, what Confirmation Signals are required in order to establish Big Move trading positions, where to establish Original Entry Points for Big Move positions, where to place Initial Protective Stops, how to utilize Trailing Stops and how to exit trades using Target Levels.

In the next chapter, we shall proceed to one of the most potentially profitable, and most frequently misunderstood, areas of commodity trading--that of Pyramiding Big Move positions to dramatically increase overall trading profits.

CHAPTER 10

PYRAMIDING THE BIG MOVES

Pyramiding is a dramatic way for the Big Move trader to increase his year-end profits with very little, if any, additional risk. The only requirements for the Big Move trader to successfully use Pyramiding are a degree of patience and application of all of the methodology described in this volume.

While Pyramiding at times can be psychologically very stressful, the monetary rewards are potentially so great that the Big Move trader, if he so chooses, can "reframe" (a concept which will be discussed later in the chapter on the Psychology of Big Move Trading), so that instead of feeling negative, anxious stress, he may elect to feel positive, exciting feelings.

Pyramiding, of course, means that after the trader has taken his Big Move position in a commodity with (X) number of contracts, he will add at different points in the future as the move progresses "one-half X" or "2X" or whatever number of additional contracts he has determined will be a part of his Pyramid.

It has been our experience that it is extremely important for the trader to determine before he enters his original position exactly whether or not the commodity he is planning to trade may lend itself to constructing a Pyramid. If so, he should know in advance, as precisely as possible, exactly when, where, and under what conditions the additional contracts will be added to his Pyramid.

The qualifications we will state for potential Big Move Pyramid positions are similar to those required for most Big Move trades.

With regular potential Big Move trading candidates, however, we are requiring that in addition to prices being at historical high, low or mid-range price levels, at least four or five of the nine Confirmation Signals be favorable to the direction of our position. With a Big Move Pyramid candidate, we will require that at least six or more of the nine Confirmation Signals be favorable to the direction of our potential position. Manda-tory among those six Confirmation Signals which must be favorable are the Long-Range Cycle and the Seasonal Pattern, both of which should be pointing in the direction of our anticipated move.

One exception to our preliminary requirements for isolating and identifying a potential Big Move Pyramid Candidate is that we will limit ourselves only to those commodities which are trading at historic high or at historic low price levels, eliminating from consideration for Pyramids those commodities trading at historic mid-range price levels. This requirement is due not only to the limited potential, relatively speaking, for commodities trading at historic mid-range price levels, but also because of their ten-dency to give false initial signals which could prove disasterous to a Big Move Pyramid position.

The following illustration shows a very likely Big Move Pyramid candidate with prices at historic levels. At the point indicated, both the Seasonal Patterns and the Long-Range Cycle are pointing in the direction in which we are considering establishing our Big Move position:

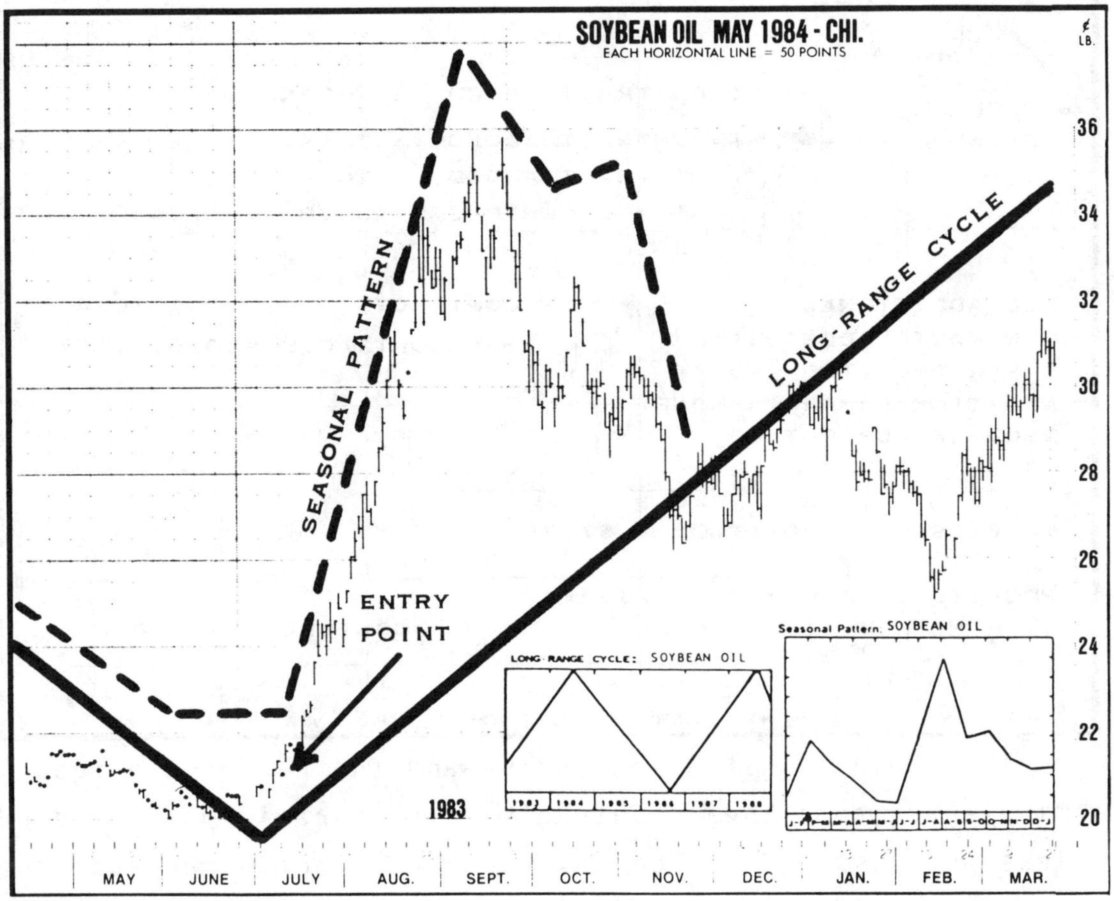

At the beginning of this chapter, we spoke of Pyramiding as requiring very little, if any, additional risk. This is because in the majority of Big Move Pyramids, we are able to use our paper profits, as the move progresses, in order to cover the margin requirements for the additional contracts added. As a result, many contracts frequently may be put into place simply by using these paper profits to cover the margin reqirements and to enormously increase the ensuing profits:

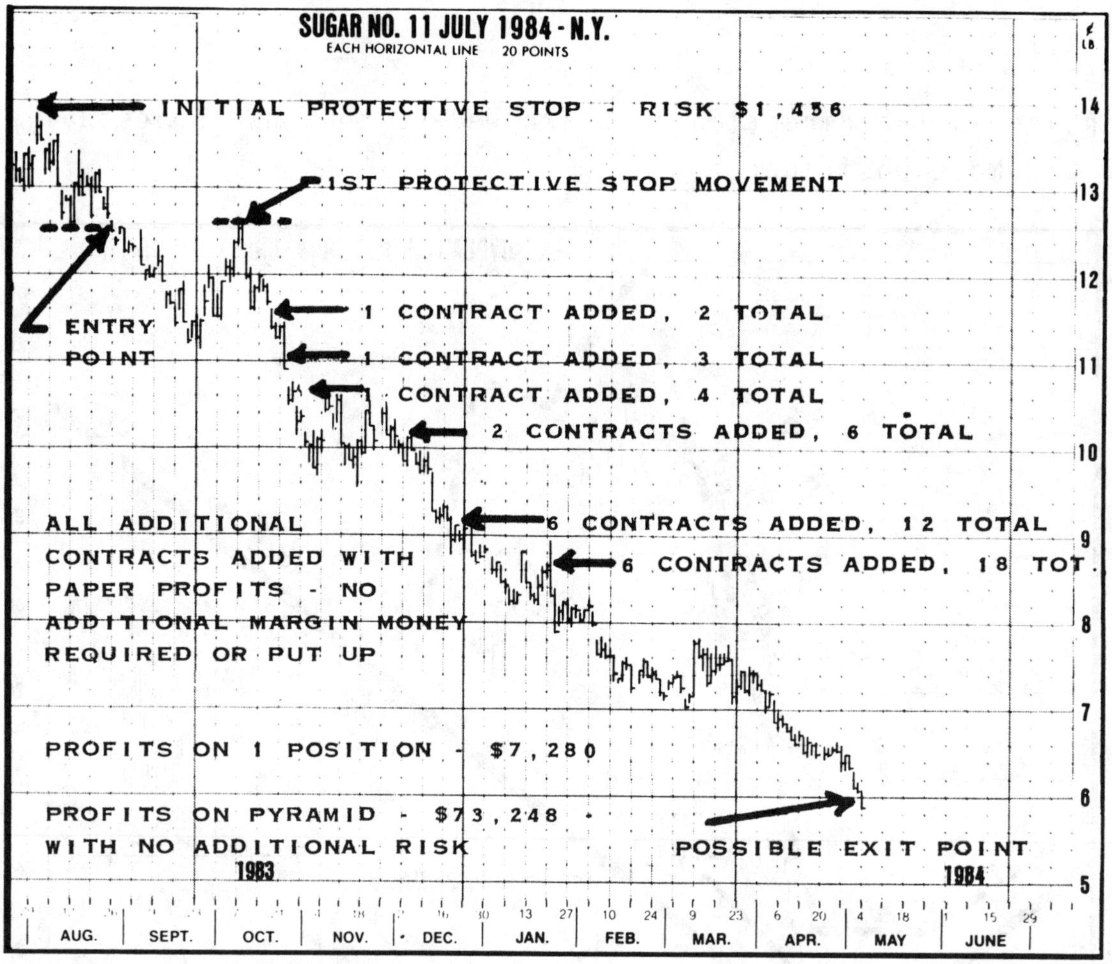

As the above illustration shows--and the reader can readily determine--each additional contract in the Pyramid may be added with less and less of a price move in our direction because the paper profits multiply accordingly as additional contracts are added to the Pyramid.

Some trading advisers argue that it is better to add all of the contracts early on in the Pyramid or that if the trader anticipates a total of 10 contracts, instead of purchasing or selling one contract to begin with, that he should establish his initial position for a total of 10 contracts. While it is true that this would increase total profits, these advisers overlook the fact that the original risk--if the signals generated were false ones or if some UFO should occur--would increase enormously. In fact, in this example, the original risk would increase by a factor of 10. As a rule of thumb, we have found that successful Pyramids following the guidelines of six of our nine Confirmation Signals and so forth as we have stated, generally give additional profits of around 500% over single-contract positions. Generally, in order to buy the number of contracts required--all at the Original Entry Point--to achieve the same amount of profits would involve about a 500% greater risk than that required to establish the Pyramid illustrated, beginning with but a single contract.

It has been our experience that Bull and Bear Pyramids are, over a sufficient period of time under examination, equally profitable. So it makes little difference whether prices are at historic high or at historic low price levels since the end results achieved will be relatively the same.

We said earlier in this volume that it generally is best to avoid establishing Big Move positions in thinly traded commodities; this is even more true of potential Pyramiding candidates. While the Big Move trader occasionally may make an exception to the rule against trading thinly traded commodities for a single position, he should never consider thinly traded commodities for potential Pyramid candidates. As a rule of thumb, we consider thinly traded commodities to be any which are exhibiting Open Interest of less than 10,000 contracts over the recent past and whose Volume on high volume days is running less than 5,000 contracts per day.

Contrary to what the reader might expect, the best way to handle Big Move Pyramids is <u>not</u> to initiate them in distant contract months, although many traders believe they should since they know that if their Pyramid is successful, it may run for many months before their trade is closed out. The problem with this distant-month approach is that the more distant months of any commodity are very lightly traded, so if the move proceeds rapidly and the trader is adding multiple contracts rapidly, he is ensured of receiving terrible fills and possibly even creating a limit situation.

It is far better to trade not the nearby month, but the next month away from the nearby month. As the nearby month reaches its first notice day, the trader should roll over his positions from the contract month he is in to the next contract month.

While the previous illustrations shows what is called a "Fully-Margined Pyramid" (since all of the trader's paper profits are being used for margin requirements), in practice, this is not a good approach to follow since market corrections could result in the trader's having to put up additional margin in order to stay in his positions--something which we advise no Big Move trader to ever do. It is better for the trader to calculate his adding additional contracts based upon 80%-to-90% of being fully-margined. This requires but a bit of simple arithmetic in order to determine where the Entry Points would be for adding additional contracts, as opposed to adding contracts on a fully-margined basis.

While there are an infinite number of ways to construct Pyramids, we will limit ourselves solely to those methods which we believe are the easiest to use--while at the same time being the most profitable--for a Big Move trading program. One of the best and simplest methods is to utilize the example previously given, though modifying it from a Fully-Margined Pyramid to a 90%-of-Margin Pyramid. The second best method, in our judgment, is to add additional contracts at predetermined points along the move, regardless of paper profits. This generally requires much more capital than the first method discussed, and if the reader is sophisticated enough to utilize this later technique, he will be aware of the additional risks involved as well as know how to determine the points at which to add additional contracts. Hence, we will not discuss this second method in detail, but will limit ourselves to the method that we personally prefer, which is utilizing 90% of the trader's paper profits to add additional contracts.

The following graph illustrates how the same contract shown as our first Pyramiding illustration would differ when using the 90%-of-Margin approach:

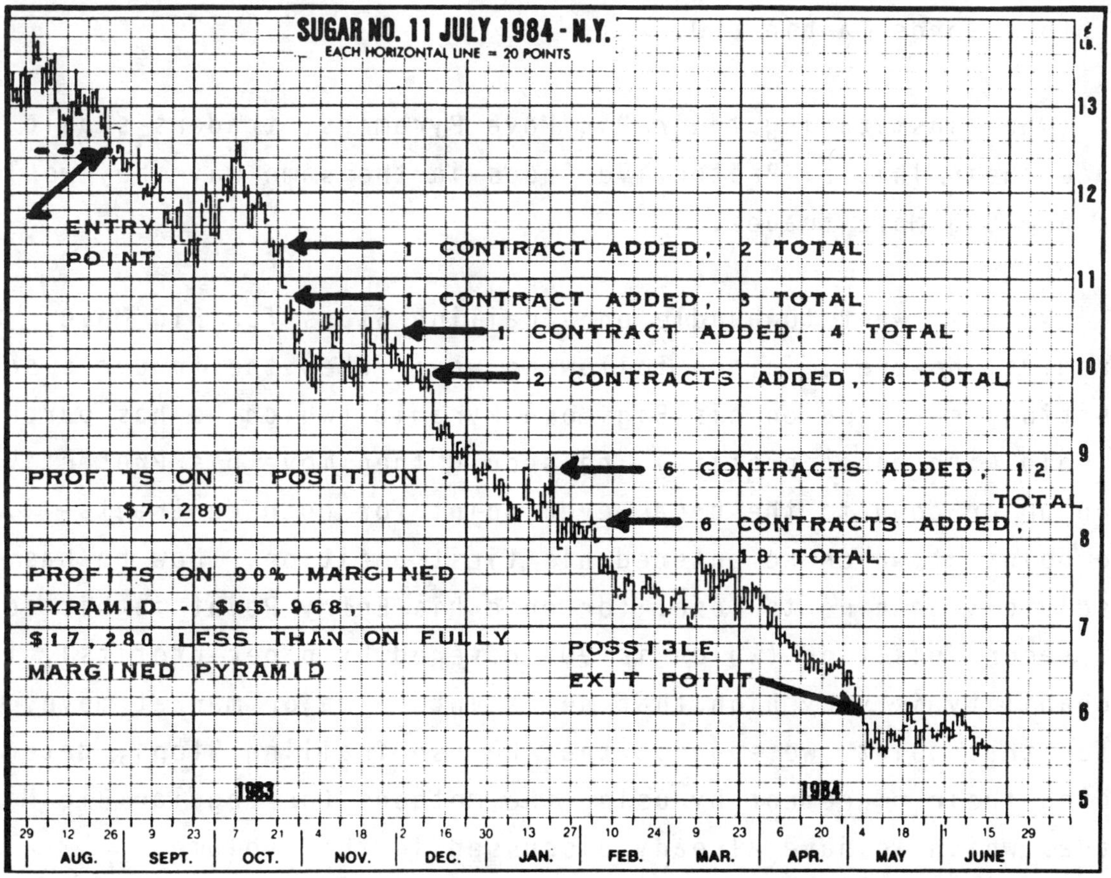

As can be seen, the total profits are somewhat reduced, but this is, in effect, an insurance policy premium which the Big Move trader is paying to protect himself from market corrections and to keep himself in his Big Move Pyramid position.

The one exception we would make to the 90%-of-Margin rule is for those Big Move traders who are very well capitalized and can afford to meet margin calls if the Big Move position should suffer a significant correction. In this case, however, we would advise such well-capitalized Big Move traders to use their judgment regarding the number of Confirmation Signals which must remain favorable even during such a correction before they ever institute such a Fully-Margined Pyramid. We also would advise not only these Big Move traders, but all Big Move traders with Pyramids, to seriously consider rapidly exiting all of their Pyramid positions should there be a sudden and dramatic change in the fundamentals--in other words, a big UFO.

When instituting their Big Move Pyramids, traders should place their Initial Protective Stops in the same way they would for any Big Move trades.

We will want to handle our Trailing Stops for Big Move Pyramids, however, in the following way: When the trader's second position is filled on his Big Move Pyramid (which he has purchased or sold with paper profits), he should then move his Protective Stop up or down to the break-even point for both contracts--i.e., the point at which he entered his first position. Now he has absolutely nothing to lose, for once his Entry Point is hit for his second position (which is 90% covered by paper profits), the probability is very high that he is into a major market move. After that point, we suggest that he use Trailing Stops, determining their placement by using the methods for regular Big Move trades which we have already discussed in this volume.

The last major consideration for Big Move Pyramids that we would like to discuss is taking profits. As the first Target Level is approached and hit, we would suggest that the Big Move Pyramid trader liquidate one-third of his Pyramid positions with an order to get out of the market at exactly the Target Level point, retaining the other two-thirds of his Pyramid position. Once that Target Level is passed on a Short-Term or approximate four-week cycle basis, then Protective Stops for all remaining Pyramid positions should be moved up to that Target Level at which he liquidated the first one-third of his positions. The remaining two-thirds positions should be liquidated in the following manner: As the second Target Level is hit, an order should be resting to liquidate one-third more of the total positions--or one-half of the remaining positions--at the second Target Level. And when prices have passed that Target Level on a Short-Term Cyclical basis, then the stops on the remaining contracts should be moved to that second Target Level and the remaining contracts should be held onto with Trailing Stops established by having them just a tic away from a tightly-drawn trendline between Short-Term Cyclical highs or lows. The following illustration shows how exiting Big Move Pyramid positions generally is accomplished:

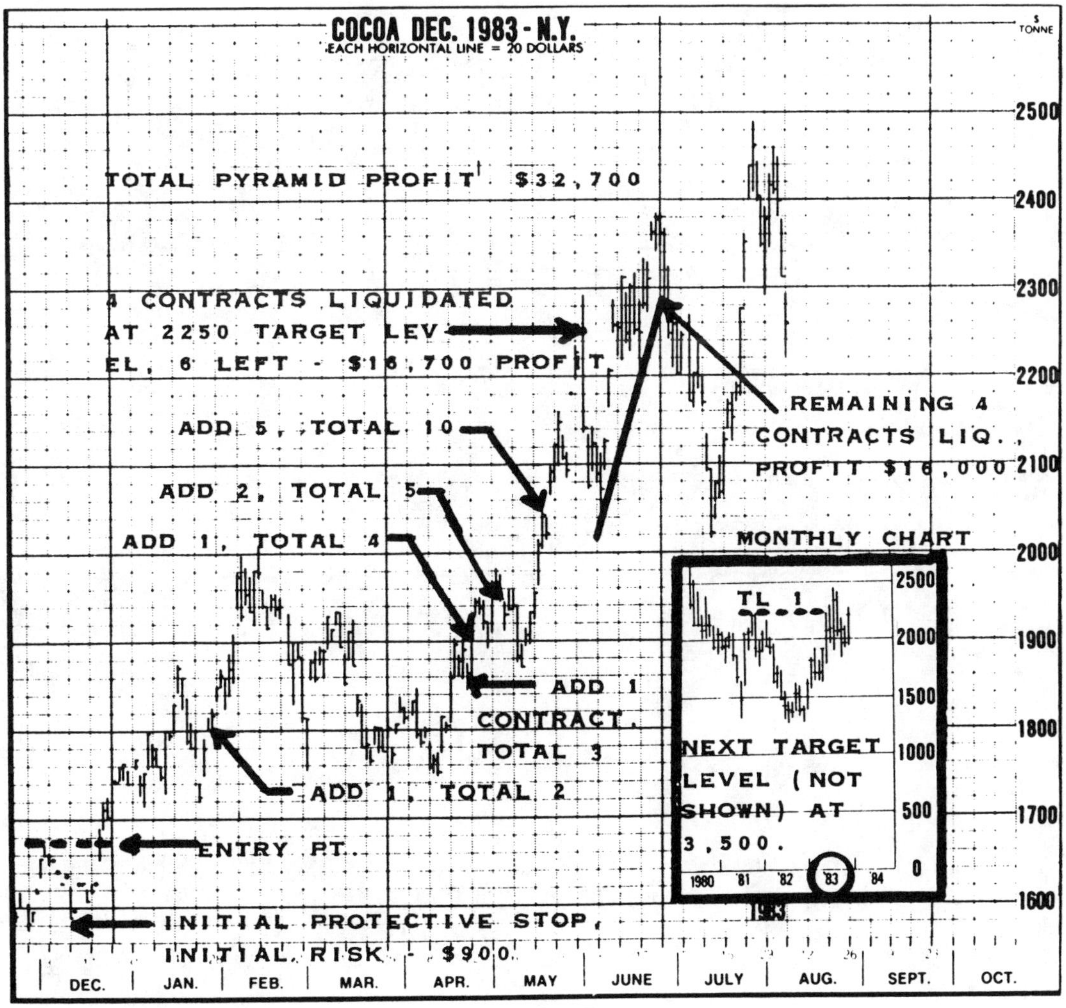

* * * * *

As the reader can see, Pyramiding is not nearly as difficult as it might seem, especially if the trader decides in advance exactly how his Big Move Pyramids will be constructed and does not confuse himself with the myriad number of different Pyramiding possibilities and combinations. As simple as this approach appears, it is a highly successful way to construct and profit from Big Move Pyramids.

CHAPTER 11

BIG MOVE MONEY MANAGEMENT

Money Management for a Big Move trading program is different in many ways--yet similar in some--to Money Management for any commodity trading program. First, it is necessary to consider how much money is required to successfully institute a Big Move trading program. We must emphasize that Big Move trading capital--despite the far greater probabilities of success of Big Move trades--is still considered as "risk capital." As such, it should never be money that a trader cannot afford to lose. After all, the commodity markets are a fickle mistress.

In addition just to the possibilities of having trades go against a trader's Big Move trading program and wiping out his equity, the trader is faced with many other possible happenings which could wipe him out--such perhaps unlikely, but still possible, occurrences as the President's being forced to invoke the Emergency Powers Act for whatever reason and shutting the markets down completely. Probably in such a situation the trader's funds would not be available to him for many weeks or even months. And then, too, there is the possibility that the UFO's to which we have previously referred could result in locked-limit moves for days in a row, thereby wiping out the trader's entire capital. While these are remote possibilities, they nonetheless serve to emphasize that no one should ever trade commodities either regularly or in a Big Move program with money he cannot afford to lose.

The minimum amount the prospective trader should have to institute an effective Big Move trading program is actually only $10,000, although $25,000 is definitely preferable. The figure of $25,000 is based on normal approximate margin requirements for trading 12 different commodities. The number 12 has been picked by us as an optimum figure for single-contract trading of two different commodities from each of six different commodity complexes.

This provides us with more than an adequate amount of diversification of risk. For simplicity, we categorize these six complexes as:

1. Grains.

2. Meats.

3. Foods.

4. Fibers, Petroleum and Woods.

5. Metals.

6. Currencies, Stock Indices and Financial Instruments.

We could, of course, break down some of these arbitrary divisions. Complex Number 6, for example, could be divided into two or three different complexes. This is a matter of the individual Big Move trader's choice. Typically, however, the commodities in Number 6 (and frequently Number 5 as well) move in the same general direction or in opposite directions at the same time. Of course, it is not always possible to have positions in each of these different complexes--although we believe the ideal is to have two Big Move positions in each of these six complexes--since some complexes frequently are not trading at historic low, high or mid-point Trading Range Levels. We do recommend, however, trading in as many different complexes as possible--assuming, of course, that they meet the criteria for Big Move trading and that enough Confirmation Signals are being exhibited which are of a favorable nature--in order to achieve maximum diversification and reduce overall risk as much as possible.

Frequently, the Big Move trader will find that virtually all of the members of the same complex, due to common Fundamentals, reach historic lows or highs or mid-range points at approximately the same time. The Big Move trader then is faced with the problem of entering positions in all of the members of the same complex--all six members of the Grain complex, for example--or choosing only one or two of the members of this complex. If a Big Move does, in fact, ensue and the Big Move trader enters positions in all of the members of the complex, he does increase his probability of success and profits dramatically because if one of the markets has a severe correction, taking him out of his position, frequently the other members of the complex will not violate his Protective Stops. And, of course, the Big Move trader--by having a number of different commodities within the same complex going at the same time--can elect to use different Protective Stop methods, different Entry Points, and so on, thereby affording additional protection. The risk, of course, is if the complex as a whole gives a false set of signals and the Big Move trader enters positions in all the members of the complex. In such an instance, unless the Initial Risk for each of the positions were relatively manageable, the Big Move trader could find his equity severely depleted by such a set of false signals in an entire complex.

The decision of the Big Move trader to enter only one or two of the members of a complex or all of the members of the complex when they issue signals at approximately the same time is more dependent upon his financial capabilities and his psychological temperament for approaching such a situation than upon anything else. We personally have used the one approach sometimes and the other approach at other times, depending upon our financial wherewithall and our intuitive feel for how genuine the complex's Confirmation Signals were.

The ideal situation is for the Big Move trader to have $60,000 equity in his account. This equity would permit him to handle the maximum number of signals which may appear at any given time, to pyramid his moves without using paper profits if he should choose to do so, and to cope with an unforeseen run of bad luck. Traders who have not traded a Big Move program before should remember that the amount of equity in a trader's account may have to be considered over a three- to 12-month period because many filled positions last that long and, in the meantime, unless he has substantial paper profits, if new positions become available, the Big Move trader may be forced to have additional capital in order to handle margin requirements.

While $25,000 is a very sound amount with which to start a Big Move trading program--and $50,000-to-60,000 is an ideal amount to handle maximum opportunities and unforeseen circumstances--a Big Move trading program <u>can</u> be initiated with far, far less than these amounts. In fact, it is possible for a Big Move trader to initiate his trading program with just enough equity in his account to enter only one Big Move trade and, since the probability of success in Big Move trading is greater than it is in normal commodity trading, there is a fair likelihood that he will succeed in this trade, increase the equity of his account and then be able to start trading more than one commodity. This is a slow and arduous process, however, and if his first position were an unprofitable one, the trader could be wiped out totally.

For the smaller investor with an account of $10,000 or less, two approaches for Big Move trading may be used. One is for him to trade one commodity per complex for only three, four or five of the different complexes, depending upon the margin requirements of those commodities which fulfill the specifications for a potential Big Move trade. The other posibility is for him to trade Mini-Contracts on the Mid-American Exchange. An ever-increasing number of commodities are available there to trade as Mini-Contracts. These commodities typically require anywhere from one-fifth to one-half the standard amount of margin required on the major exchanges.

Going this route is, of course, a slow process. But for traders with very limited funds, this may be the only viable alternative. Unfortunately, sometimes it is difficult to locate a broker who is familiar with Mini-Contracts or willing to work with investors on them. If the reader finds this to be the case, he may contact us, as stated in Appendix E at the back of this book, for a copy of our recommended broker list which includes those who are more than willing to work on Mini-Contract Big Move trading programs.

The next topic to be considered is examining potential Big Move trading candidates as to the amount of dollar risk they involve. The risk, of course, is the amount between the trader's Original Entry Point and his Initial Protective Stop. It is not a bad idea for the trader to add another 5% to whatever this dollar amount is to make up for "slippage," or his order's not getting filled exactly at the point specified. Also, the trader should add the amount of commission required per trade to his risk on the trade itself in order to get the total amount of money he is risking.

We believe that a good guideline is for the trader not to risk more than 10% of his total account on any individual trade. If his funds are limited or he is an aggressive trader, he might increase the figure to 15% or 20%, but we would not recommend going beyond 20% in any case. On the other hand, if he is a particularly conservative trader, 5% of his total equity on any single Big Move trade would be more appropriate.

Next we will look at what percentage of margin requirements in terms of dollar value a trader should risk on any particular potential Big Move trade. In other words, if the margin for a particular commodity is $2,000, what percent of that amount should the trader risk between his Original Entry Point, his Initial Protective Stop, adding 5% for bad fills and tacking on the broker commission? We have found over the years that it is best to try to limit the amount of risk percentage-wise to margin to 50% and to try to avoid wherever possible any trade which requires the risking of more than 100% of Orinial Margin.

This, of course, is but a guideline which can be changed, depending upon the amount of potential reward. The trader can determine the Risk/Reward factor by dividing the dollar value in potential profits between his Original Entry Point and his first Target Level into the amount of dollar risk, which is the dollar value between his Original Entry Point, etc. The lower, of course, the the Risk-Reward Ratio is, the better the potential trade. Hence, if the potential reward (given that the Target Level has been realistically determined) and enough Confirmation Signals are favorable, then the trader may choose at times to go significantly above the recommended limit of 100% of Original Margin as his initial dollar risk.

Another way the trader can utilize the Risk/Reward Ratio is when his capital is not sufficient for him to trade all of the potential Big Move trades available at that point in time. By calculating the Risk/Reward Ratio for each potential Big Move trade, he can isolate the Big Move trading candidate with the best potential by entering those with the lowest Risk/Reward Ratios. He should do this keeping in mind the necessity to diversify, so that if all of the lowest Risk/Reward Ratio candidates were in the same complex, he would take positions in other complexes on the lowest Risk/Reward Ratio candidate in each complex.

Generally, any trade with a Risk/Reward Ratio higher than 0.50 indicates that the potential Big Move trade candidate is either not a sufficiently rewarding one or the trader has calculated his Initial Protective Stops, his Initial Entry Point or his Target Levels in an incorrect manner.

Often we are asked about how much money a Big Move trader should keep in reserve. We believe the best way to consider this is to remember that we are talking about risk capital--money which the Big Move trader can afford to lose without seriously hurting himself. Considering, too, that Big Move trades typically have a relatively high rate of success, it is our belief that the Big Move trader should keep virtually no reserve in his account, but that he should be fully committed financially, assuming that there are enough potential Big Move trades. This does not mean, however, that if there is only one Big Move trade available to him, he should use all of his capital, buying and selling multiple contracts of that particular commodity. Rather, this means that if there are sufficient potential Big Move trading opportunities, the Big Move trader should commit himself to as many of them as the equity in his account will permit.

During those periods of time when it is not possible for the Big Move trader to commit all of his--or most of his--equity to actual positions, it is probably best for him to have his brokerage house keep the excess funds invested in Treasury Bills or the brokerage house's money market fund, assuming that the brokerage house is set up in such a way that the funds can be transferred easily back and forth between the investment accounts and the trader's own commodity account.

* * * * *

Money Management procedure in a Big Move trading program is relatively simple to follow, as are most of the other aspects of Big Move trading. By following the guidelines in this chapter, the Big Move trader will find that it is no more difficult to manage the financial aspects of a Big Move trading program than it is for any other type of commodity trading program. In fact, the principles described in this chapter can be applied to any type of commodity trading program, whether it is of a Big Move type or Short-Term type. The basic principles of Risk/Reward Ratio, percent of total equity committed and--perhaps most importantly of all--<u>diversification</u> are easy-to-follow principles which every commodity trader should be using in his program.

CHAPTER 12

PROJECTED PRICE GRAPHS

One of the newest and most exciting developments in Big Move Trading Analysis is that of the Projected Price Graph (PPG) technique. The concept of the PPG developed from an attempt to predict with as much precision as possible the future direction of prices for a given commodity over a 12-month calendar year period. Considering this type of attempt may seem, at first, to be somewhat of a grandiose project. Nonetheless, we feel that the goal of such price prediction is desirable enough for us to make at least an attempt at it.

By way of background, the development of the PPG concept came from the observation that Seasonal Patterns were skewed in the direction of Long-Range Cycles. When a Long-Range Cycle was heading up, the Seasonal Pattern was much more pronounced on the Bull side of the seasonal move and less severe on the Bear side of the seasonal move. The converse was true when a Seasonal Pattern took place during a Long-Range Cyclical Bear move.

It also was observed that when a Long-Range Cycle was due to top or bottom within a given calendar year, this had a profound effect on the Seasonal Pattern for that given year. When the Long-Range Cycle was due to bottom at approximately the same time-

-or within a month or so--as the Seasonal Pattern, then the Seasonal Pattern behaved relatively predictably in terms of its phasing--i.e., the time frame during which the seasonal low occurred was in "phase," or happened at the same time, as the Long-Range Cycle bottomed.

But if the Long-Range Cycle were due to bottom in, say, the summertime and the Seasonal Pattern were due to bottom in the wintertime, a complete distortion of the Seasonal Pattern took place.

Upon close examination, however, it was found that there must be other factors influencing the skewing of the Long-Range Cycle's reaching its climax or bottom and the Seasonal Pattern's reaching its seasonal high or low.

It was further determined that shorter cycles--such as the Intermediate-Term Cycle which typically lasts about six months and even such shorter cycles as the approximate eight-week cycle and approximate four-week cycle--all had influence upon the Seasonal Pattern and the Long-Range Cycle.

When all of these cycles and the Seasonal Pattern were combined mathematically, there was still a great degree of imprecision in the final results.

We concluded that even Longer-Range Cycles than the ones we were examining and which are given in Appendix B of this book were involved--those such as the Kondratieff wave. Any examination of these very long cycles seemed to be a virtually impossible task, so we limited our development of the PPG concept to the Long-Range Cycles we have listed in Appendix B, to the Seasonal Patterns and to shorter cycles--those all the way down to the approximate eight-week cycle.

If this were a perfect world, it would be possible--by the combining of all of the different known cycles for any commodity and the Seasonal Pattern and perhaps the adjusting of the overall results for even Longer-Range Cycles--to come up with a graphical representation of future price movement over any given period of time. Unfortunately, however, this is not a perfect world, either in the commodity markets or in any other phase of life, so this is not possible.

When we constructed our PPG's, we elected to go with the calendar-year time frame for three reasons. First, the Seasonal Pattern is a calendar-year cycle. Secondly, for us to take any shorter period of time than a full year would not be particularly useful for our purposes in Big Move trading. Thirdly, for us to take a period of time longer than 12 months would make such analysis more subject to distortion because we would be going further out in time and such Projected Price Movement in excess of 12 months would not be particularly useful to the Big Move trader.

So, if our cyclical analysis were reasonably accurate and our Seasonal Pattern were relatively exact, then we should be able to come up with a good representation of future prices by mathematically adding or combining all of these different cycles. The one difficulty, however, is the appearance of Unexpected Fundamental Occurrences. Such a sudden UFO as an embargo, a war or a strike would be sufficient to significantly distort and invalidate even the most exact Cycles and Seasonal Patterns.

The occurrence of these UFO's, however, does not relegate PPG Analysis to the scrap pile because whenever there are no UFO's which affect a particular commodity, having a PPG Analysis done for it is a very valuable tool for the trader to predict not only when to enter a market, but also approximately when to exit the market. A PPG Analysis also is valuable as an aid to Pyramiding positions and to determining the magnitude of price moves, thereby helping to establish Target Levels.

Another way a trader can utilize PPG's is to be aware of the fact that when a particular market is not behaving particularly in line with its PPG, then fundamentals must be taking place to alter the PPG. Generally, these fundamentals would be of the UFO nature and everyone in the trade would be well aware of them.

Sometimes, however, when the commodity's price movement is not mirroring its PPG, it is indicative that fundamental forces are at work which either are unknown to the public or, if they are known, whose impact has been discounted by the public at large.

While the ideal way to construct such PPG's is with the aid of a computer, we realize that the majority of our readers will not have the capabilities of following this approach. Hence, we have developed a rather simplified method--one which does not require the use of an elaborate computer system or program and which can be done by the average trader with a little bit of practice and instruction.

Appendices A and B at the back of this book contain all of the information the reader will need for many years into the future in order to construct his own PPG's in combination with determining the Intermediate-Term Cycle and the approximate eight-week cycle which commodities are following.

The first thing the reader should do is to combine the Seasonal Pattern with the Long-Range Cycle.

The following illustration shows a Seasonal Cycle superimposed upon a Long-Range Cycle for a particular commodity:

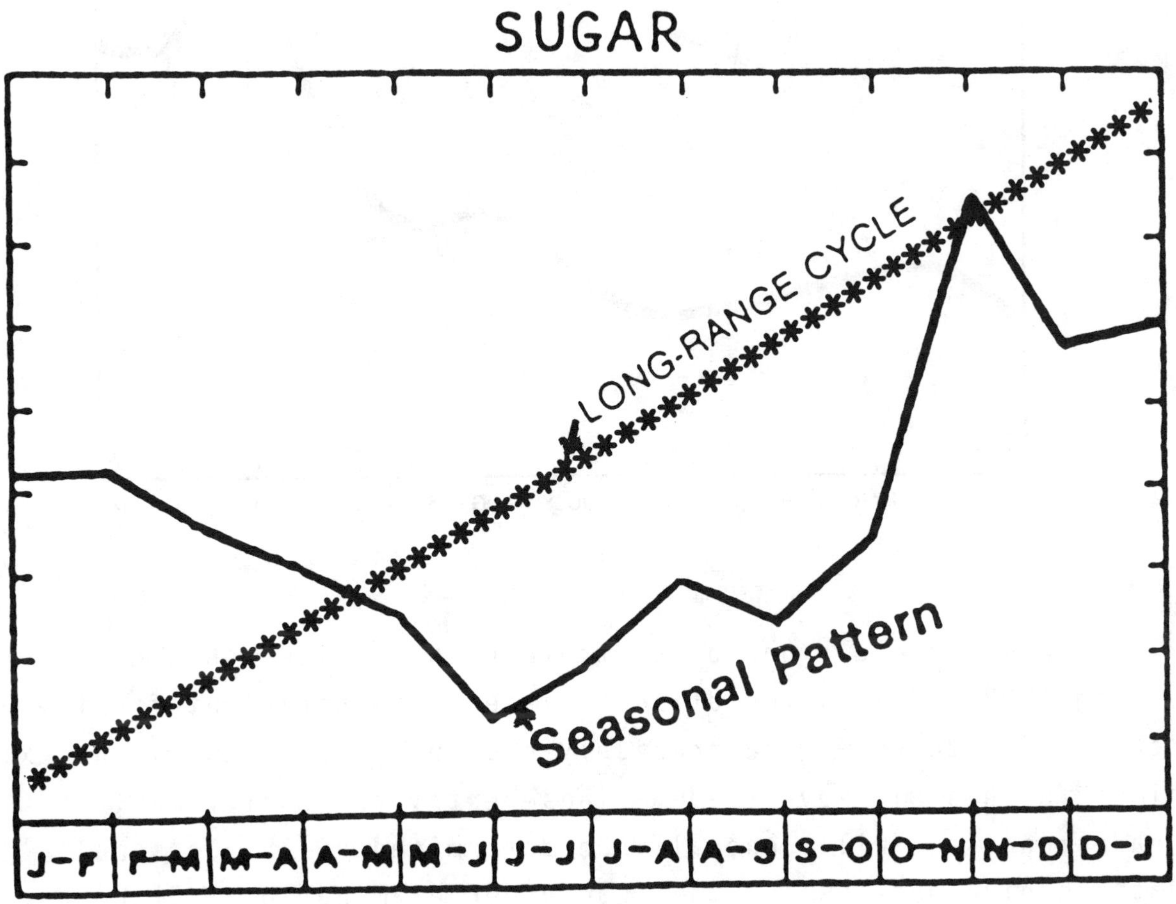

These two cycles are then mathematically summed, which can be done precisely by using any series of arbitrary values on the vertical axis. The addition of this Long-Range Cycle and the Seasonal Pattern is shown accomplished in the illustration below:

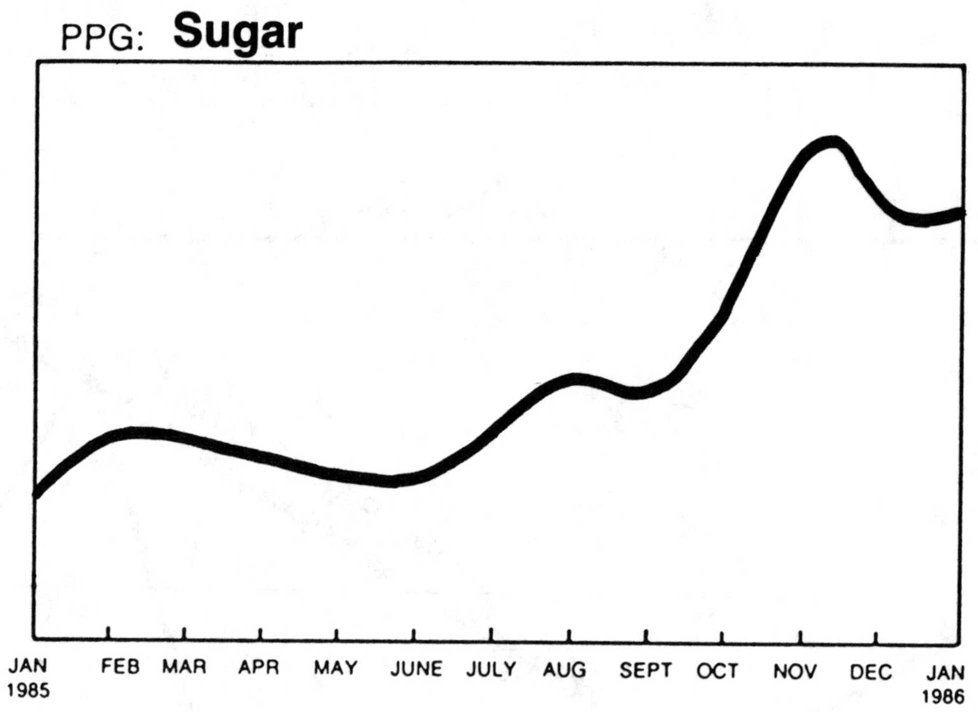

Now we have a broad brushstroke of how prices should behave during 1985. This information by itself is sufficient for the Big Move trader to know more precisely his approximate entry and exit times for his Big Move trade. These entry and exit times, as the reader can see, will generally be determined by the Seasonal Pattern high and low for the year under examination. Of course, the Big Move trader should already know his approximate entry and exit times simply from examining his Seasonal Pattern charts.

In the case of a commodity with a Long-Range Cycle which is heading down: if the Long-Range Cycle is not due to bottom during the particular calendar year under examination, then the low for the Seasonal Pattern most likely will not reach the all-time historic low levels seen on the monthly charts for the commodity under examination. Hence, the Big Move trader can well assume that his first or second Target Level will be hit, but that, most likely, an extreme Target Level at or near the all-time historic lows will not be reached during this calendar year. Conversely, if the Long-Range Cycle is due to bottom during the calendar year under examination, then the likelihood that the all-time historic lows, or extreme Target Level, will be reached--or broken--greatly increases.

The illustration which follows shows an example of the former case where the Long-Range Cycle is not due to bottom during the upcoming calendar year. It shows that Target Levels one and two will be the ones most likely achieved. If, however, the Long-Range Cycle had been due to bottom in this calendar year, then Target Level three most likely would have been reached or exceeded:

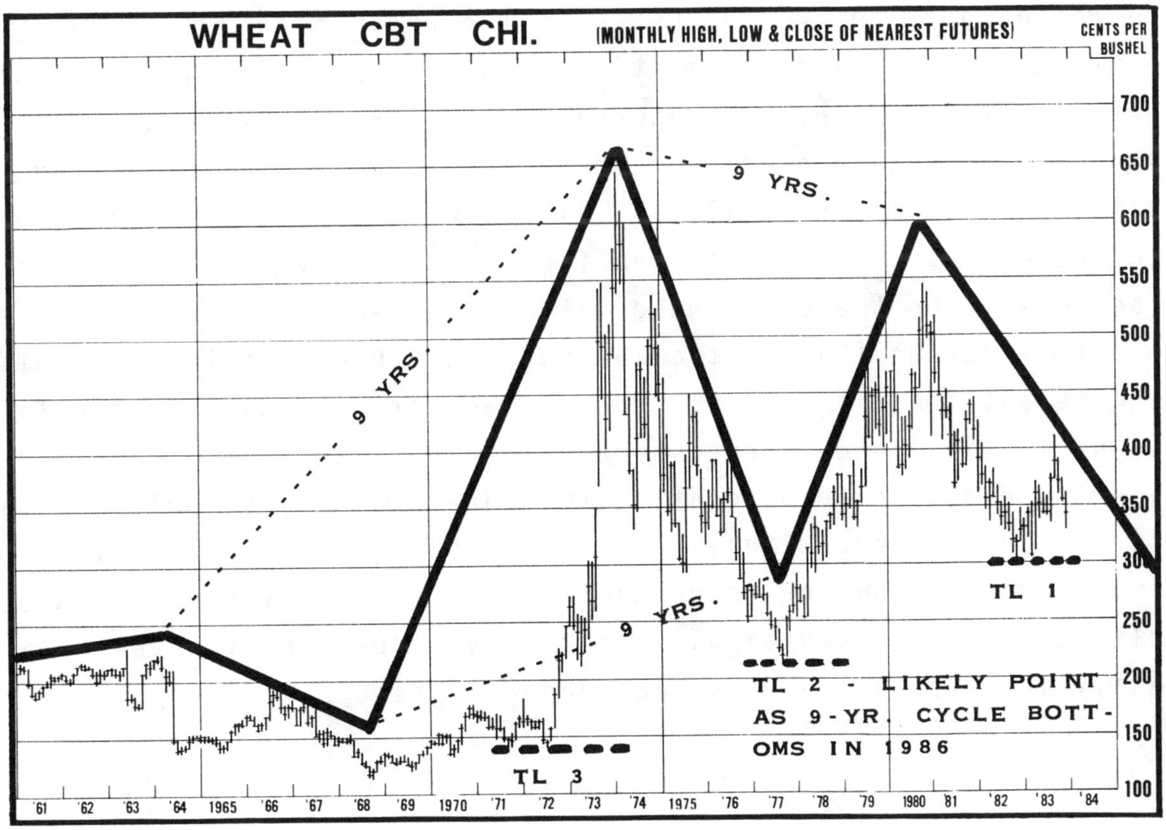

The Big Move trader can utilize this information very readily in deciding when to take his profits by the way he adjusts his Trailing Protective Stops. In the first case where the Long-Range Cycle is not due to bottom, it behooves the Big Move trader to use one of the Trailing Stop techniques which keeps his protective stops even closer to the current price action than he normally might as prices approach the first Target Levels. If, however, the Long-Range Cycle were due to bottom during this calendar year, we most likely would see prices drop on down to the extreme Target Level or beyond. In this case, the Big Move trader would most likely want to keep his Trailing Protective Stops back farther than usual as the first Target Levels are reached in order to protect his position from any market price corrections and to thereby stay in his position until the extreme Target Level is reached.

This information is valuable also to the trader who has Pyramided and is holding multiple contracts as the Target Levels are approached. As we discussed in the chapter on Pyramiding about exiting portions of multiple-contract positions, as the different contract levels are approached, the Big Move trader who has Pyramided--if the Long-Range Cycle is not due to bottom during this particular year--will most likely want to exit a higher percentage of his positions at the first Target Level than he otherwise would. On the other hand, if the Long-Range Cycle were due to bottom during this particular year, the Big Move trader would be more apt to exit a smaller percentage of his multiple positions as the initial Target Levels are hit. This may seem like a precise and exacting adjustment of trading methodology, but, let us assure you, the additional profits which can be reaped from such a simple examination and adjustment of how to vary the percentage of multiple-contract positions exited at various Target Levels can vastly increase a trader's year-end profits.

We all are aware of how difficult it is sometimes to look at any given daily price chart and see the fluctuations, patterns and cyclical behavior of the commodity in question due to Intra-Day price volatility on the bar chart and skewing of the various cycles. By adding in the Intermediate-Range Cycle, which often is an approximate 26-week cycle, the Big Move trader can further fine-tune his PPG.

The graph which follows shows how an Intermediate-Term Cycle can be determined:

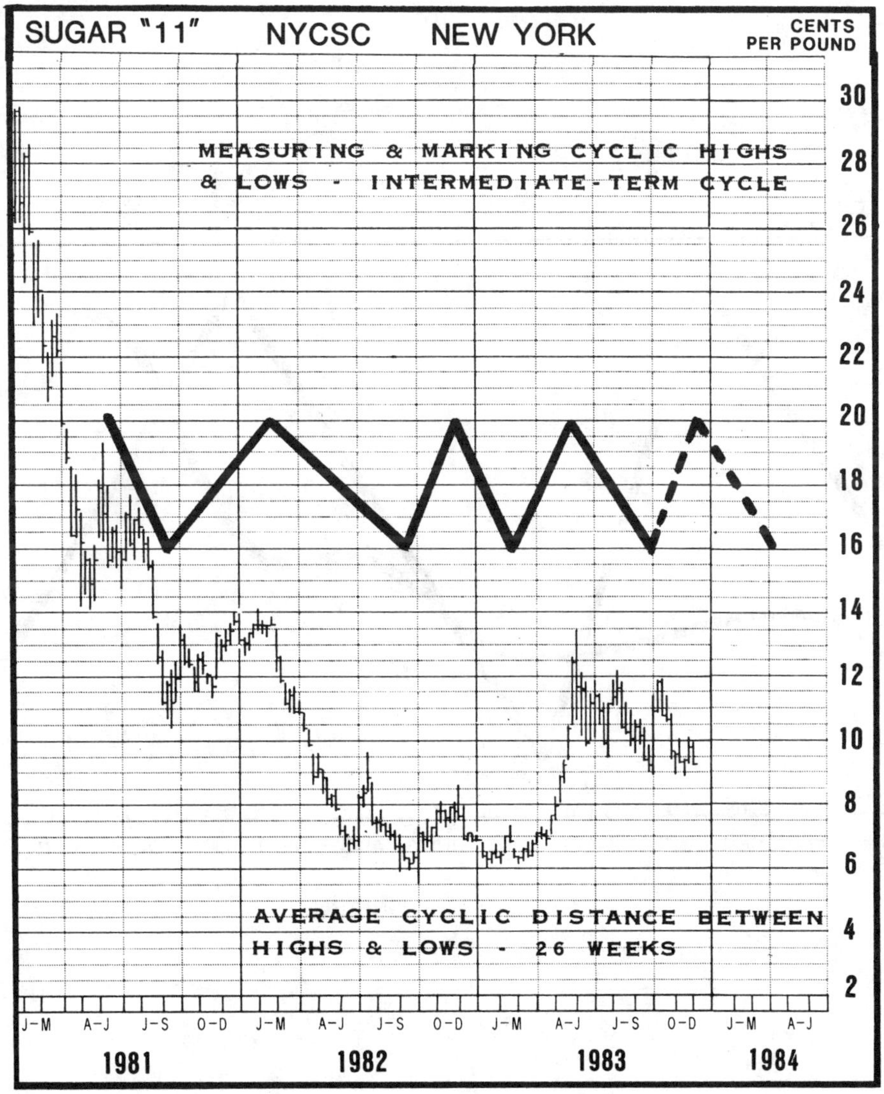

By taking the previous PPG which was developed from combining the Long-Range Cycle and the Seasonal Pattern for the given commodity and adding in this Intermediate-Term Cycle, a more exact picture of predicted price action can be obtained.

The illustration which follows shows our formerly developed PPG overlaid with the Intermediate-Term Cycle:

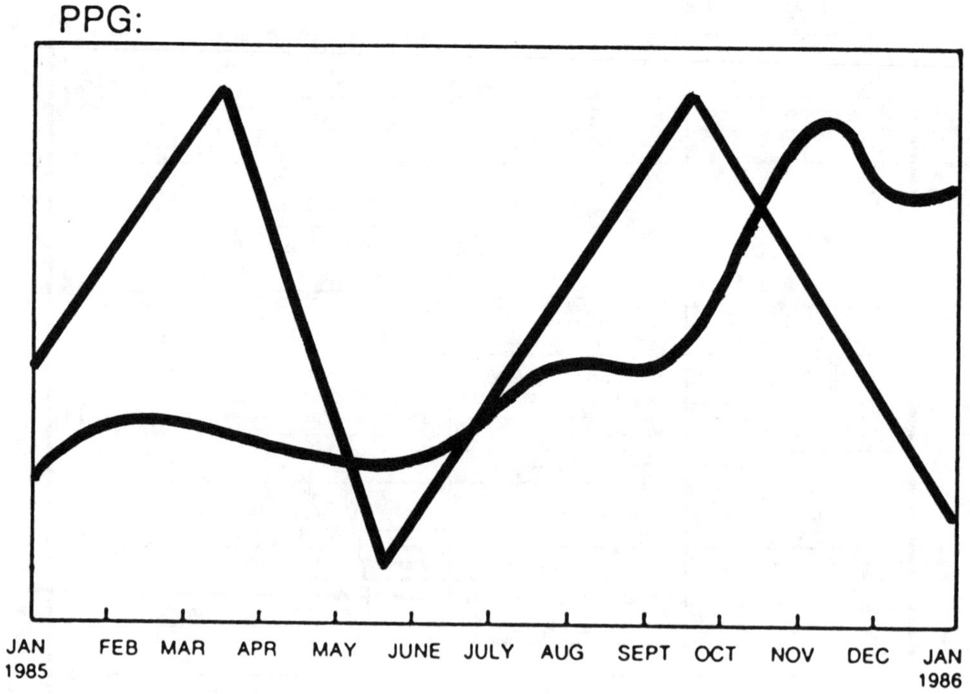

When these two are added together, the result would look like:

PPG: **Sugar**

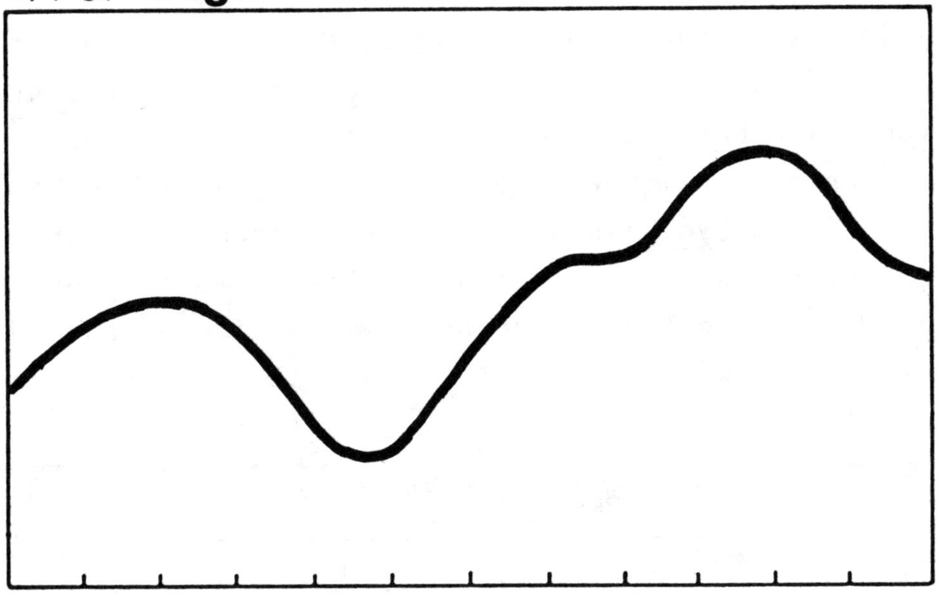

The reader can see now that the resultant PPG is beginning to look more and more like an actual price chart, with its infinite variations, for a real-time commodity (though not a bar chart, but rather, perhaps, a chart of closing prices which would be drawn as a single line). To continue using our former Bear market example: if the Intermediate-Term Cycle were due to bottom at the same time as the Long-Range Cycle and/or the Seasonal Pattern, then the magnitude of such bottoming would be magnified in terms of price amplitude--i.e., the move would carry farther downward than might otherwise be expected. This information gives an even clearer picture of whether or not various Target Levels will, in fact, be breached or whether the Target Level will stop the move. A trader can utilize this information in the same manner as he did previously in terms of placing Trailing Protective Stops and deciding percentages of numbers of multiple-contracts to exit at various Target Levels when Pyramiding.

If a trader chooses to, he also may add in such Shorter-Term Cycles as the approximate eight-week cycle in order to get an even clearer picture of the predicted price action for the coming year. Since we have said approximate eight-week cycle, and since this is due to variation between commodities and variation for any given commodity during a calendar year, if the trader wishes to include this Shorter-Term Cycle in his PPG, it is necessary for him to take the most recent price action for the commodity, on a daily chart, and determine the length of this particular commodity's approximate eight-week cycle. An illustration of how this is done is shown below:

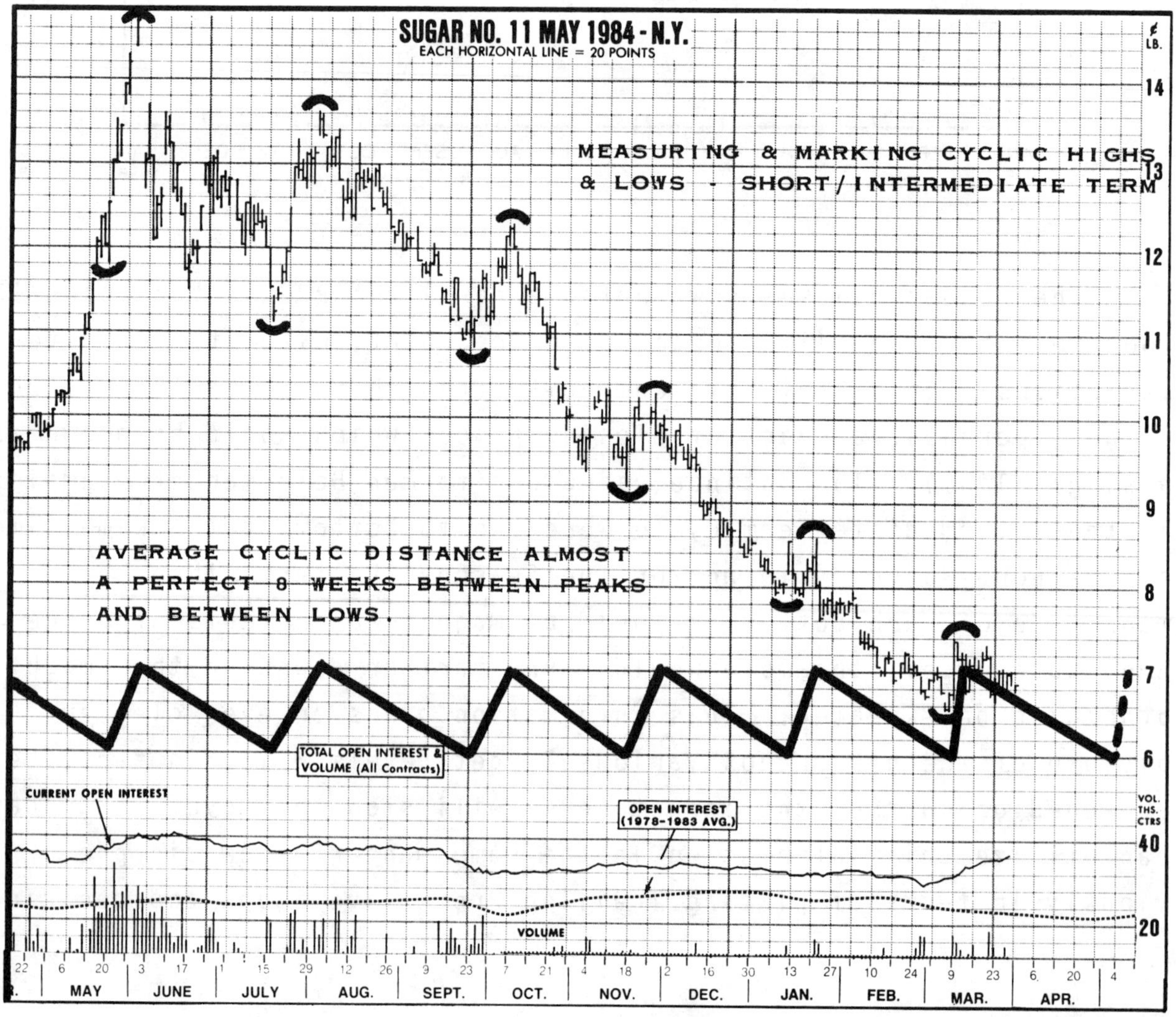

Then the trader, having this information, can further refine the PPG to incorporate this Shorter-Term Cycle by adding the Short-Term Cycle into the already developed PPG.

The following illustration shows our example PPG with an overlay of the Shorter-Term Cycle.

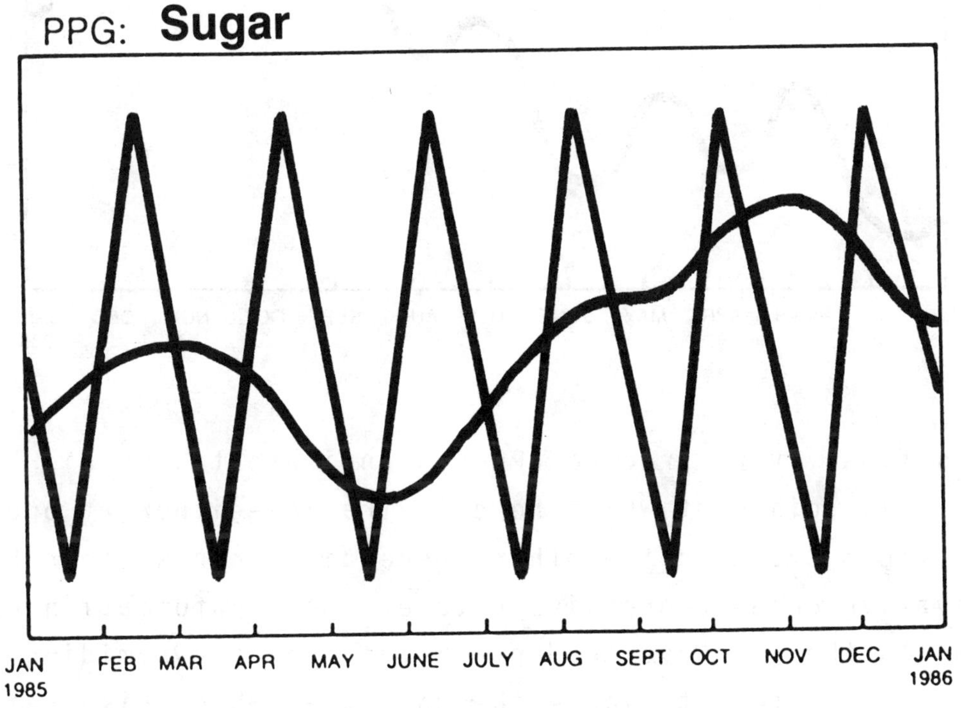

When these two are added together, the more precise PPG would look like the following:

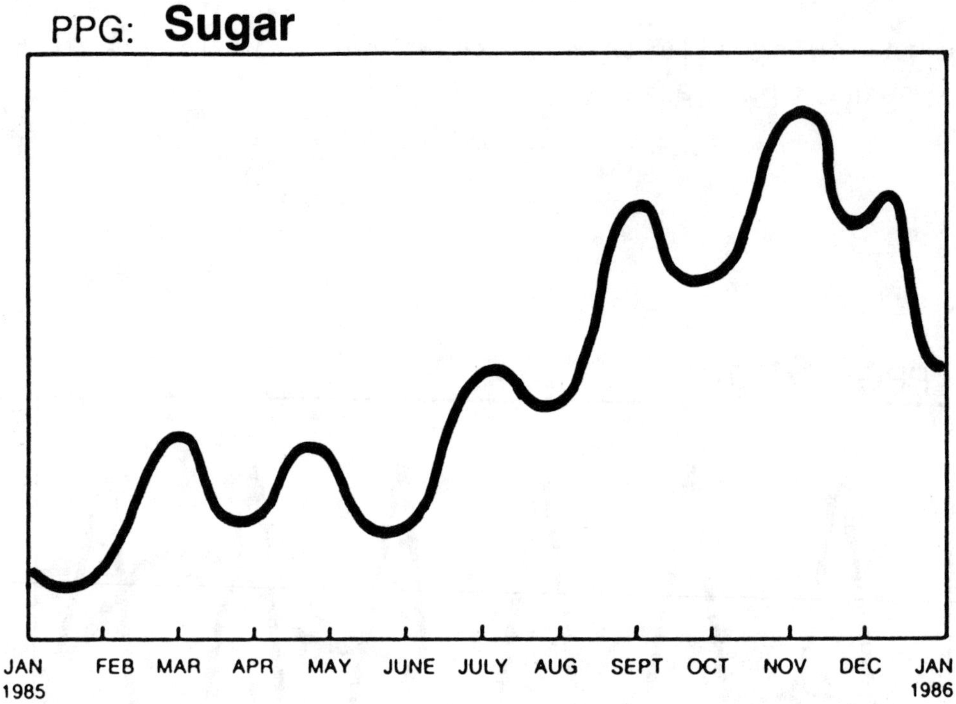

This final, very precise PPG can indicate to the Big Move trader likely points at which he can Pyramid--either at one end of the Short-Term Cycle or the other, depending upon whether he is of a conservative or an aggressive nature. This information can also be useful to the Big Move trader--whether he is Pyramiding or not--by enabling him to anticipate the points at which his Trailing Protective Stops may be endangered and to adjust his stops accordingly--to move them in closer only after these combined cyclical highs (or lows, in the case of a long position) have been established. This can be done, in the case of a short position, if the trader waits until these PPG highs have been formed and the market moves down away from them and then adjusts his stops to just above the PPG high. He would use the reverse procedure, of course, in the case of a long position. Many traders who have been experimenting with or using PPG's have told us that they have found that trendlines drawn on a PPG can tend to be even more valid than trendlines drawn on the actual daily price action charts. When using trendlines with PPG's, however, the trader should heed one caveat: he should make ones stops on a Close-Only basis.

It would be possible, of course, to continue with the even Shorter-Term Cycles--such as the approximate four-week cycle--to try to paint an even more precise PPG.

We feel, however, that to go to this extreme--given the changes in the market place caused by day to day changes in traders' perception of the existing fundamentals--would be carrying the development of the PPG to an extreme that is neither particularly accurate nor particularly useful utility for the Big Move trader.

Needless to say, everything we have said about a market with the Long-Range Cycle heading down applies in just the opposite fashion to a market with the Long-Range Cycle heading up.

We mentioned earlier that the PPG for any commodity can be coordinated with historical price information in order to determine--albeit in an approximate fashion--the levels, high and low, of each point on the PPG under construction and analysis.

This is accomplished by examining the price levels of the preceding three years on a monthly chart for the given commodity and marking the respective high and low points for that commodity.

If the Long-Range Cycle _is_ due to top or bottom during the coming 12 months or period for which the PPG is being constructed, then the trader would assign for the lowest price level on his PPG the point of the historic low of the preceding seven years.

Conversely, if the Long-Range Cycle is due to top during the period of time for which the PPG is being constructed, he would assign the numerical high value for his PPG as that point.

If the Long-Range Cycle is _not_ due to top or bottom during the period under examination, then the high and low points for the PPG would be arbitrarily selected from one of the other Intermediate Target Levels--such as TL1 or TL2. The decision on whether to use TL1 or TL2 should be made as a result of how nearby or how far into the future, in terms of years, the Long-Range Cycle is due to top or bottom.

If the Long-Range Cycle is due to top or bottom in the 12 months following the period of time for which the PPG is being constructed, then the trader should use TL2 as the extreme point on his PPG. If the Long-Range Cycle is due to top or bottom farther away into the future, he should use TL1 as the extreme point on his PPG.

When the extreme high or low point value has been thusly determined and entered on the PPG under construction, the approximate current level of prices can be marked on the PPG at the extreme left side of the PPG.

After this has been done, a measurement can be made on the left axis of the PPG graph and a numerical value per eighth-inch inch or quarter-inch can be determined and the rest of the PPG can be filled in with numerical values such as:

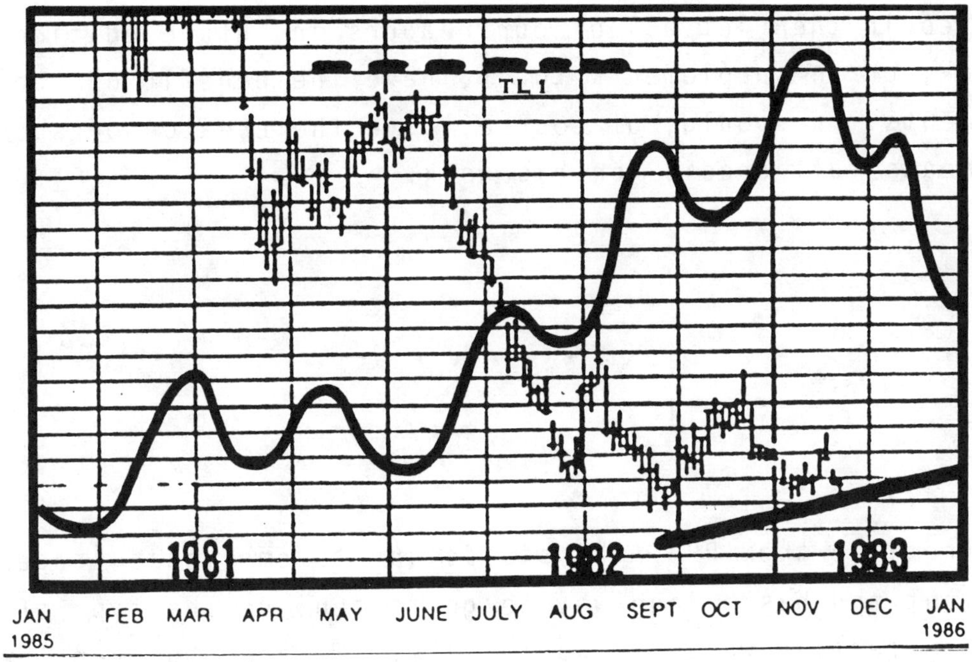

We are constantly attempting to refine our own PPG methodology, examining as many other factors as possible which might influence the PPG under construction.

We are doing this by examining as many former years as possible for as many commodities as possible and constructing PPG's for the following 12 months, without examining what the markets really did in the following 12 months.

We anticipate that many readers will apply their own creativity to PPG Analysis and possibly come up with many factors or techniques which have escaped our own analysis.

We would greatly appreciate any reader with different or original approaches to improving upon PPG Analysis contacting us and, if he is willing to, sharing his refinements so that we can incorporate them in our own PPG Analysis.

We could then let all of our readers in future editions of this book, or in supplements to it, have the benefit of such improvements. We would, of course, give the creator of such improvements full credit for his work.

* * * * *

We realize that PPG Analysis is in its embryonic stages of development and has a long way to go to achieve the type of predictive perfection which we would like. We are, however, pragmatic enough to realize that the relatively constant influx of UFO's for all markets--as well as the effect of very Long-Range Cycles which may be totally unknown to us--have a profound bearing on market price action.

Hence, it is almost a foregone conclusion that PPG Analysis--like all other areas of commodity analysis--will never be a perfect methodology, but an imperfect, and, at the same time, very useful tool for the Big Move trader to help him increase his profits dramatically for any given calendar year. Appendix C at the back of this book gives our own PPG Analysis for all the major commodities that Mega-Trades follows for its subscribers.

These PPG's for 1985 should provide those readers who wish to use them as "ready-made" with a valuable tool for their Big Move trading programs. For the Big Move trader who wishes to construct his own PPG's in the future, the examples in Appendix C will serve as an "answer sheet" to help him check his own construction of PPG's.

CHAPTER 13

WINNING TRADE ANALYSIS

This, in our opinion, is perhaps the most important chapter in this entire book. If not the most important, it certainly ranks as the next most important to Chapter 14: "Losing Trade Analysis." It is amazing how few traders ever take the time to analyze their trades after they are completed. The tendency seems to be that if a trade is a winning one, the trader's exuberance or satisfaction from having the profitable trade is such that he very rarely, if ever, goes back and examines exactly what the components were that did, in fact, make this particular trade a successful one for him.

The converse also seems to be the case. In conversations with numerous traders and subscribers, we have found that it is extremely rare for a trader to go back and make a detailed analysis of his losing trades to find out what went wrong. From a psychological perspective, this is probably due to the trader's discomfort at examining a trade which cost him money, his own inability to admit mistakes and the general sense of discomfort which such an analysis would evoke.

In this chapter on analyzing profitable trades, we will examine an actual _Mega-Trades_ recommendation from 1983, a representative Big Move trade. We selected this particular trade at random, and in our subsequent analysis, we found that in some respects it was a "flawed" Big Move trading candidate in that, while it was successful, it did not meet necessarily meet all of the criteria we have set for positioning ourselves in Big Move trades. Since this position was selected at random from our winning trades, however, we will examine it in detail to find out why this particular trade did, in fact, work.

We believe it is of the utmost importance that every Big Move trader who wishes to be as successful as possible analyze each and every winning trade in order to determine why it was profitable. By so doing, the Big Move trader can learn from and reinforce his successful Big Move trading techniques. And when a Big Move trade is of a marginal nature--i.e., it does not necessarily fulfill all of the criteria for a Big Move trade to the degree we would normally wish--such analysis will provide the Big Move trader with insight into the key components which made such a marginal trade profitable.

It would have been quite simple for us to have carefully selected a Big Move trade from all of our Mega-Trades recommendations in order to find an "ideal" potential Big Move trade--one which fulfilled all of the criteria that we have established in this book to an extraordinarily high degree. There were a few such trades over the past years, but since this is an imperfect world, it is very rare to find any given potential Big Move trading candidate which possesses all of these criteria in its favor to such a high degree.

In February of 1983 we issued a recommendation to buy July, 1983 Sugar. At that particular point in time, many of the commodity markets were trading at neither historical high nor at historical low price levels, but instead were trading in a mid-range area. Sugar, however, was an exception. It was trading at that point in time at historically low price levels, as can be seen from the accompanying monthly graph of Sugar.

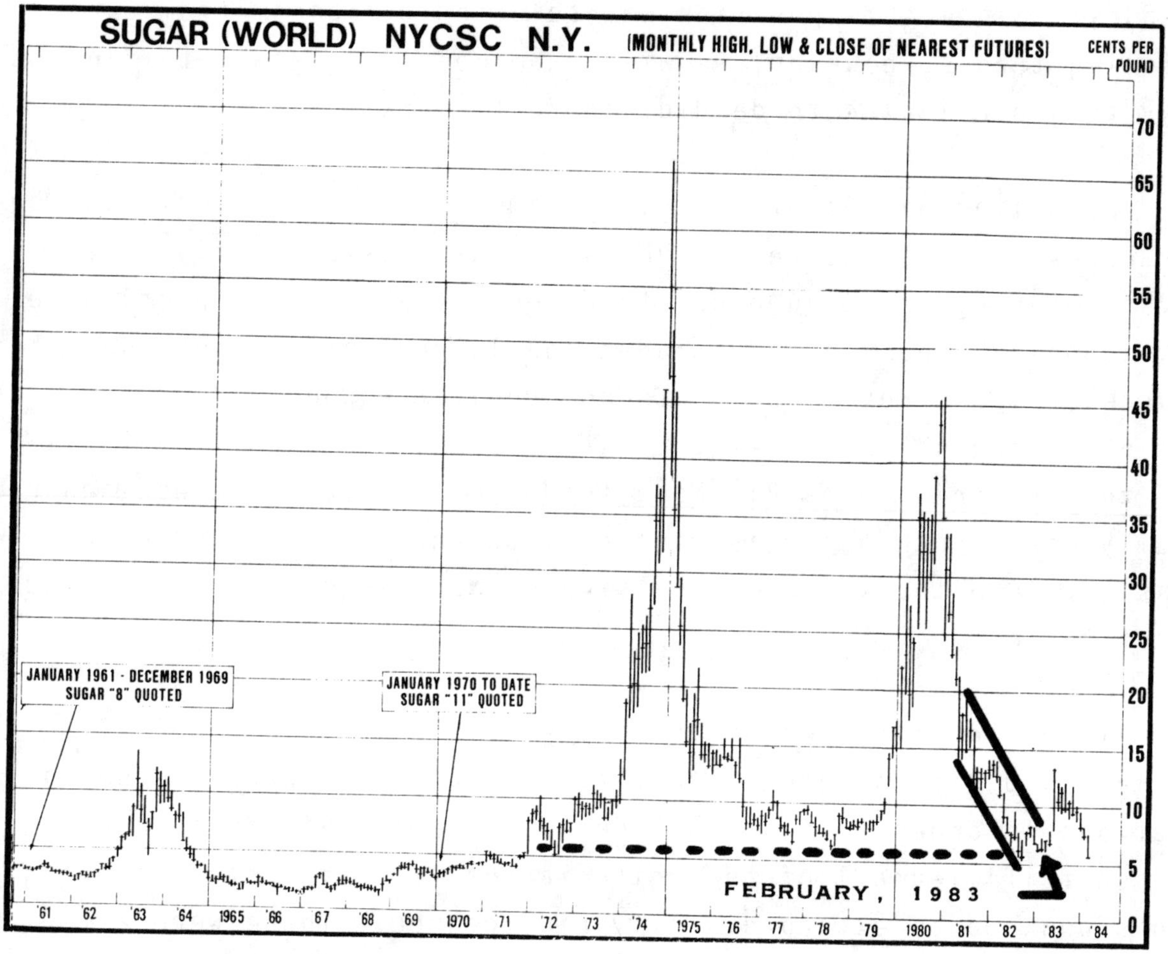

From this standpoint, Sugar certainly qualified as a potential Big Move trading candidate. Prices throughout 1981 had been falling rapidly from their highs at 45-cents and, throughout the later part of 1982 and early 1983, prices essentially had been moving sideways, as is readily observable on the monthy graph. This sideways trading pattern with a slight downward cast which Sugar had been exhibiting can be readily seen more easily on the following weekly chart:

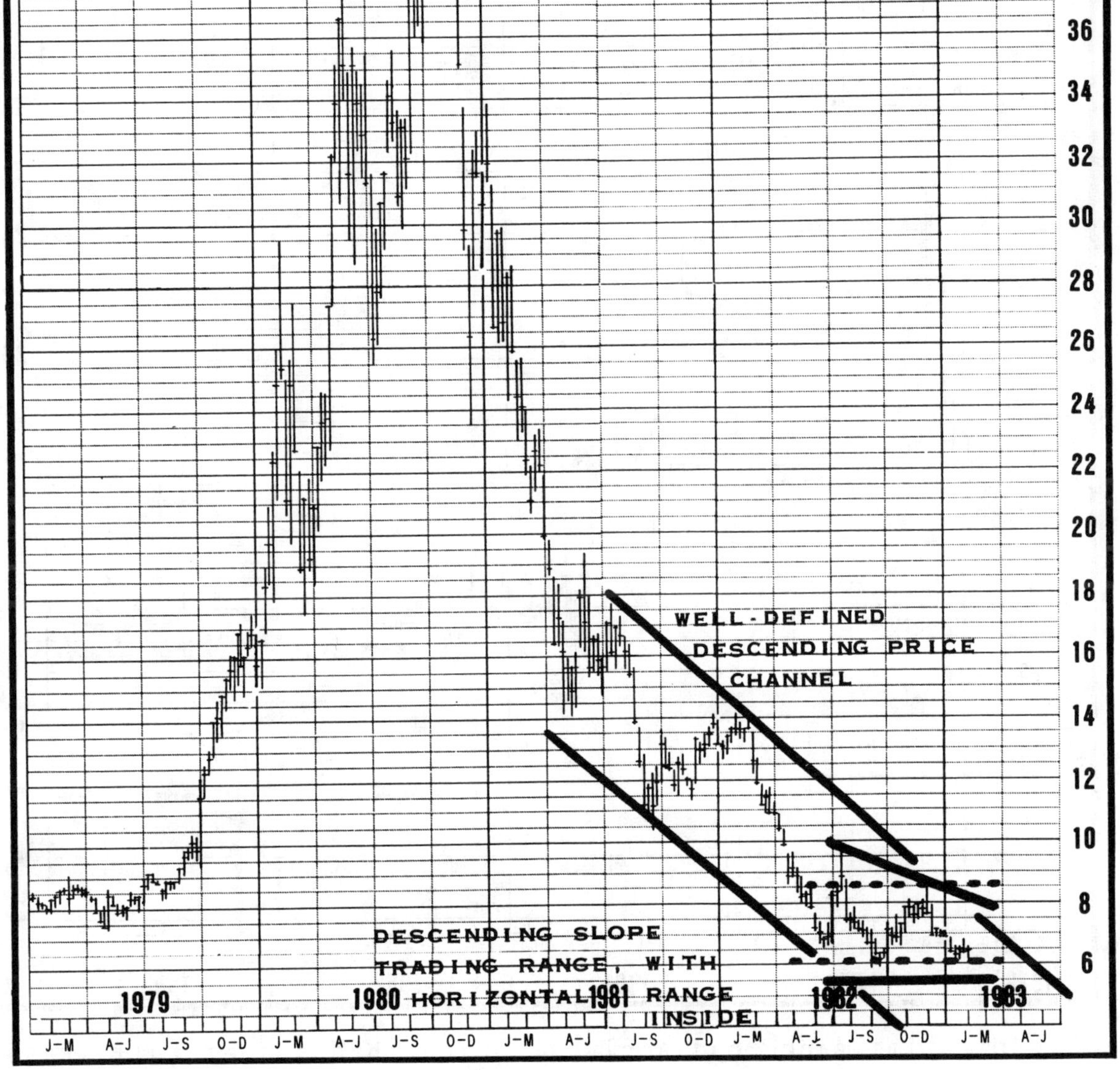
SUGAR "11" (WORLD)
NEW YORK
cents per pound
46
44
42
40
38
36
34
32
30
28
26
24
22
20
18
16
14
12
10
8
6
WELL-DEFINED
DESCENDING PRICE
CHANNEL
DESCENDING SLOPE
TRADING RANGE, WITH
HORIZONTAL RANGE
INSIDE
1979
1980
1981
1982
1983
J-M
A-J
J-S
O-D

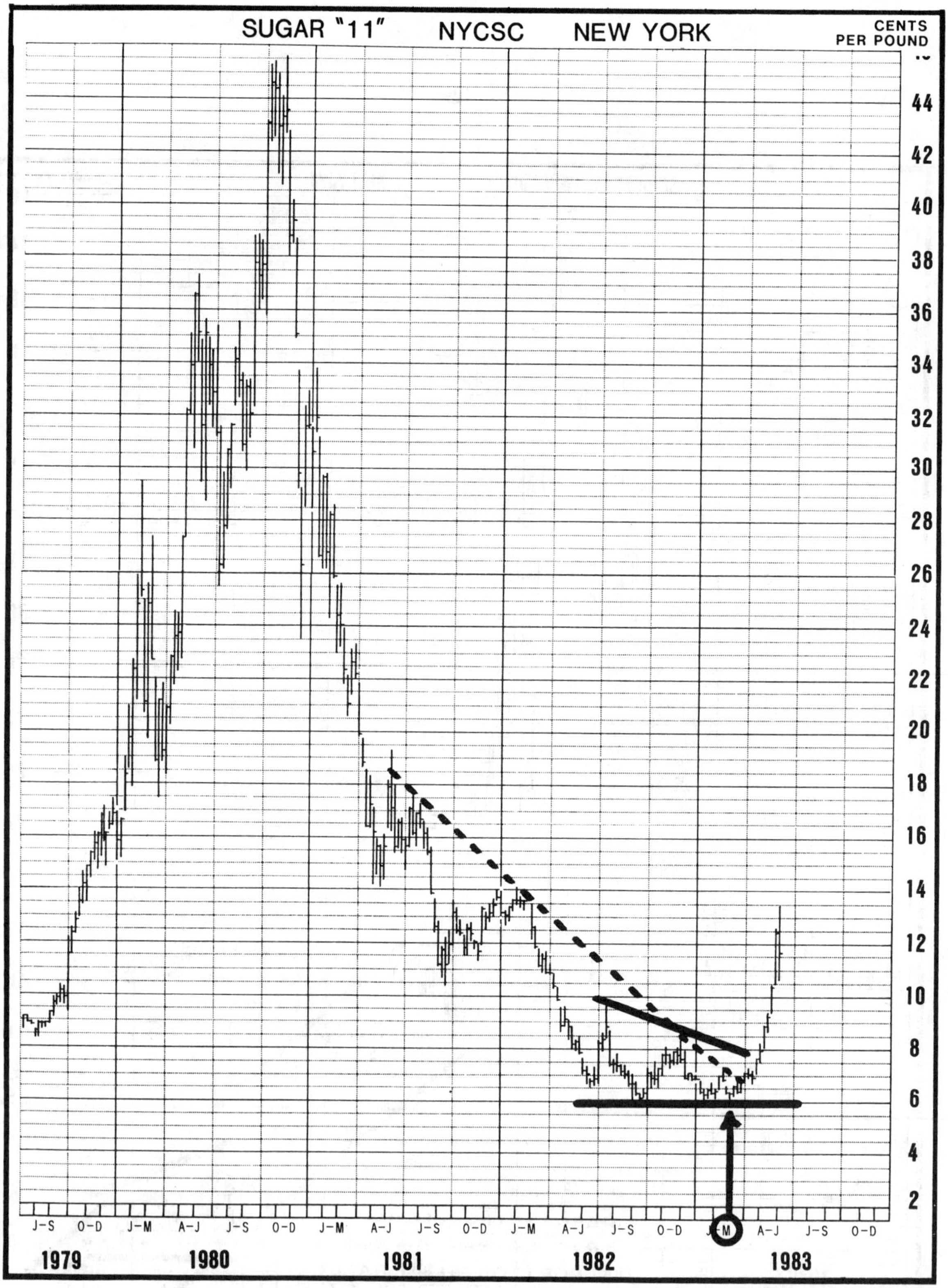

By the time March had arrived, prices had successfully resisted an attempt to again break through the six-cent level and, instead, bounced off what then appeared to be a key support level. This holding of the six-cent support level, coupled with the historically low price levels for Sugar, both were significant and quite positive indicators that the next move in prices would be up. A thorough study of all the Confirmation Signals we have discussed in this volume, however, was required in order to validate establishing a long Big Move position. The previous illustration of another weekly graph of Sugar, actually a time point after which we had established our long positions, shows well the breakout from the bottoming pattern.

First, we'll examine our Confirmation Signal for the Seasonal Pattern for Sugar during the upcoming time period during which and after which the trading position would have been established. Sugar typically bottoms in the month of June and then seasonally proceeds upwards until November, at which time it typically crests and then proceeds back down again until the following June. The Seasonal Pattern, such as those shown in the back of this book in Appendix A, shows this seasonal tendency, and, in the case of a potential Sugar trade, the pattern does not look particularly favorable for the long side until the month of June arrives--several months away from the time we were considering entering the market. Therefore, we received no Confirmation Signal of a positive nature for establishing long positions in Sugar at this time.

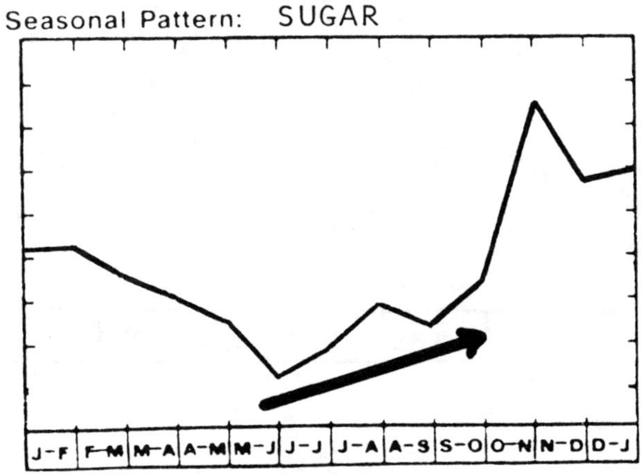

The next Confirmation Signals that we will look at are the Long-Range Cycles which affect Sugar. The most important cycle from our standpoint, of course, is the Long-Range Cycle, although we realize fully that Intermediate and Shorter-Term Cycles also are important. Our analysis of the Long-Range Cycle for Sugar determined that our conclusion regarding the bottoming of the Long-Range Cycle for Sugar in 1983 was not accurate because subsequent skewing appeared most likely due to even Longer-Term Cycles, as we have discussed earlier in this book. But at that point in time, the Long-Range Cycle appeared to be bottoming in early 1983 and then heading up through the latter part of 1986. The reader will notice in Appendix B at the back of the book that we have revised the Long-Range Cycle for Sugar from the one which we use in the following illustration to reflect this skewing caused by these Longer-Term Cycles. But in the late winter of 1983, all indications were that the Long-Range Cycle was, in fact, bottoming and getting ready to start up. This appeared to us to be a validation that Sugar would begin an up-move despite the fact that the Seasonal Pattern was not calling for an up-move to occur until early summer. The Long-Range Cycle which we were using for Sugar for February-March 1983 follows:

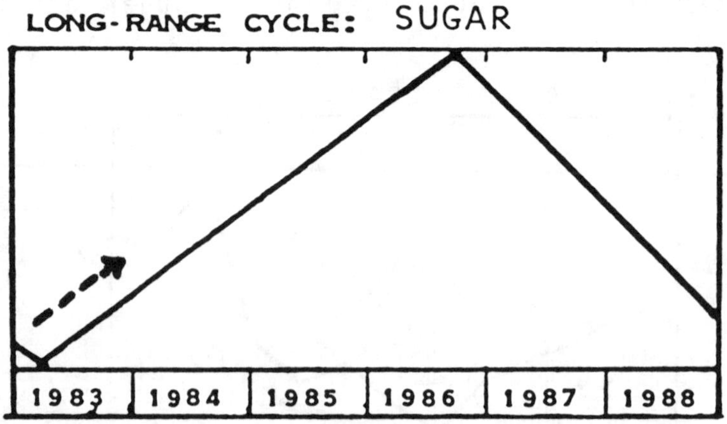

Our next Confirmation Signal--Bullish Consensus--assured us that prices were getting ready to move up since, during the month of January, the market had become very oversold, with the Bullish Consensus figure dropping below the 25% level for most of the month of January. The Bullish Consensus figure then began an upward move, with dipping in March and then resuming its upward climb. This was a very positive indication that the Sugar market was, in fact, getting ready to turn up. This is an example of how an indicator often will "lead" the actual market action by a period of even as much as two months, since the oversold condition of the Bullish Consensus--when it was below 25%--occurred that much before the market actually turned up.

The reader will notice that the Bullish Consensus in early May reached an overbought level in excess of 75% and 80%, which foreshadowed the violent market correction which took place the last week of May and the first week of June. Here, the Bullish Consensus led the market by just about one month--a valuable signal that when the market became so overbought, it was time to use Trailing Stop techniques that would move a trader's stops in closer than they had been up to this point in time.

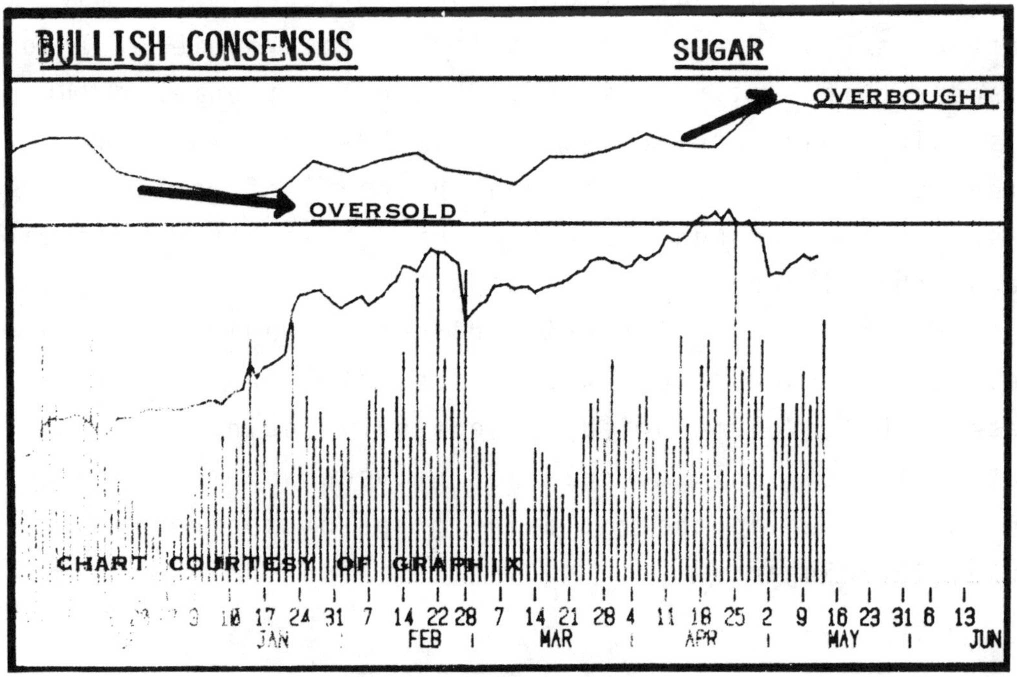

The Bullish Consensus for this market illustrates another good point regarding this Confirmation Signal: A Big Move trader could simply have bought his positions the moment the Bullish Consensus dipped below 25% in mid-January, which would have been a very safe and good place to have bought into the market; but, on the other side of the coin, if the Big Move trader had liquidated his positions in early May, when the Bullish Consensus moved above 80%, he would have lost a lot of his profits, or if he had assumed a short position market at that point, he would have exposed himself to unnecessary risks due to the wide Initial Protective Stop placement which would have been required. Hence, as can be seen, Bullish Consensus is a very valuable Confirmation Signal tool when it is combined with other Confirmation Signals. By itself, it works remarkably well sometimes; but, at other times, using Bullish Consensus alone without these other Confirmation Signals can cause disasterous results.

Our next Confirmation Signal, Volume of Trading, initially gave us some contradictory signals, as can be seen in the next illustration. While prices dropped during the latter part of February, Volume stayed very high. But as prices fell in March, Volume started drying up. Then as prices began their move through the latter part of March and into April, the Volume of Trading increased significantly. Since we had not yet entered the market at this point--our entry point being 7.99-cents--we felt that--with the Volume increasing through the month of April as prices increased up and through their high of 7.80-cents set in mid-February--this increase in Volume was a very Bullish indication, suggesting that the ensuing price direction would continue on the upside. By the same token, when prices stalled in early April and decreased a bit, Volume dried up somewhat--again a very Bullish indication to us. This correlation between Volume and price motion can be seen in the following graph of the daily price chart for July, 1983 Sugar:

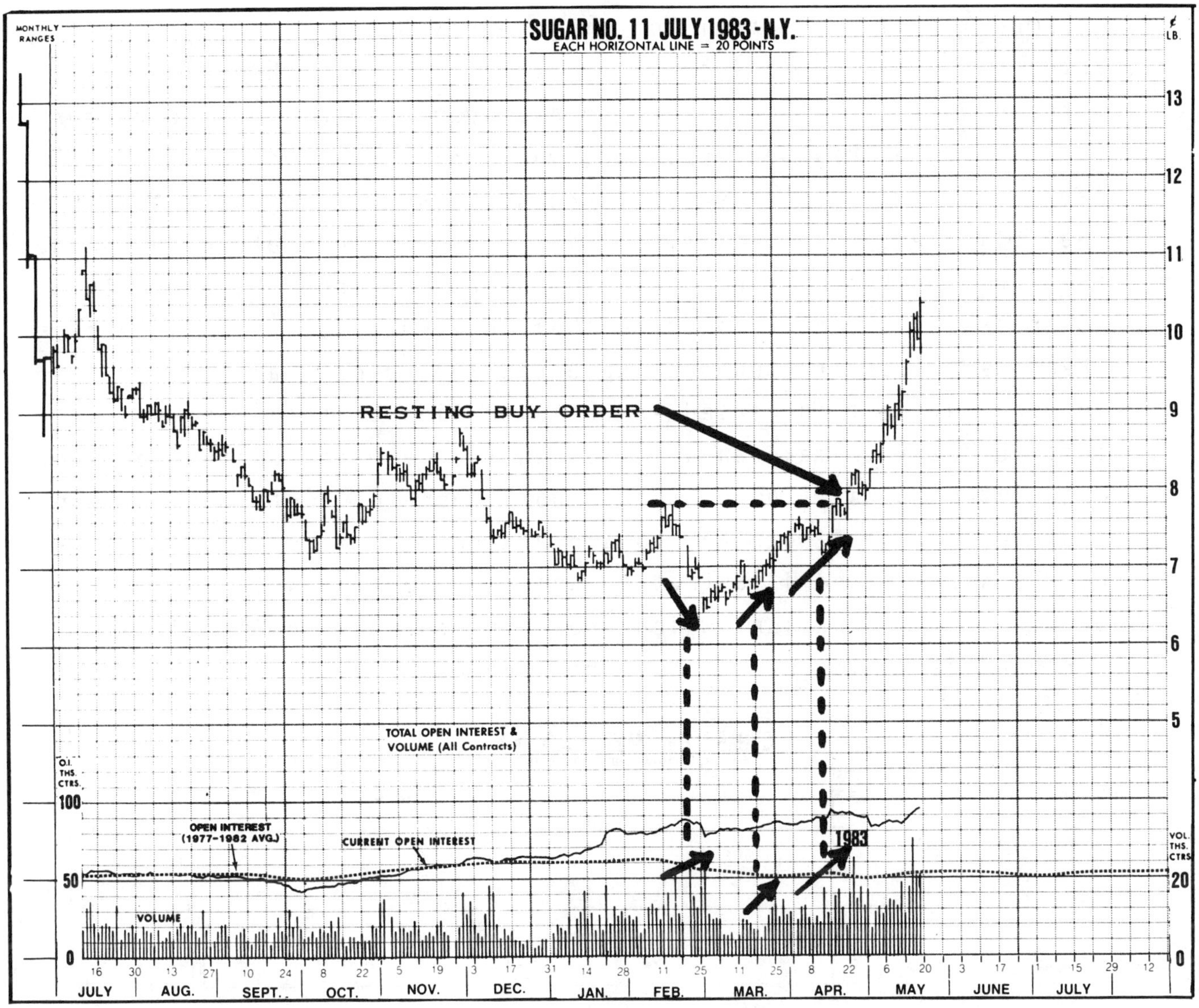

So, of the first four Confirmation Signals we examined, three were positive from the standpoint of predicting an up-move in Sugar. Now we will examine Open Interest. Throughout the summer of 1982 as prices declined dramatically from 11-cents on down to the 7-8-cent area, Open Interest remained relatively flat. Then in October of 1982, Open Interest started moving up as prices rallied through October and November. This was the first indication that the market was perhaps getting ready to turn. But other factors prevented the early October low of just above 7-cents from being the bottom of the market, and as prices decreased from early

December until the actual bottom in early March of 1983, Open Interest continued to increase--a Bearish sign. The reader will note, however, that in late January, Open Interest bulged up for one week as prices went up, and, when prices perked up again in late February, Open Interest increased its angle of assent. The real clincher, however, came during the last week of February and the first week of March when Open Interest dropped by about 10,000 contracts as prices crashed to their contract lows at 6.4-cents. Then, as prices started back up again throughout March, the rise in Open Interest increased--a definite sign that the market was getting ready to make an up-move, whether a major up-move or not. Open Interest was a good, though not concrete, Confirmation Signal that we were getting ready to see a nice Bull move upward. This can be seen in the illustration which follows as well as in the preceding illustration, which shows the changes in Open Interest through the months of March, April and May:

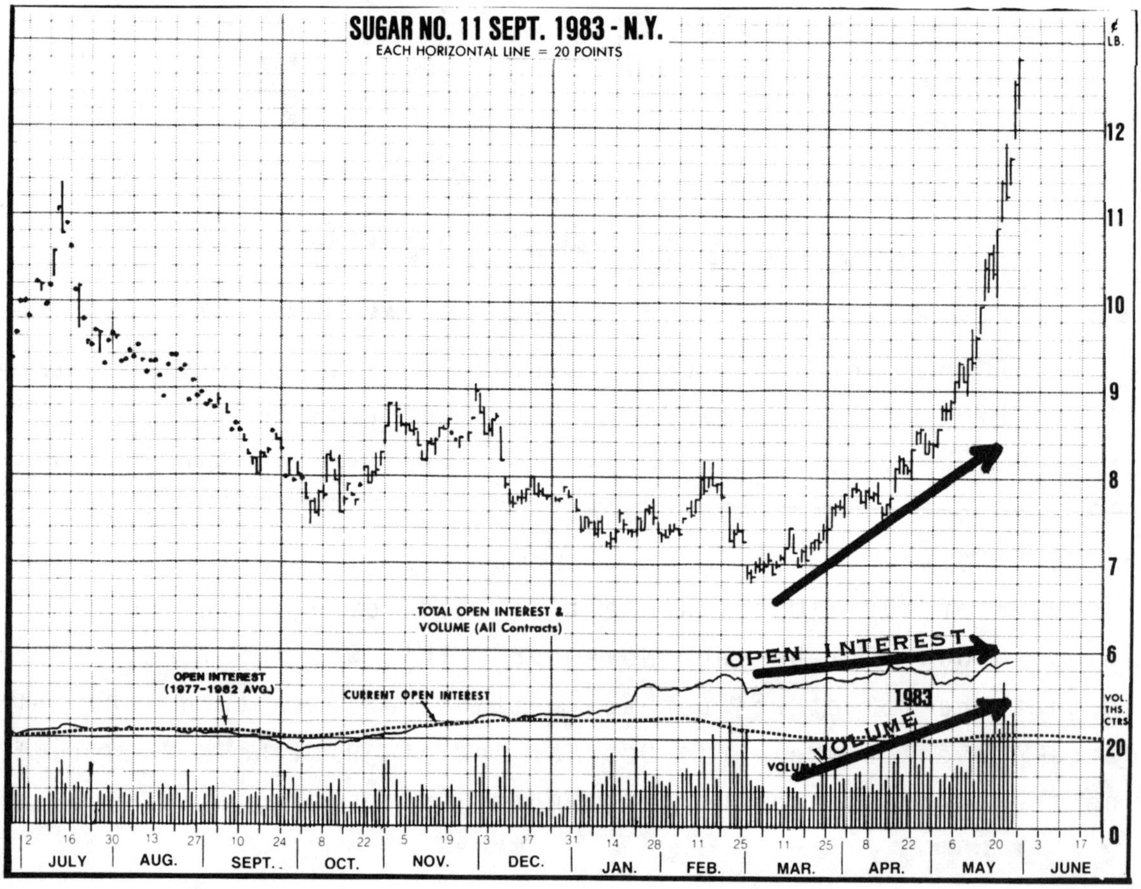

Our next Confirmation Signal is Moving Averages. By the time we were considering entering our Big Move position on the long side, the closing price of Sugar was below the 10-day and 40-day Moving Averages and had been ever since December of 1982, with the exception of a brief blip upwards in February. Our Entry Point at 7.99-cents would be such that the closing prices would definitely be above both the 10-day and 40-day Moving Averages if we were to get a fill. So from that standpoint, the Moving Averages as a Confirmation Signal were Bullish for our position, considering the fact that for our position to even fill in the first place, closing prices would have to move above these two key Moving Averages. The following illustration shows how the Moving Averages were positive for a Bull Move in Sugar:

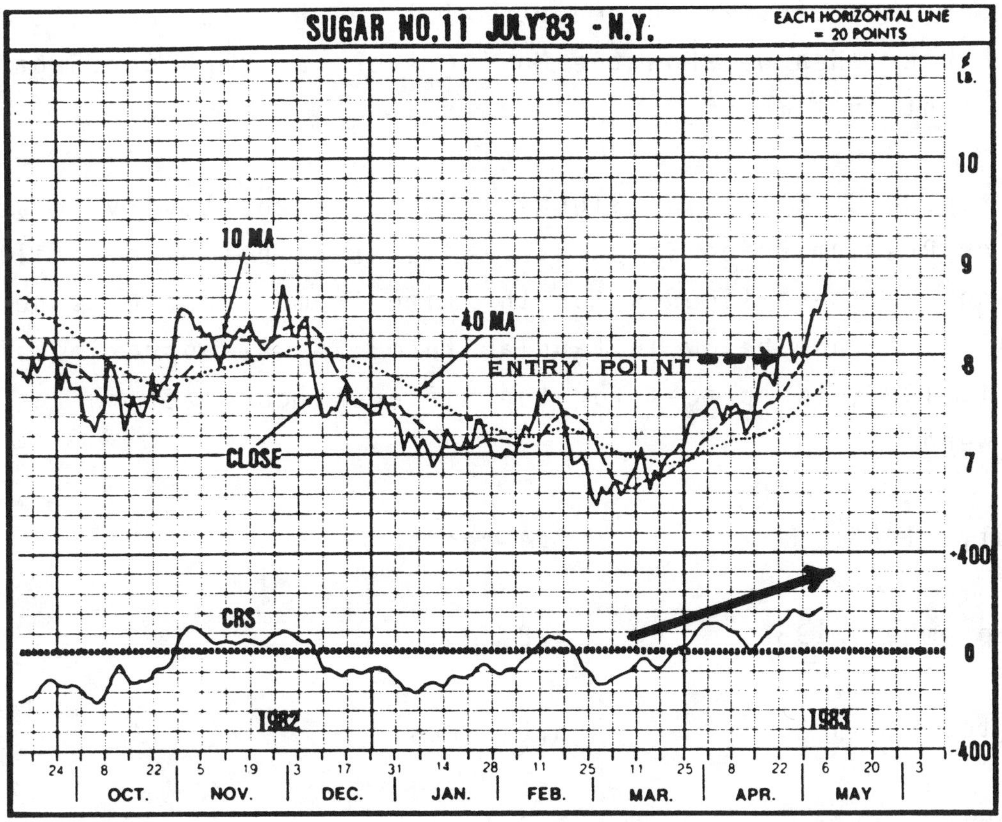

Also shown on this chart from Commodity Research Bureau is the Current Relative Strength (CRS), which is one type of Relative Strength Index we have not discussed in this volume as a Confirma-Confirmation Signal. We could have added any mathematically-derived Relative Strength Index which has been tested and proven over a sufficient period of time to our list of Confirmation Signals, but we have chosen not to do this. Besides a Relative Strength Index, we could have included a number of other factors as Confirmation Signals, but we wanted to keep our approach as simple as possible, so we did not include any type of Relative Strenght Index as one of our Big Move Confirmation Signals. We will note, however, that the Relative Strength Index at the end of February had, in fact, turned down--not a particularly Bullish indication. The Relative Strength Index, or the CRS, did, in fact, become positive just about the time we entered our long positions, however, as the reader will be able to see later in this chapter when we show the Moving Average graph for Sugar at a later point in time.

Our next Confirmation Signal is that of Positivity or Negativity, or Premium Price Spreads. While we do not have an illustration showing these figures for the time frame under consideration, we will list them below in tabular form. As of approximately April 1, 1983, the prices for the different contract months of Sugar were:

July, 1983:	7.4-cents
September, 1983:	7.8-cents
October, 1983:	8.2-cents
March, 1984:	9.2-cents

May, 1984: 9.4-cents

Hence, the more distant contract months of Sugar each showed an increasing price level, indicating a strong amount of Positivity. We certainly were not dealing with a commodity that was exhibiting any degree of Negativity. So, our Positivity/Negativity Confirmation Signal also indicated that Sugar would continue to increase in price.

Our eighth Confirmation Signal is the Commitments of Traders. The most recent figures available to us at the time we were considering the trade--since they are only published at the end of each month--were those as of January 31, 1983, and our recommendation was originally made in the month of February:

COMMITMENTS OF TRADERS—LARGE HEDGERS, SPECULATORS AND SMALL TRADERS

Open Interest Positions Shown in Percent (Rounded) as of January 31, 1983

MARKETS	LARGE HEDGERS				LARGE SPECULATORS				SMALL TRADERS			
	Long	Short	Net	△	Long	Short	Net	△	Long	Short	Net	△
Cattle (Live)	23	35	-12	- 1	13	3	+10	+ 6	59	57	+ 2	- 5
Cocoa	32	68	-36	-15	32	3	+29	+ 6	36	29	+ 7	+ 9
Coffee	50	46	+ 4	- 2	7	20	-13	0	42	33	+ 9	+ 2
Copper	12	72	-60	- 6	19	11	+ 8	+ 1	66	13	+53	+ 5
Corn	43	56	-13	+ 1	11	2	+ 9	+ 4	43	39	+ 4	- 5
Cotton	37	57	-20	- 4	9	8	+ 1	- 6	52	33	+19	+10
Gold (Comex)	33	64	-31	-10	17	9	+ 8	+ 5	41	18	+23	+ 5
Heating Oil #2	59	28	+31	0	7	31	-24	+ 3	27	34	- 7	- 2
Hogs	25	13	+12	- 4	21	10	+11	+ 2	48	72	-24	+ 1
Lumber	12	48	-36	- 1	18	4	+14	+ 1	68	46	+22	0
Oats	22	51	-29	-24	3	4	- 1	- 2	74	45	+29	+25
Orange Juice	28	60	-32	+ 4	7	8	- 1	- 3	55	22	+33	0
Platinum	7	78	-71	- 4	33	8	+25	+ 2	59	12	+47	+ 3
Pork Bellies	12	14	- 2	- 2	15	22	- 7	-14	66	56	+10	+17
Silver (Comex)	5	39	-34	- 1	15	4	+11	0	75	51	+24	+ 3
Soybeans	28	60	-32	-22	13	3	+10	+10	54	33	+21	+12
Soybean Meal	41	58	-17	+ 1	18	2	+16	+ 8	39	37	+12	+ 1
Soybean Oil	33	65	-32	-43	13	7	+ 6	+16	49	24	+25	+26
Sugar "11"	53	75	-22	- 6	10	11	- 1	+ 2	33	10	+23	+ 4
Wheat (CHI)	11	50	-39	-27	12	7	+ 5	+ 5	72	38	+34	+22

As can be seen on the graph above, in the period of time under examination--January, 1983--large speculators were short more positions than they were long. But however Bearish that might appear to have been, that factor was at least neutralized by the next column--the Delta--which showed that with a plus 2, the large speculators were actually less Bearish than they had been in the preceding month, since the plus-2 figure indicated that the net figure as of December 31, 1982, would have been a minus 3. Hence, this Confirmation Signal was of a neutral cast and was neither particularly favorable nor unfavorable to our intended long position.

Now we come to our ninth and last Confirmation Signal--Fundamentals. During the period of time we were considering the trade, we aquired our basic information primarily from data in the Wall Street Journal, Consensus and Futures Magazine. The essence of the Fundamental information was that the majority of all available data was favorable to the Bullish case.

The Fundamentals included: inclement weather in the form of torrential rains in Cuba, the prospects of a new International Sugar Agreement, a drought in Austrailia which was cutting back output, wet weather and flooding in Europe which was delaying beet sowing, the reduction of EEC acreage, and drought in both the Philippines and Thailand.

In fact, very little--if anything--was of a Bearish nature in the Fundamental information available to us in the February-March time frame of 1983, with the exception that current supplies of Sugar on hand were somewhat excessive. Hence, our last Confirmation Signal--Fundamentals--was almost overwhelmingly of a Bullish nature.

So in March, 1983, between our regular monthly issues of Mega-Trades, we made the following recommendation on our twice-weekly telephone hotline update:

BUY JULY, 1983 SUGAR AT 6.90 STOP, WITH INITIAL PROTECTIVE STOPS AT 6.39 ON AN INTRA-DAY BASIS.

TARGET = 20¢

INITIAL RISK = $571

RISK % OF MARGIN = 19%

POTENTIAL PROFIT = $25,760

RISK/REWARD RATIO = 0.022

Before we get into our discussion of our Initial Entry Point, Initial Protective Stop, Trailing Protective Stop, Target Levels and Exit Points, we would like to point out that besides meeting our primary qualification of prices being at an historic extreme or mid-range level, Sugar's Confirmation Signals were favorable to a Bull move for seven of the nine signals we utilize, and one of the two remaining signals was not Bearish, but neutral.

On paper then, everything seemed at that point to ensure a profitable Big Move trade, and this, in fact, did occur.

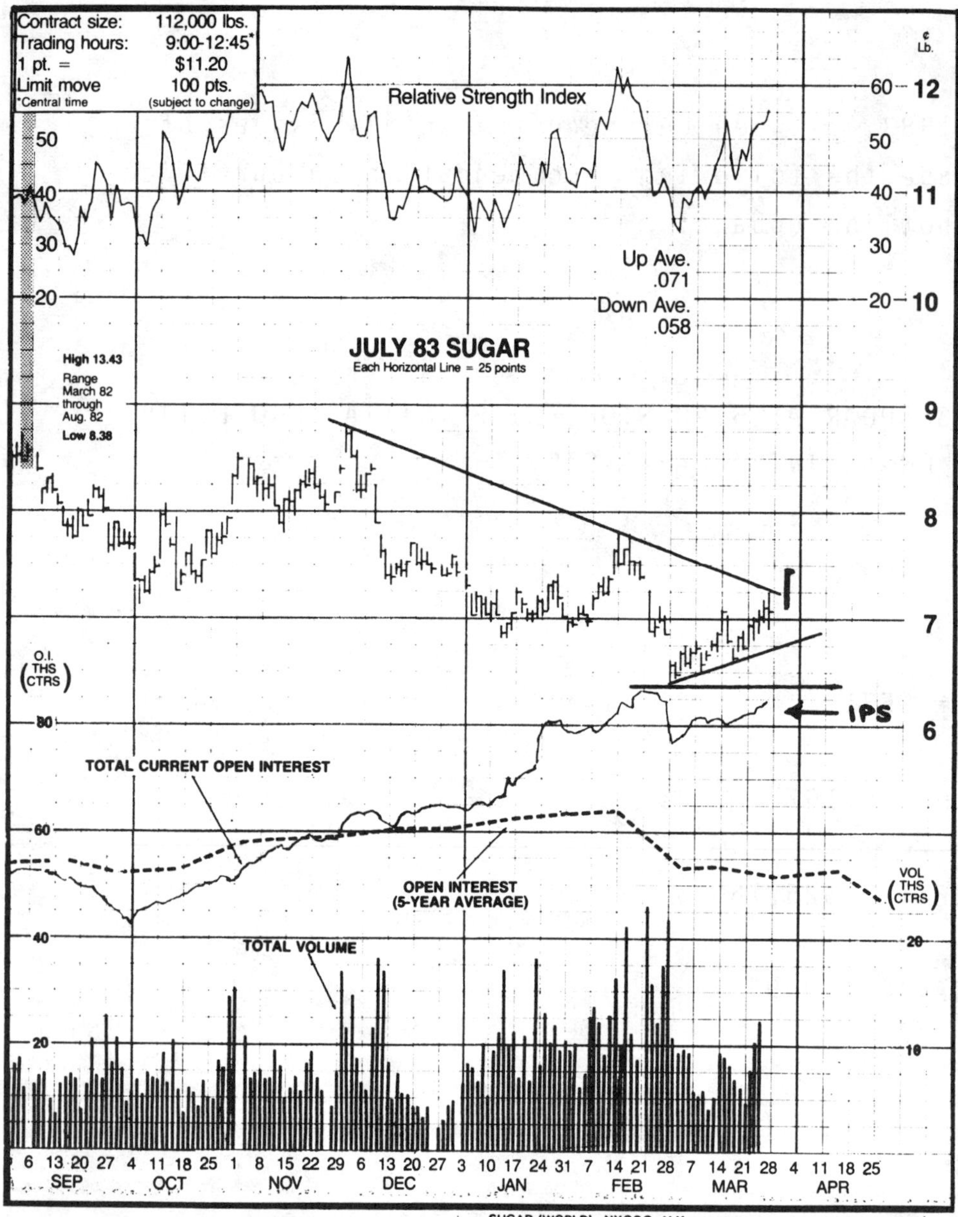

SUGAR - JULY

CURRENT SITUATION:

PRICES REALLY GOT A NICE "SHOT IN THE ARM" ON THURSDAY OF THIS PAST WEEK AND THIS MOMENTUM SHOULD BE HELPFUL TO OUR BULL POSITIONS.

TECHNICAL ANALYSIS:

THE BREAKING THROUGH ON THE UPSIDE OF THE DESCENDING TRENDLINE ON THE ACCOMPANYING DAILY CHART IS AN ENCOURAGING SIGN THAT OUR ORIGINAL ANALYSIS OF THIS MARKET IS CORRECT. GIVEN THE EXTREMELY DEPRESSED CONDITION OF THIS MARKET, IT LOOKS AS IF WE WILL BE PYRAMIDING OUR POSITIONS, MOST PROBABLY AT 8¢ AND 9¢ LEVEL OR IN THAT GENERAL VICINITY VIA INSTRUCTIONS ON THE WEEKLY RECORDER. BREAKTHROUGHS OF THESE LEVELS WILL BE POTENT SIGN, THO WE DO ANTICIPATE A CORRECTIVE DROPBACK SOMETIME SOON.

CYCLICAL ANALYSIS:

INTERMEDIATE-TERM CYCLES ARE DUE TO TOP NEAR THE END OF 1983, BEGINNING OF 1984, HENCE OUR PROJECTION OF TARGET ACHIEVEMENT AT THAT POINT OR VERY NEAR TO IT.

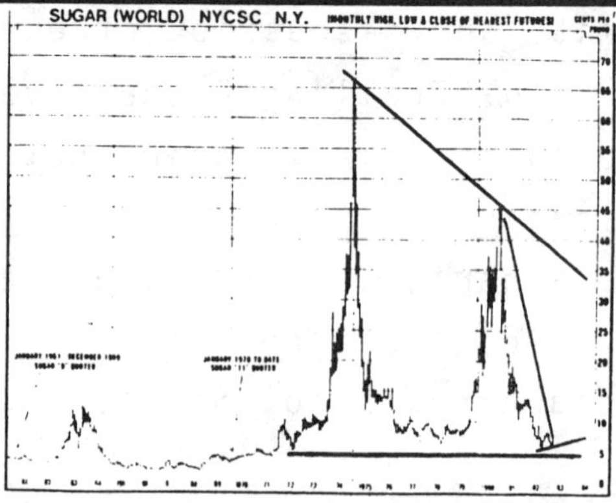

FUNDAMENTAL ANALYSIS:

SEASONALLY PRICES TREND DOWN UNTIL MAY/JUNE, BUT THEN INCREASE THRU JAN/FEB, TYING IN WITH OUR CYCLICAL ANALYSIS WELL. DUE TO THE COMPLICATED NATURE OF THE SUGAR MARKET IT IS DIFFICULT TO ANALYZE FUNDAMENTALS INTELLIGENTLY, BUT EARLY SIGNS OF PLANTING CUTBACKS AND THE IMPROVING U.S. ECONOMY ALL BODE WELL FOR AN IMPROVEMENT IN SUGAR PRICES.

RISK/REWARD ANALYSIS:

CURRENT RISK = $571
RISK % MARGIN = 19%
PRO. PROFIT = $25,760
RISK/REWARD = 0.022

TIME FRAME:

ANALYSIS NOW INDICATES THE TARGET AREA WILL PROBABLY NOT BE REACHED UNTIL EARLY 1984.

RECOMMENDATION

HOLD LONGS BOUGHT AT 6.90, KEEP PROTECTIVE STOPS AT 6.39
TARGET = 20¢

In the preceding illustration, we have reproduced the exact recommendation page from the April, 1983, issue of Capricorn (the original name for Mega-Trades). This page shows the information which was given to our subscribers in printed form, as a followup to the actual recommendation itself, which, as we said, was given over our twice-weekly telephone hotline update.

First, we would like to examine our determination of our Original Entry Point at 6.9-cents. As can be seen from the reproduction of the original recommendation, we elected to use the very Short-Term cyclical top and gap point as determinants of our Original Entry Point. The reason we went with a very Short-Term set of signals was due to the fact that such an overwhelming majority of our Confirmation Signals--seven out of nine--indicated an upcoming Bull move, which, combined with the changes in Volume and Open Interest during this period of time, appeared to heavily validate an upturn in prices.

We placed our Initial Protective Stop just a bit below the contract low of Feb. 28, as can be seen on the original recommendation page. We were fortunate that by using such a Short-Term entry signal--thereby getting our position in at a relatively low point--our initial dollar risk was relatively very low, only $571--and we were still able to put our Initial Protective Stops below the lowest point which prices had reached for this contract month in Sugar.

We will not take the reader through a day-by-day examination of our movement of Trailing Protective Stops. The following illustration, however, will show the reader how we utilized ever-ascending, steeper trendlines in order to determine the placement of our stops, which we reported on our twice-weekly telephone update. We used this method for Sugar because of the near asymptomatic climb in prices, instead of utilizing eight-week or four-week cyclical low points below which to put our stops. It has been our experience that whenever a market climbs in a near-vertical fashion, the market is going to turn just as quickly and head downward. Seeing this type of price pattern, we elected to keep our stops extremely close to the market, finally moving them all the way up to 11.89-cents, where the steepest trendline would have intersected prices after the blowoff past 13-cents.

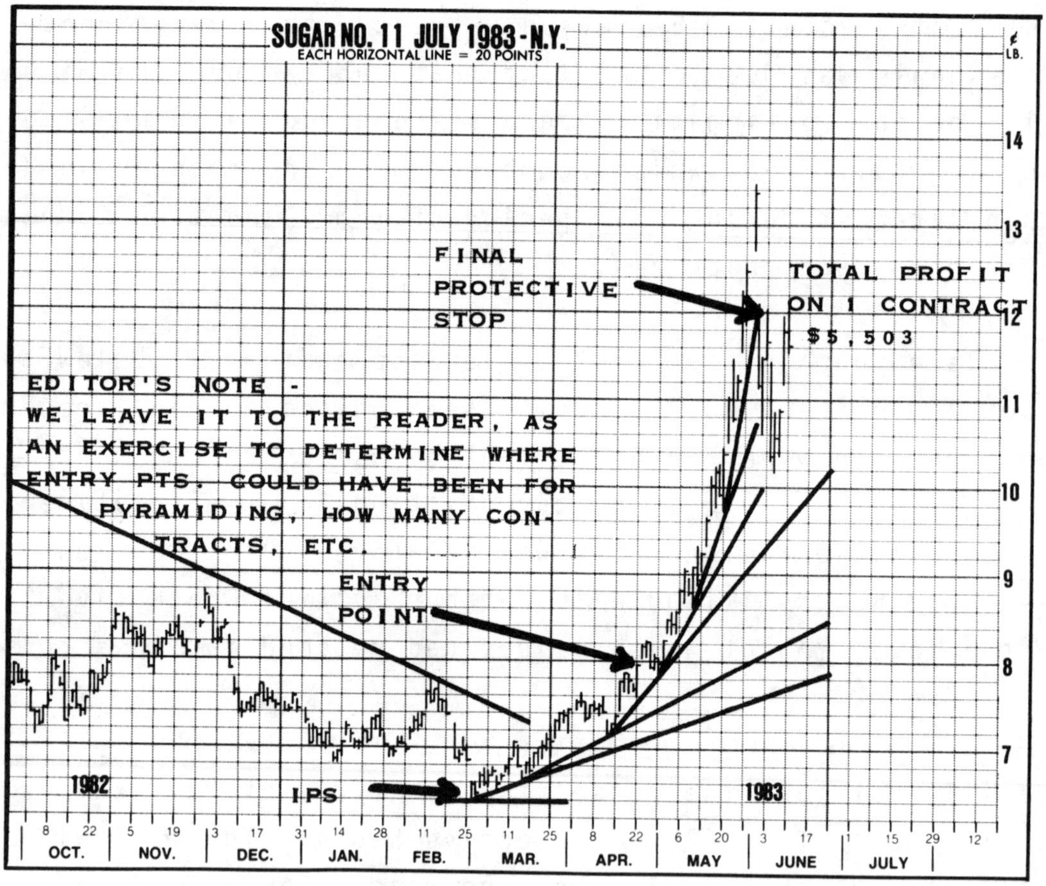

We actually were filled on our own positions at 11.81-cents, losing .08-cent due to slippage. Actually, considering the volatility of this market, the fill was quite a good one, ending up netting us profits for this trade of $5,503.

The Target Level of 20-cents which we had selected obviously was never achieved. This fact was due to a number of changing Fundamentals which took place within the market place during the months of May and June. If the reader refers to the first illustration in this chapter, the monthly chart of Sugar, he will see how we determined our Target Level of 20-cents as being a viable Target Level. Prices, however, reached only the first Target Level of approximately 13-cents. Had this level of 13-cents been approached in a more gradual fashion, or if the Fundamentals had not changed, the 13-cent level very likely would have been broken through and the prices would have continued on up to 20-cents.

We could have elected to take our profits at the 13-cent level (because it was our initial Target Level--though not the one that we had published) since it was our belief that prices would continue up to Target Level 2. But, given the explosive blowoff when prices went through the 13-cent level, we believed there was a reasonable probability that prices would continue to rocket upward. Unfortunately, however, this was not the case, and we did sacrifice a bit over one-cent in profit by using tightly-drawn trendlines instead of taking our profits at the predetermined Target Level 1 of 13-cents.

For every time that we lose a cent in profits--such as in this case--there will be another case in which prices do continue on up to the 20-cent level in an extremely explosive fashion, thereby more than recouping for us the one-cent in profits which we lost on this particular trade.

* * * * *

This was a remarkably simple trade which netted us more than $5,000, with an Initial Risk of less than $600. All of the elements were in place for this trade to be profitable. We had prices at historic low levels, we had an overwhelming number of Confirmation Signals in favor of our move and we had a remarkably low Initial Risk. We selected a low risk Initial Entry Point based upon very Short-Term Cycles. But the position would have been almost as profitable had we entered it where the descending resistance trendline was broken through. The Short-Term indicators which we used to enter this market increased our profits by approximately 0.40-cents and involved some highly sophisticated and very technical calculations, which are beyond the scope of this book. For the Big Move trader, however, any of the techniques we discussed earlier in this book as being the simplest and most pragmatic ways to determine Initial Entry Points would have worked remarkably well and increased the Initial Risk only slightly, leaving the Risk/Reward Ratio at a very favorable figure. We shall now proceed to examining a less pleasant subject--a Big Move losing trade.

CHAPTER 14

LOSING TRADE ANALYSIS

In this chapter we will approach a far less pleasant, but even more important endeavor: Finding out what went wrong with our losing trades in order to try to prevent ourselves from making the same mistakes in the future--if, of course, we can find the reasons that the trades we are examining failed.

Quite frequently, unfortunately, no single explanation can be pinpointed for the failure of a Big Move trade. In such instances, if the trader ascertains that most of the Confirmation Signals were favorable to his position; that the basic Big Move requirement for prices to be at historic highs, lows or mid-range levels was satisfied; and that there was no UFO, he is forced sometimes to conclude his examination of the losing trade by scratching his head and still wondering what went wrong.

While we are well aware of the unpleasant psychological components of losing trade analysis, we wish to reemphasize how vitally important it is for a trader to learn from his mistakes if at all possible.

It is fun and relatively easy for a trader to analyze his winning trades to see why things went right, but it is enormously important that he exercise an equal amount of care, diligence and conscientiousness when he is examining his losing trades--and they should all be examined thoroughly.

In this chapter, we will take another actual Mega-Trades recommendation from 1983--a representative Big Move trade.

Unlike the winning trade in the preceding chapter, which was selected at random, this losing trade, however, was chosen particularly because of the enormity of its loss and a number of other reasons which will become evident to the reader as we proceed through this chapter.

Here, too, it would have been very easy for us to have carefully located a losing Big Move trade from among our Mega-Trades recommendations in order to find an easily explainable losing example.

Instead, we have elected to analyze the losing recommendation which we made for December, 1983 Gold.

In July of 1983, we issued an OCO recommendation to buy or to sell December, 1983 Gold at that particular point in time. With many markets trading at their historic mid-range price levels rather than at their historic high or historic low levels, Gold was a fairly typical representative of the markets in general.

As the reader can see on the following monthly graph of Gold, where we have marked the approximate point of our recommendation, Gold historically was trading at almost a mid-range price level--depending, of course, upon how many years back in time we cared to research.

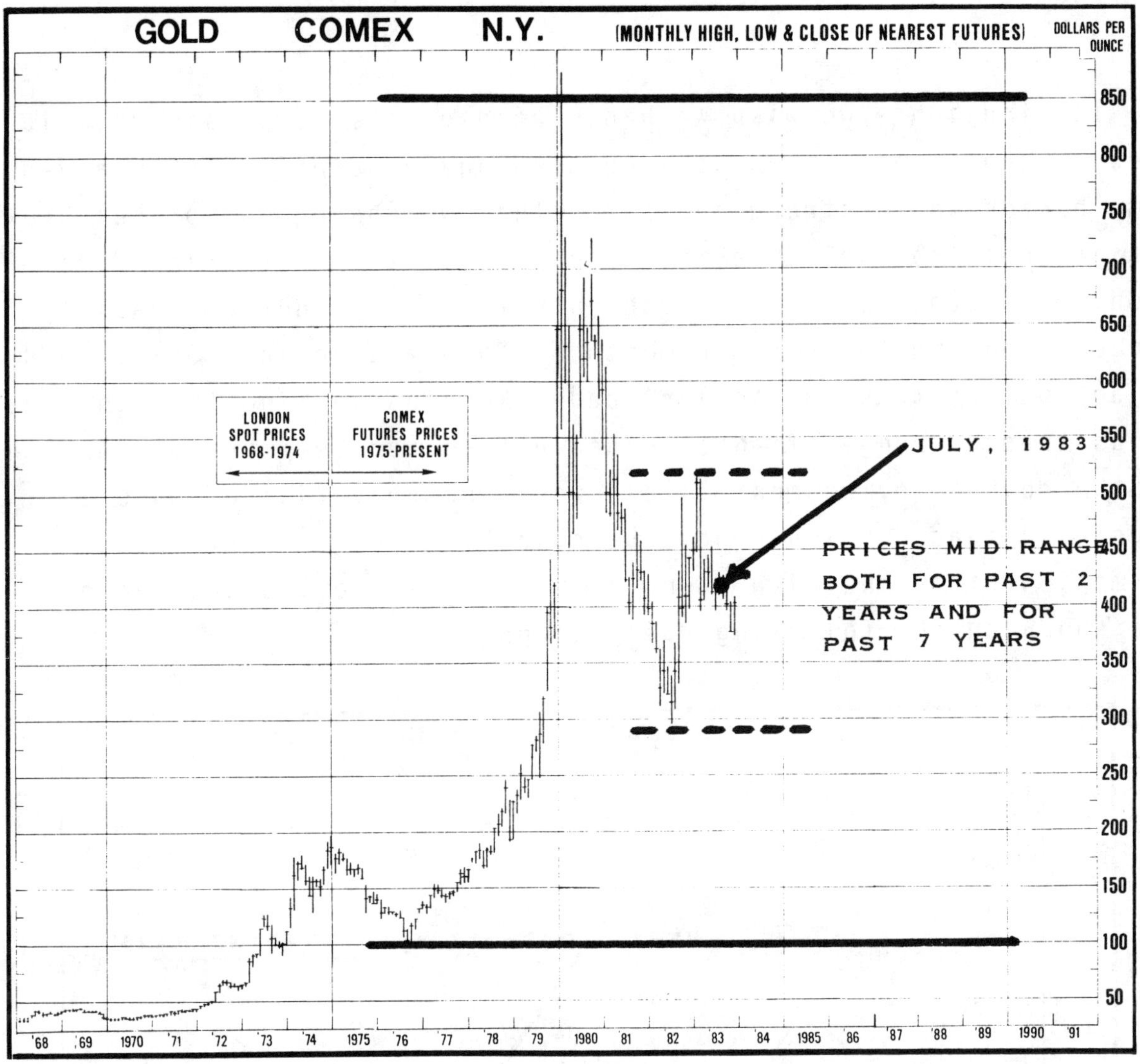

From this standpoint, Gold qualified as a potential Big Move trading candidate. Since we did not wish to "take a gamble" and by-pass a trade with significant potential in either direction, we elected to go with our OCO order. While at this point in time--early July--December Gold was trading at around $440, the nearby contracts were trading more in the vicinity of $420, the point we have indicated on the monthly graph.

Gold had been in one trading range through the months of March, April and May and finally had broken out on the down side and formed another trading range extending through June. This was a point we overlooked at the time.

In hindsight, we wish we had placed greater emphasis upon it because the three-month extended trading range of the February-May time period was a strong indicator that whichever way prices broke out of that trading range would constitute the next price direction. Instead, we chose to concentrate on the shorter trading range extending through the month of June and on into July. Had we approached this particular trade, keeping in mind that the previous trading range of an extended nature had been broken through on the down side, we most likely would not have issued an OCO orde. Instead, we would have been looking to go short upon confirmation of another leg down in prices. These trading ranges are shown on the following daily graphs:

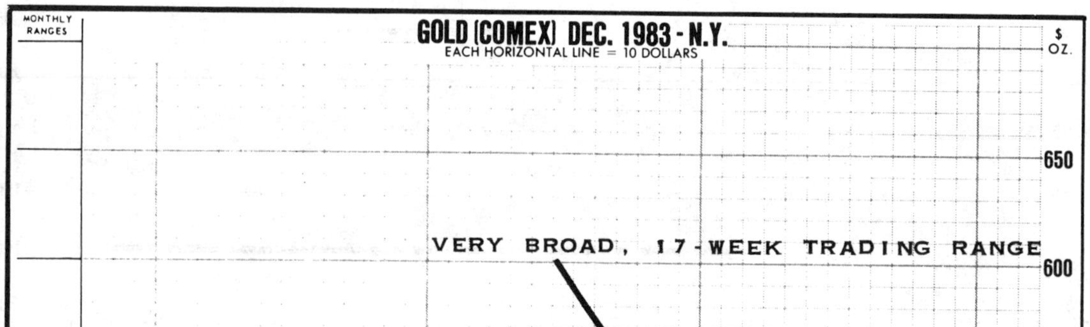

Typically, the way a trading range of a minimum of five weeks is broken out of is sufficient to indicate the next price direction. But we have found that a trading range composed of approximately 14 weeks is a far better indicator of Longer-Term price direction than a five-week trading range is. So our bias should have been on an order to the short side from the very beginning instead of on an OCO order with its possibility of being filled on the long side by a false upward breakout of the trading range.

Another point which we missed in this trade--which can be seen in the previous weekly graph of Gold through early June--is that the price rally from late February through mid-May of from approximately $400 to $450 represented almost a 50% retracement back up to the $515 highs of the January-February time frame. This almost perfect 50% retracement back towards these significant highs should also have made us suspect of a resumption of the up-move that had begun in August of 1982.

Now, let's look at our Confirmation Signals to see what they showed us during this period of time.

The Seasonal Pattern for Gold during the period of time we were preparing to enter the trade showed that Gold typically declined in price between June and July, rose between July and August, and then declined again from August through September. With such a zig-zag, this was not exactly the type of pattern with which a trader should have felt completely comfortable.

We would be more inclined to rate the Seasonal Patterns as neutral in this case (as opposed to being Bullish) because even though prices typically rose from June to some point in July, they turned down again in August--hardly what we should have desired for a Big Move, Long-Term trade:

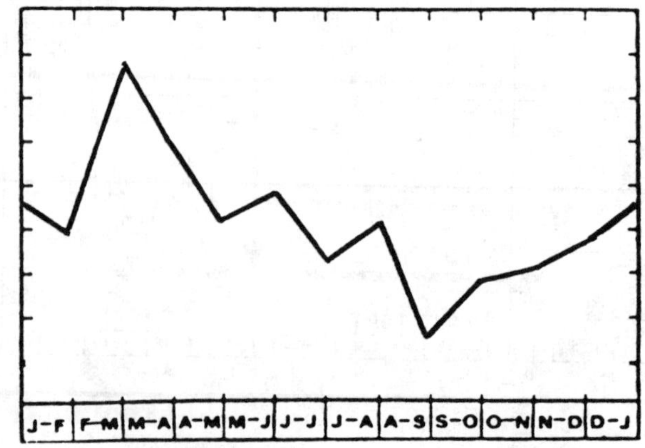

Our next Confirmation Signal is the status of the Long-Range Cycles. The first--and obviously the most important--cycle for any Big Move trade is the Long-Range Cycle. Although subsequent analysis determined that our conclusions regarding the phasing of the Long-Range Cycle for Gold in July, 1983, was not accurate--due to its subsequent skewing most likely because of those even Longer-Term Cycles we have been discussing throughout this book--at that point in time, the Long-Range Cycle appeared to have bottomed in 1982--much as in the case with our earlier example of Sugar in the preceding chapter--and to be heading up until early 1986. This was one of our most positive Confirmation Signals, justifying the potential establishment of a long position in Gold and the use of an OCO order as opposed to an outright resting sell order:

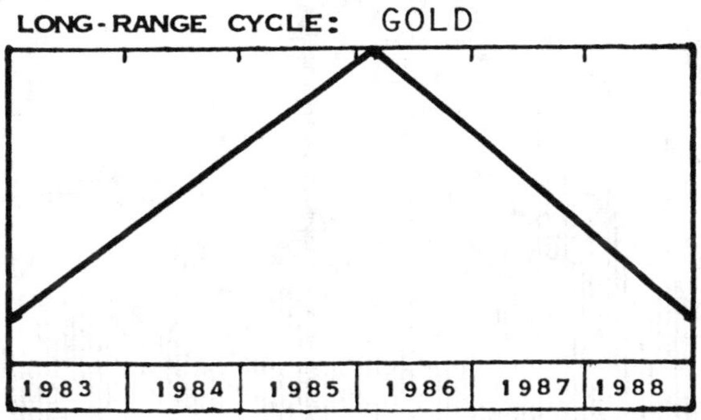

The next Confirmation Signal, Bullish Consensus, did not give us any particular indication one way or the other as to the next direction for Gold price movement. Hence, we would evaluate it to have been relatively neutral in this case. It can be seen in the following illustration that throughout May, Gold, ranging around the 70% figure, had been bordering on the overbought, although it had not been totally overbought. During the early part of June as prices themselves had dropped, the Bullish Consensus had dropped down to 30%, but it had not broken that figure. It then had proceeded back up again as Gold prices rallied toward the latter part of June. This increase in Bullish Consensus throughout the second half of June was a slight indication of a potential up-move in Gold. But the rise had been so gradual--only to top towards the latter part of June and begin down again into July--that by the time our recommendation was made in early July, the Bullish Consensus was resting at 30%--not exactly the oversold condition we should have been looking for to indicate a market turn.

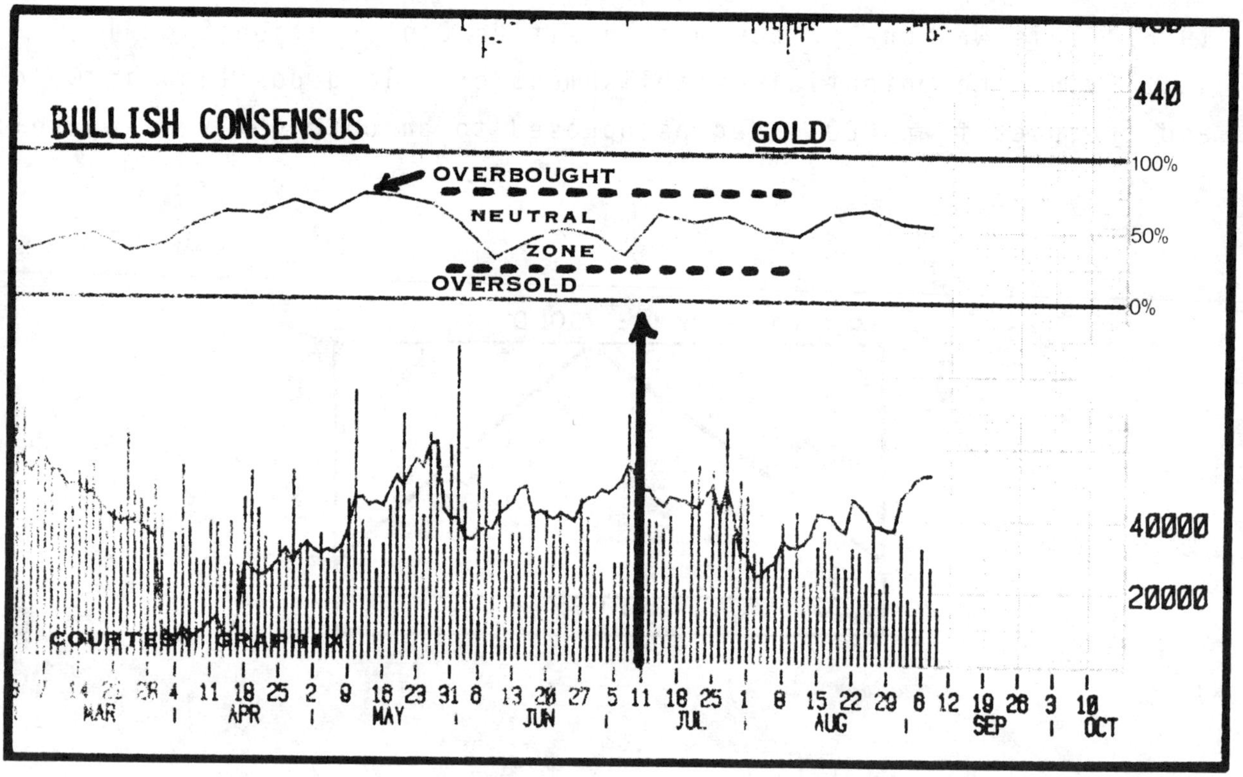

When we look at our next Confirmation Signal, Volume of Trading, we find that back in early March, when prices had crashed severely from the $550-level on down through the $450-level, the Volume of Trading had increased significantly, a Bearish signal. As prices had moved sideways through the remainder of March and April and into May, the Volume of Trading had remained relatively flat. There had been, however, a couple of key days--such as those during the first week of June--when we had had a very high trading Volume of almost 90,000 contracts. This had come as prices roared out of their first trading range and moved from approximately $460 down to $425 in the course of two days--a very Bearish Volume indicator. As prices had attempted to rally slightly through June back up to the $440 level, the Volume of Trading had remained relatively flat. Also, there had been one false signal in Volume in early July--the last Volume shown on the chart below--when prices had moved significantly upward in one day and Volume had totaled almost 70,000 contracts. This, of course, was a Bullish signal.

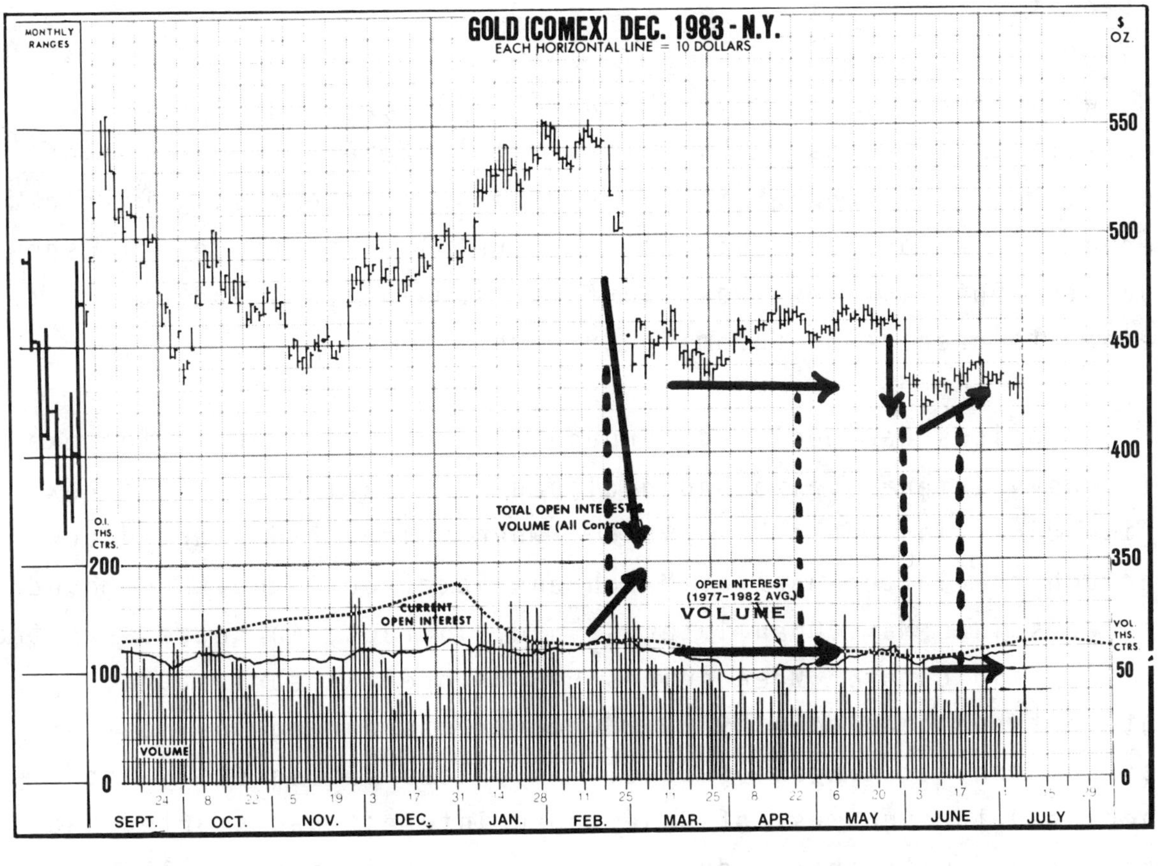

In essence, then, we have a mish-mash of Volume interpretations. We would be more inclined now to ignore that single last high Volume trading day--which is shown on the graph just given--and instead look at the overall patterns of the Volume during the period from March 1 through July 1, which, if anything, indicated a somewhat Bearish cast to the market. Then, however, we placed an inordinate amount of significance on the high Volume of this one day during the first week of July.

When we look at our first four Confirmation Signals for Gold, we find that two of them are neutral, one is Bullish, and one is Bearish. Let us now examine our next Confirmation Signal--Open Interest.

While the illustration which we will be using is of such a scale that it is just a bit difficult to determine the changes in Open Interest--although they could be seen more easily with a different scale for Open Interest--a careful examination will show that the Open Interest was, in fact, somewhat misleading as it tended to predict an upcoming Bull move.

As prices had declined through the month of March, for example, Open Interest also had declined, indicating that the next price direction would be upward. When prices had started upward through the latter part of March and into April and then moved sideways into May, Open Interest had, in fact, increased--another Bullish indicator. When prices had dropped in early June, Open Interest had gone down by 20,000 contracts during the last week of May and the first week of June. As prices subsequently had increased through most of June, Open Interest had started back up again. And with the gradual increase in prices overall through June and July, Open Interest, while it had moved partially sideways, had been inclined somewhat upward--another Bullish signal. The following daily price chart shows the correlations between Open Interest and price motion that proved to be so misleading in the case of Gold:

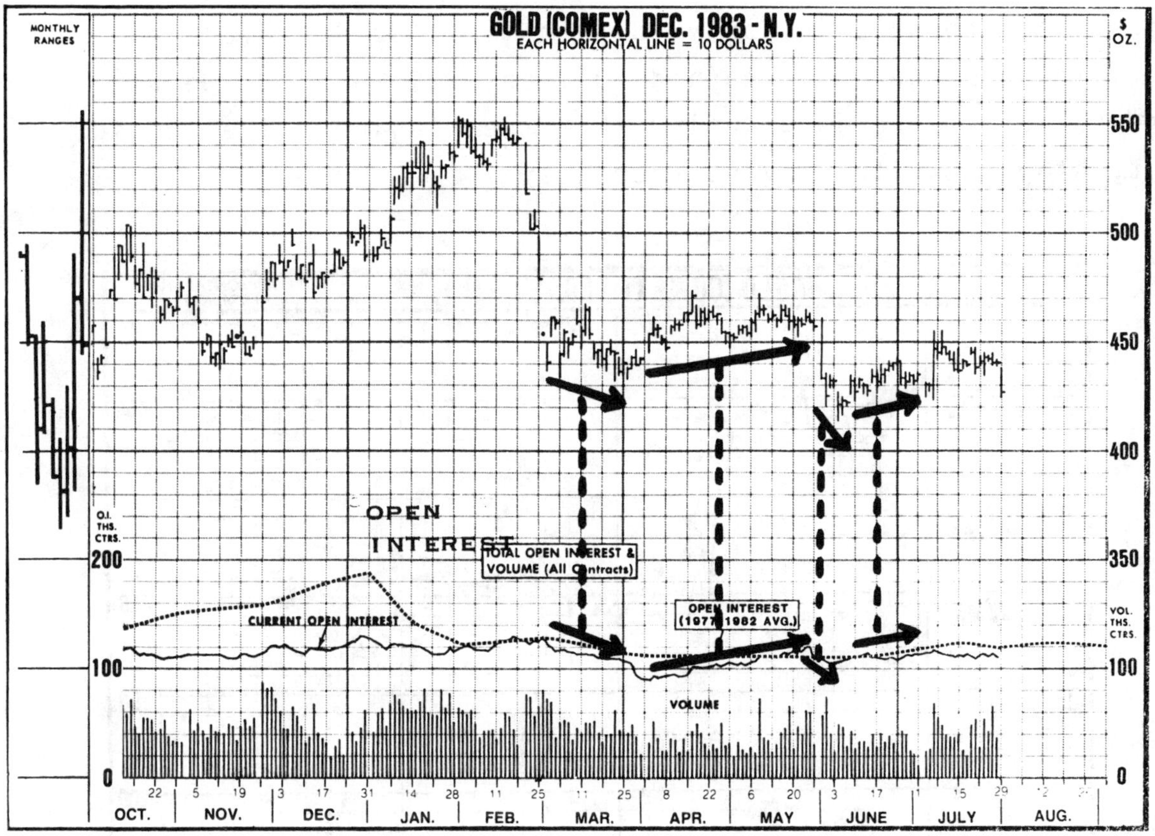

When we examine the Moving Averages through June and July, the period of time we were considering establishing our position, we find--as shown in the following illustration--that while closing prices had moved up sharply through the 10-day and 40-day Moving Averages, the slope of the 40-day Moving Average itself had not turned up. Just because the closing prices had moved above these two sets of Moving Averages was not a conclusive indicator that prices had, in fact, reversed, however, because the period of time that they had been above the averages was very brief. Another week or two of prices being above the Moving Averages would have been far more conclusive. It has been our experience that, most frequently, when there is a false move beyond the Moving Averages, it rarely lasts for more than one or two weeks. So while on the surface it appeared in early July that the Moving Average Confirmation Signal had turned Bullish, it had not. We were somewhat premature in assuming that the closing prices would, in fact, stay above the Moving Averages.

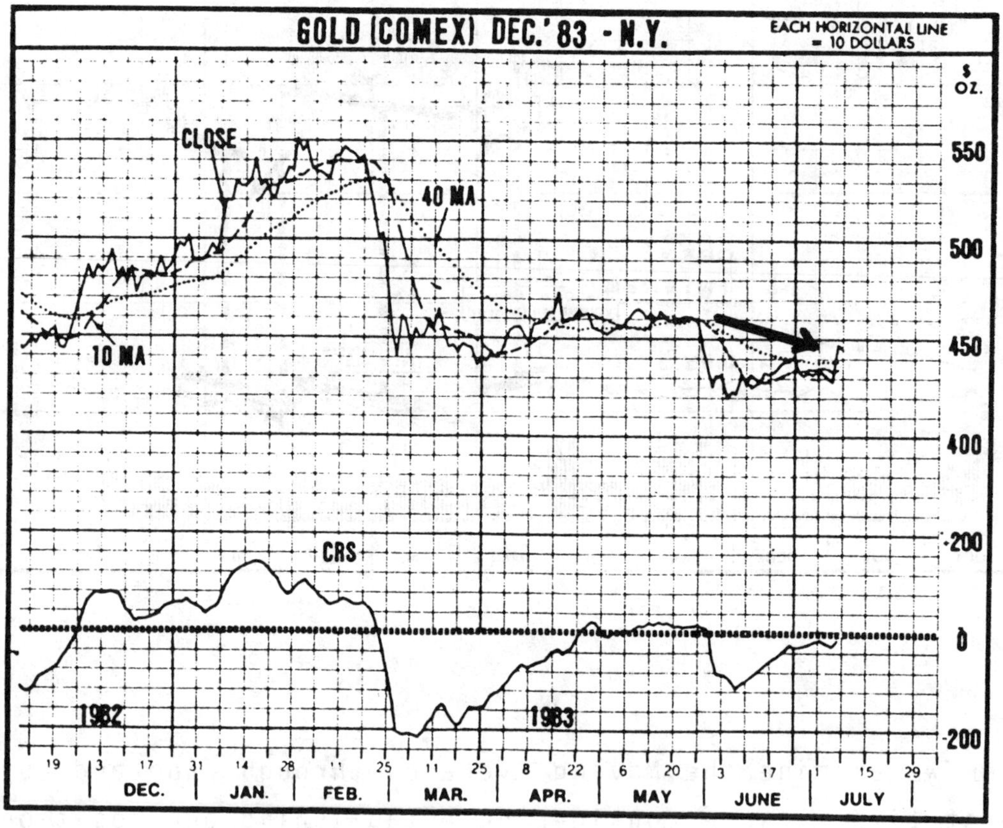

The reader will notice, too, that the CRS indicator at the bottom of the Moving Average illustration shows that prices were still in a Bearish mode even though closing prices had turned above the Moving Averages. We do not mean to imply that the CRS should overrule the use of our Moving Average Confirmation Signal, but we do wish to point out that if we had noted more prudently that the CRS was still Bearish, we might have questioned our potential long position a bit more carefully.

When we look at our next Confirmation Signal of Positivity/Negativity--we find that prices were exhibiting some degree of Positivity, as is shown by the following listing for the the different contract months of Gold as of July 1:

August, 1983:	$421
October, 1983:	$428
December, 1983:	$432
February, 1984:	$447

Since the more distant contract months of Gold each showed an increasing price level, there was a relatively strong degree of Positivity. From a Fundamental standpoint, this was due probably more to investors' anticipation of increasing inflation levels than anything else. But, for our purposes, this Confirmation Signal was Bullish, and it helped to lead us astray.

The next to the last of our Confirmation Signals is that of Commitments of Traders. As can be seen in the following illustration: As of June 30, a few more large speculators were holding long positions than short positions. But when we turn to the Delta column, we find a minus 2 reading, which indicates that from the preceding month, there had been an increase in Bearish sentiments despite the fact that a very slim majority of large speculators were long as opposed to being short. This Confirmation Signal could be read in either one of two ways: First, that the fact that more large speculators were long than short was a

Bullish indicator or, second, that since the Delta had changed and large speculators were less Bullish than they were in the preceding month, that this was an impending Bearish signal. So looking at both possibilities, we do not have a clear-cut, strong Confirmation Signal one way or the other.

COMMITMENTS OF TRADERS—LARGE HEDGERS, SPECULATORS AND SMALL TRADERS
Open Interest Positions Shown in Percent (Rounded) as of June 30, 1983

MARKETS	LARGE HEDGERS				LARGE SPECULATORS				SMALL TRADERS			
	Long	Short	Net	△	Long	Short	Net	△	Long	Short	Net	△
Cattle (Live)	18	37	-19	-14	8	8	0	+5	71	52	+19	+9
Cocoa	48	70	-22	+14	26	9	+17	-11	25	20	+5	-4
Coffee	33	61	-28	+24	14	8	+6	-21	50	29	+21	-4
Copper	29	73	-44	+2	14	12	+2	-3	54	12	+42	+1
Corn	53	50	+3	-8	5	4	+1	+5	39	43	-4	+3
Cotton	24	74	-50	+9	19	1	+18	-1	55	24	+31	-9
Gold (Comex) ●	51	58	-7	+8	10	9	+1	-2 ●	25	18	+7	-5
Heating Oil #2	46	57	-11	-14	19	9	+10	+14	27	26	+1	0
Hogs	21	9	+12	+6	17	12	+5	+22	56	72	-16	-26

Looking at our last Confirmation Signal--Fundamentals--we find that upon reading through back issues of the Fundamental reference sources which we utilize, there were more Bearish Fundamentals than Bullish Fundamentals at the time we placed our recommendation.

Among the negative Fundamentals were: the belief that any precious metal sales by nations in need of foreign exchange would be from their Gold reserves; the economic summit conference held in Williamsburg which emphasized the U.S.' high interest rates, thereby causing a steady influx of funds into the U.S. and depressing Gold prices; the fact that the jewelry manufacturing industry--the largest consumer of Gold--normally takes a long vacation during the month of July; and continuing rumors that the IMF would be forced to sell some of its 103-million ounces of Gold reserves. All of these factors numbered among other Bearish pieces of news.

When we examine now the Fundamentals as they existed in the June-July period of 1983, we are very disappointed in ourselves for using an OCO order instead of an outright resting sell order for Gold.

Nevertheless, in our July, 1983 issue we unfortunately made the following recommendation:

BUY DECEMBER, 1983 COMEX GOLD AT $451 WITH INITIAL PROTECTIVE STOPS AT $424, OCO, SELL AT $413 WITH STOPS AT $430. STOPS CLOSE ONLY.

TARGETS = $520/$350

INITIAL RISK = $2,700

RISK % OF MARGIN = 77%

POTENTIAL PROFIT = $6,900/$6,300

RISK/REWARD RATIO = 0.39/0.428

In essence, what happened was that we entered a very untenable potential Big Move trade because of our own overemphasis of certain Confirmation Signals.

Even though prices did meet our one criterion for establishing a Big Move trade--that of trading at a historic mid-range price level--the Confirmation Signals were anything but clear-cut.

The following table illustrates our interpretation, in hindsight, of how the Confirmation Signals should have appeared to us at that point in time:

BULLISH	NEUTRAL	BEARISH
Long-Range Cycles	Seasonals	Volume
Open Interest	Bullish Consensus	Fundamentals
Positivity/Negativity	Moving Averages	
	Commitments	

In the following illustration, we have reproduced the exact recommendation page from the July, 1983 issue of Capricorn showing the information which was sent to our subscribers.

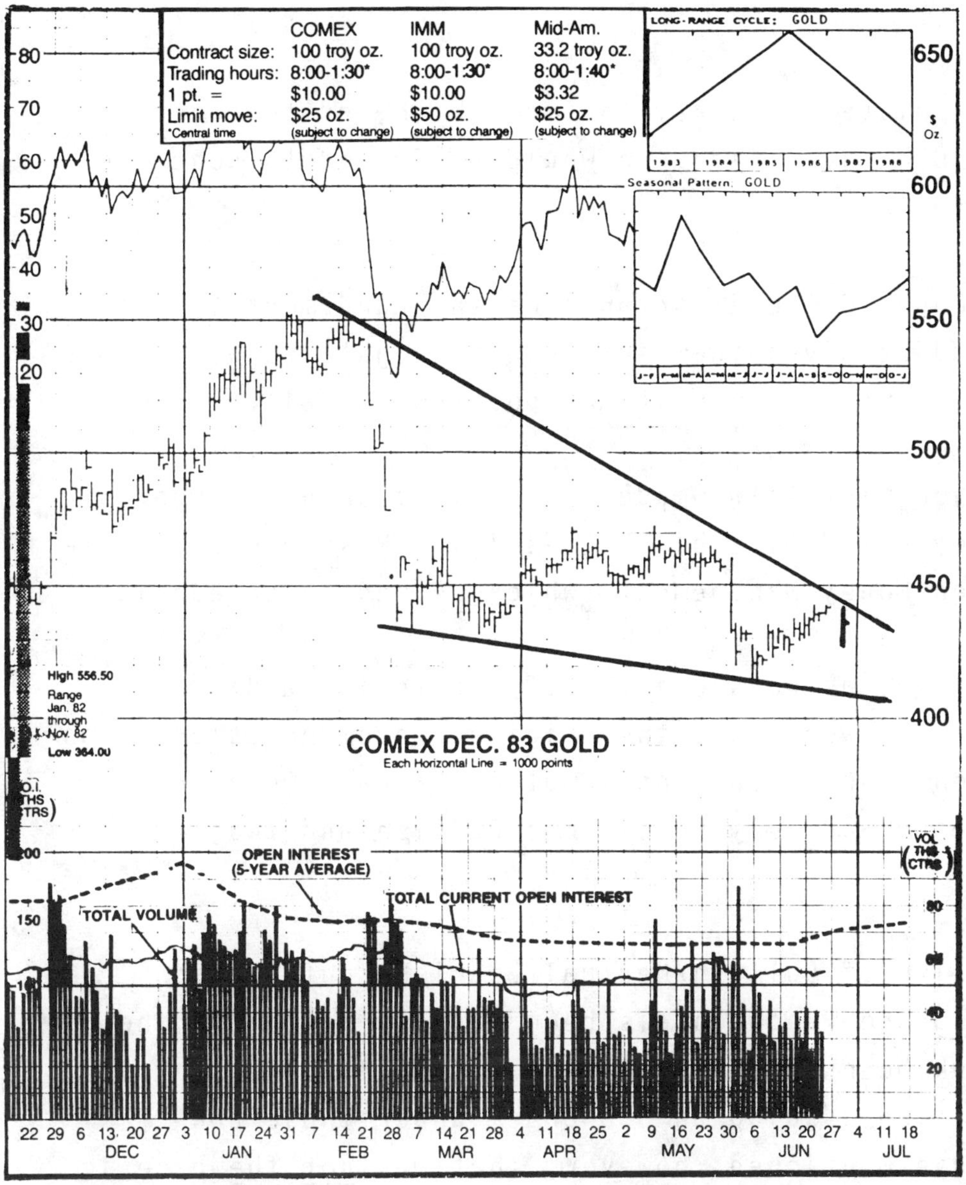

GOLD - DECEMBER

CURRENT SITUATION:

BULLISH CONSENSUS = 47%
PRICE CONSOLIDATION IS MOST LIKELY THE CALM BEFORE THE STORM AS PRICES ARE GETTING READY TO BREAK OUT IN A BIG WAY.

TECHNICAL ANALYSIS:

PRICES ARE COILING IN A MAJOR WAY ON THE MO. CHART BELOW, BRACED BETWEEN MAJOR ASCENDING AND DESCENDING TRENDLINES. ON THE DAILY CHART, THE COIL IS NARROWING TOO, AND GIVEN THE CONFUSING FUNDAMENTAL SITUATION PRICES COULD BREAK IN EITHER DIRECTION ONCE THE FUNDAMENTALS AFFECTING GOLD PRICES BECOME MORE CLEAR. EVEN THO THE TREND LOOKS DOWN ON THE DAILY CHART, WE ARE OPTING FOR AN OCO ORDER AS WE HAVE THIS NARROWING OF PRICES, ESPECIALLY ON THE MONTHLY CHART, AND OPPOSED TO THAT ARE THE LONG-RANGE CYCLES.

CYCLICAL ANALYSIS:

SEASONALS SOMEWHAT MIXED AND THO THE LONG-RANGE CYCLE POINTS UP, THE INTERMEDIATE CYCLE MAY BE SKEWED AND NOT YET HAVE BOTTOMED, WHICH WOULD FILL US SHORT SIDE.

FUNDAMENTAL ANALYSIS:

THE KEY, WE BELIEVE ABSENT A WORLD CRISIS, IS WHAT THE FED DOES AND HOW IT AFFECTS INFLATION, I.E. IF RATES DECLINE, INFLATION GOES UP, GOLD FOLLOWS (OR LEADS), AND VICE VERSA. CONFUSING PICTURE.

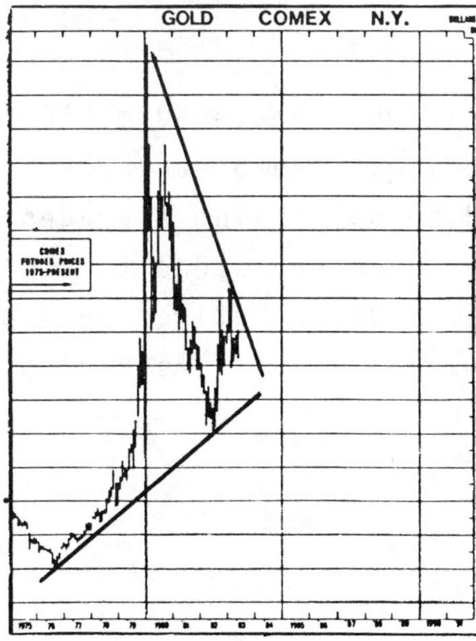

RISK/REWARD ANALYSIS:

INITIAL RISK = $2,700
RISK % MARGIN = 77%
PRO.PRO.=$6900/6300
RISK/RE.=0.39/0.428

TIME FRAME:

IF SHORT, POSSIBLY A MONTH OR TWO, IF LONG PROBABLY FIVE TO SIX MONTHS TO TARGET.

RECOMMENDATION

BUY AT 451 STOP WITH STOPS AT 424, OCO SELL AT 413 WITH STOPS AT 430. STOPS CLOSE ONLY.
TARGETS=520/350

If we had to isolate three key factors which, quite frankly, made this a lousy Big Move trade, we would be forced to conclude that they are as follows:

First, we discounted the importance of the Fundamentals tremendously. Had we given them sufficient weight, we would have established a short position if any position at all.

The second major mistake we made was risking such a large amount of money--$2,700. This huge Initial Risk violates some of our rules on Money Management, which we mentioned earlier.

Our third mistake, as we see it, was in entering a Big Move trade--even though we issued the original recommendation as an OCO order--when four of our Confirmation Signals were pretty neutral in status and only three were Bullish and two, Bearish.

Had this division of Bullish/Neutral/Bearish Confirmation Signals existed <u>and</u> the Fundamentals been equally mixed and the Initial Dollar Risk been substantially lower, then we could quite readily have justified issuing an OCO order under those conditions. As we have mentioned, however, that was <u>not</u> the case in this instance.

Let us look now at what happened to the Moving Averages as the month of July progressed. The breakthrough by closing prices above the 10-day and 40-day Moving Averages of early July was short-lived as prices then proceeded to dip through the Moving Average lines and then subsequently move sideways. Then we got into a very choppy market insofar as Moving Averages and closing prices were concerned:

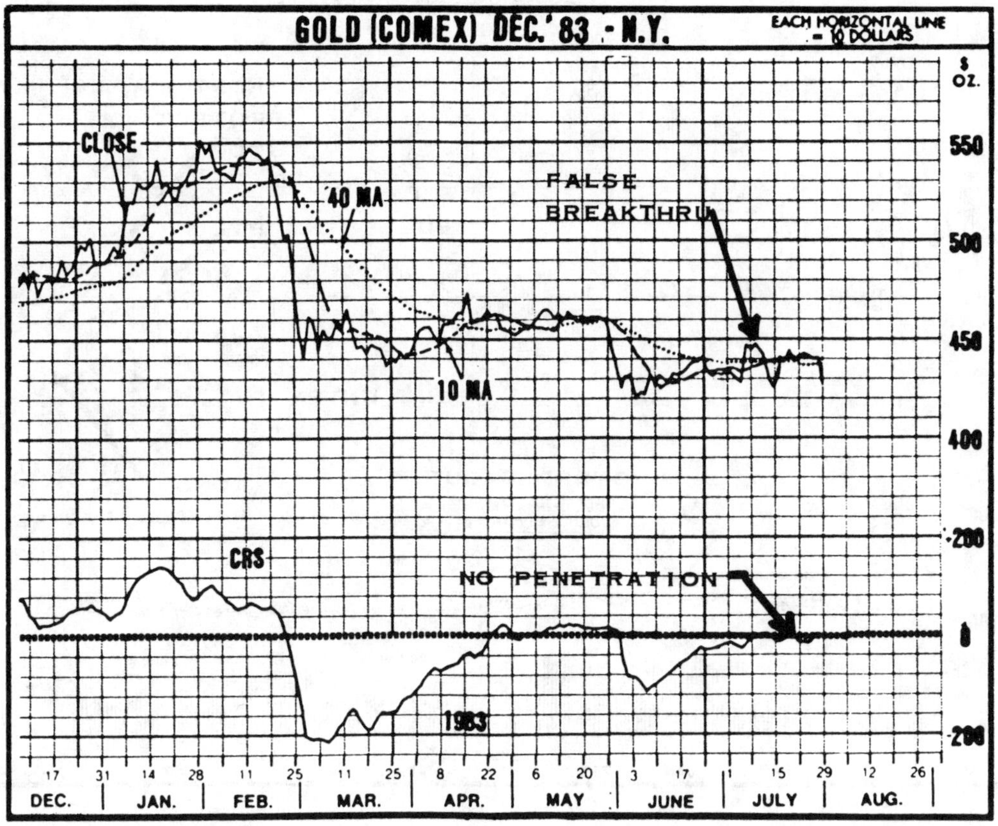

The next graph of daily prices throughout the month of July shows what happened to our position as prices dropped down and hit our Initial Protective Stops. Our Entry Points, incidentally, for both our long and short positions, were established, as the reader may have guessed, by a breakout of the trading range formation as previously drawn on the daily graphs. In other words, a upside breakout of the trading range would initiate a long position for us, while a downside breakout of the trading range would establish a short position for us.

Unfortunately, the upside breakout of the trading range was a false signal caused by UFO's and aided and abetted by our own obtuseness of the entire situation.

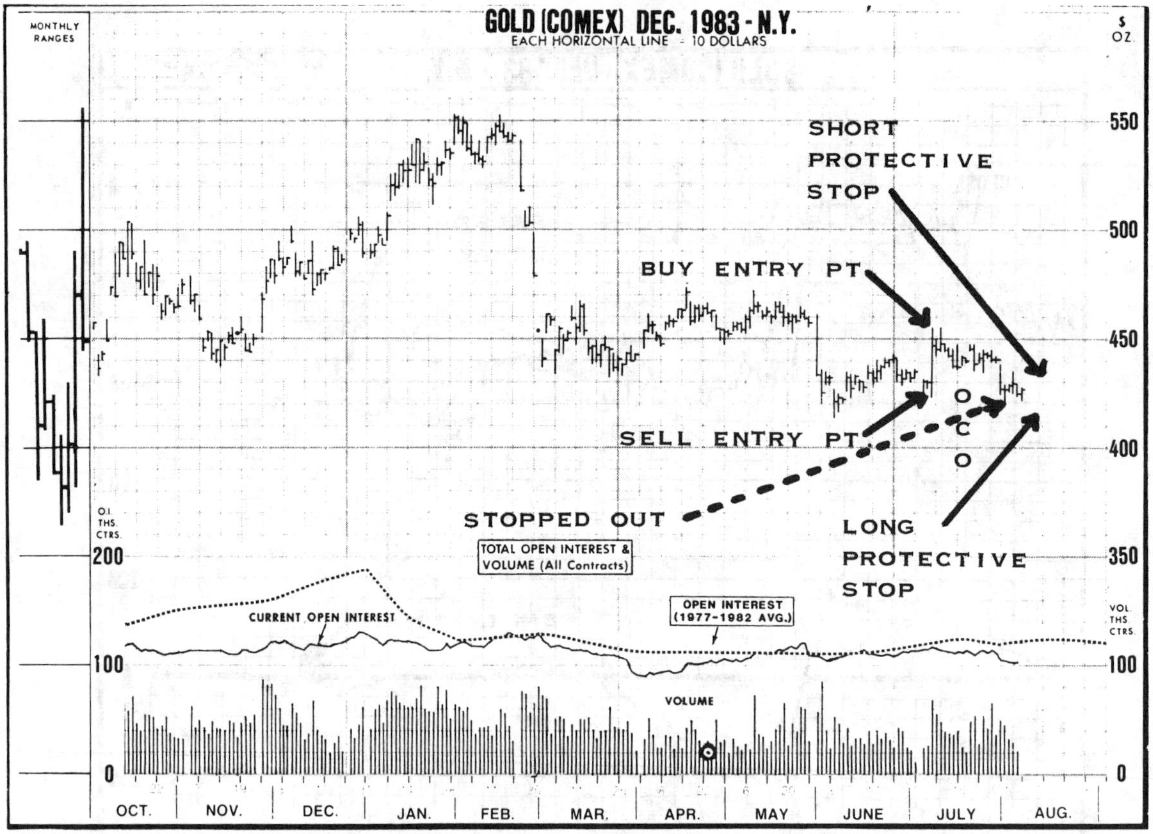

Ideally, of course, our Initial Protective Stops would have been placed beyond the extreme point of the trading range. But to do so in this case would have forced us to put our Initial Protective Stops back down at $413, thereby increasing our risk to an exorbitant $3,800 for a long position. Instead, we elected to place our stops just below the Short Term Cyclical low of mid-June, which seemed to us at that point in time to be a reasonable place to have our stops. We used Short-Term Entry and Protective Stop methodology since we believed that if prices did break out of the upside of the trading range, they would move upwards rather quickly.

Instead, of course, prices dipped down at the end of August and hit our Initial Protective Stop, where we got an actual fill for our own positions at $423.50, losing only 50-cents due to slippage. As with Sugar in the preceding chapter, it actually was a rather good fill.

The reader could argue that after our position was filled at $451 and prices dipped back down the following week, we could have moved our Protective Stops up to approximately $433, thereby eliminating $900 of the Risk. But given the slowness with which the market was appearing to move, we did not feel that having our stops that close was safe if, in fact, a major Bull move was about to take place.

Incidentally, our Target Levels can be seen in the first illustration in this chapter. The Long Target Level 1 that we gave in the actual recommendation was just a hair below the peak in 1983 prices. However, the Target Level on the downside as a part of our actual recommendation was not the low of 1982 since we believed that if we were filled on the short side, the inflationary pressures which seemed to be building up at that time in the economy would prevent prices from dropping all the way to the $300-level. This is another example of poor judgment on our part since the $300-Target Level makes much more sense scientifically than relying upon our own interpretation of future prospects for inflation did.

This entire recommendation was fraught with mistakes in interpretation and judgment on our part. Our recollection is that at the time we made the recommendation, it seemed to make perfectly good sense to us to use the same OCO approach, Entry Points, Initial Protective Stop Points and the Target Levels that we actually did use. In retrospect, however, we are amazed at how klutzy we were in our overall analysis since it cost not only our subscribers, but also us ourselves, very dearly.

* * * * *

As psychologically painful as it has been for us to examine such a terrible recommendation that we made as this, it has been useful to us to do so. We hope that the reader has also found it helpful and instructive. Above all, we hope that our analysis of this losing trade emphasizes to the reader the importance of performing just such analysis as this on all of his losing trades.

It is ironic--but seemingly factual--that the more mistakes a trader makes in a losing recommendation, the greater the dollar risk he suffers.

We are glad that we chose this particular example for this chapter because of the multiplicity of misjudgment and mistakes which went into our analysis. We hope that this example will dramatically illustrate how easy it is--especially when a trader has been going through such a period of successful trades as we had been during the months preceding this recommendation--to become sloppy and overlook very important points.

CHAPTER 15

THE PSYCHOLOGY OF BIG MOVE TRADING

A chapter on psychology always seems out of place in a book on trading commodities. The fact should not be overlooked, however, that a Big Move trader's success or failure in the market place is every bit as much--if not more so--determined by psychology as it is by his rigorous adherence to all of the Big Move trading methodology we have discussed.

If the reader has gotten this far in this chapter and is experiencing a vague sense of discomfort, or if he is thinking something along the lines of "I really don't need to read this," then the likelihood is extremely high that he, in fact, does need to read this chapter very carefully. A trader's discounting the need to examine himself or his feeling uncomfortable or ill-at-ease about it, generally is a very good indication that psychological processes are at work in him which can--and frequently will--sabotage even the best-constructed and most carefully laid-out Big Move trading program.

This chapter's purpose is not to provide a detailed, diagnostic guide as to how traders subconsciously defeat themselves. Nor is this chapter intended to be a "do-it-yourself," psychological "fix-it" treatise.

In our earlier work, THE TAURUS METHOD, we devoted 26 pages to such diagnoses and "fixing-it," and another of our books, GAMES INVESTORS PLAY, is entirely concentrated in these areas. The chapter in THE TAURUS METHOD entitled "How Your Mind Affects Your Trading" is, in effect, a condensation of GAMES INVESTORS PLAY. Since many readers of this current volume already own copies of one of these two other books of ours, we do not feel it is necessary to repeat that material in this chapter.

Our major purpose in this chapter--just in case the reader does not have either of these other books or he has chosen not to read the material on psychology in them--is to enable the reader to determine honestly whether or not any of his own subconscious psychological patterns are getting in the way of his trading success, and then to suggest in a broad way what steps he may take to alleviate these roadblocks.

Our book, GAMES INVESTORS PLAY, grew out of a survey we took of our Taurus newsletter subscribers some years back. After we had had a very successful year in making recommendations in the commodity markets, we noticed in our correspondence a number of letters from subscribers complaining about how poorly they had done in the markets during that same year. Interspersed among those letters were a few exulting at how very well their writers had done. In many cases, some of them had made greater profits with our Taurus recommendations than we had.

We had read for years that 90% of all commodity traders, according to government surveys, either lose all of their money or drop out of the markets during their first 12 months of trading because their funds deplete to almost nothing. Only 10% of the traders in any given year show a profit in the commodity market, and the fact is that these winning traders tend--to a very high percentage degree--to be "repeaters" year after year--i.e., this same 10% of the commodity trading population makes money year-in and year-out. What fascinated us after receiving this correspondence from our subscribers, however, was that all of these subscribers had been receiving identically the same recommendations from us. Yet some had won, and some had lost.

We decided to conduct a survey among our subscribers, and so we sent out questionnaires with business reply envelopes. The results literally astounded us insofar as we had believed that the reason that 90% of all commodity traders lost money over any given year was because they had bad information, did poor analysis, listened to bad advice from brokers, or some such other factor. But the results of our survey of subscribers who had been getting Taurus for the entire 12 months under examination showed that approximately 90% of them had had losing years, while approximately only 10% of them had had very successful years. (Our profits for the year under examination exceeded $100,000 trading single-contract positions.)

Our immediate hunch--since we had been schooled in psychology for many years--was that psychological factors must account for the difference in actual performance between the 90% of traders who were unsuccessful and the 10% who were successful.

We subsequently selected a number of these unsuccessful traders and spoke with them--as well as some of the successful traders--on the telephone. Our conversations bore out our conclusion that the only differences between the winners and the losers in this survey were attributable to psychological issues.

While this was not a scientifically conducted survey, it must be remembered that all of the subscribers being surveyed had been receiving identical recommendations at approximately the same time throughout the year, that all of them were generally of the same educational background and approximately the same income level, and so forth. In essence, we could find no real difference in any other factors to determine which traders would fall into the 10% winning category and and which into the 90% losing category, other than in their psychological make-ups and psychological approaches to the markets.

Having determined this, it became obvious to us that a book on the psychology of trading--really a book on the psychology of living--was badly needed for our field, and, as a result, we published GAMES INVESTORS PLAY.

It is our firm belief that any commodity trader with at least average intelligence, average income and average physical health can succeed--and will succeed--unless his own subconscious psychological issues sabotage him. It is important for the reader to note that we are talking about subconscious psychological factors and to understand that if a trader is not successful in his commodity trading program due to his subconscious psychological issues, he is not really responsible for that lack of success in the respect that the self-defeating causes of his failure are literally out of his awareness and unbeknownst to him.

But the moment the trader is given the information which we have just given him--that if he is not successful in his life, given an average set of circumstances, then his failure is due to psychological difficulties--then he immediately becomes responsible for his lack of success in commodity trading or in any other field of investment.

As long as a person does not understand that he is responsible for something he is doing because he is not even aware of doing it--because it is of a subconscious genesis--he is not blameworthy. But once he is made aware of the fact that there <u>is</u> a problem which causes him to engage in self-defeating behavior--even though he does not at that time know what the problem is--he <u>is</u> immediately responsible for his behavior from that point on, since by knowing that there is a problem, he can now take steps to do something about it.

So, if a trader has not been successful in his commodity trading program--whether it is of a Short-Term or a Big Move variety--and has never considered that it might be due to his own subconscious instead of to the vagaries of the market place, he should not blame himself for having incurred the losses he has suffered over his period of trading. But if he has been unsuccessful in his commodity trading program--or less successful than he honestly believes he should have been--knowing now that it is due to something taking place within his own subconcious mind, he can now take steps to correct this problem. If he chooses not to do anything about examining, dealing with and correcting these psychological issues, then he has only himself to blame for his continued lack of success.

For many commodity traders who have not been schooled rigorously in analytical techniques and methodology, the concept that their subconscious mind--or factors within their own minds that they are not even aware of--can create problems in their trading of the markets, may at first blush seem like a lot of mystic mumbo jumbo. Having been schooled personally in mathematics, science, and psychology, however, we can assure the reader that there is nothing mystical about the fact that each trader's psychological factors have an enormous impact upon his trading success or lack thereof.

If a trader has been unsuccessful in the markets in the past, or less successful than he believes he should have been, what really does he have to lose by at least examining the possibility in an open-minded manner that there may, in fact, well be something to the psychological aspects of success versus failure in any kind of investment program? The only thing he has to fear is that he will learn something about himself which is unpleasant or painful.

It is perfectly OK for a trader not to engage in a psychological examination of himself in order to avoid such potential discomfort, as long as he does so with the realization that by not performing such a self-examination, he may well be significantly hurting himself in a financial manner--not to mention causing himself potential unhappiness or lack of happiness in other areas of both his professional and personal life.

What options then are available to the trader who has been less that totally successful? Of course, the simplest and "easy way out" is for him to do nothing. He can simply continue doing what he has been doing. We ran across a saying recently which seems very applicable to this situation: "If you always do what you've always done, then you'll always get what you've always gotten."

If that is the case for the reader, then it makes little sense for him to spend an enormous amount of time mastering the principles of Big Move trading. True, he may be marginally successful, depending upon the significance of his unresolved subconscious psychological issues, but he will never realize his full potential in Big Move trading or in any other type of investments.

We feel that the intelligent Big Move trader--or any trader, for that matter--who genuinely and sincerely wishes to improve his financial success--as well the successes in all other areas of his life--does have a number of very viable options open to him.

Regardless of which of these following options he elects to follow, we believe that it is important for him--once he has realized that his psychological issues may be sabotaging his investment program--to dramatically scale back his trading, or drastically reduce his financial exposure, or, better yet, to simply "paper trade" until he has the opportunity to make a thorough psychological examination of himself.

Many readers will lament over how many potential Big Moves they might miss by scaling back their trading or by merely paper trading. This, of course, is true. But the flip side of the coin is that if a trader is sabotaging himself unconsciously in the first place, his Big Moves will either not be successful because of his unconscious sabotaging of them, or they will be only marginally successful and not reap the financial rewards that the winning 10% of Big Move traders realize. The markets have been around for a long, long time, and they will continue to be around for many decades to come. It is far better, we believe, for a trader to miss some large potential Big Move trades, than it is for him to sabotage them and not resolve his psychological issues.

Once the Big Move trader--if he is really sincere about finding out how he sabotages his investing program--has decided to take concrete action in this psychological arena, there are basically two approaches that he may utilize. The first is to conduct this self-searching examination on his own, utilizing such a "do-it-yourself," self-help psychological book as GAMES INVESTORS PLAY or many of the other such books listed in the "Suggested Reading List" at the end of GAMES INVESTORS PLAY.

It has been our experience that for more than half of those commodity traders who fall into the 90%-of-unsuccessful-traders category, this do-it-yourself approach can and will work--if the trader has the ability to be diligent in his efforts and to be excruciatingly honest with himself. As with any growth process, however, this procedure does take time. For some, it may be as short a period of time as a week or two of reading, self-examination, self-honesty and effort. Other traders--while they can do it on their own--may find that this procedure takes several weeks or even months. We invite the reader to ask himself, however, if spending such a period of time in this effort is not far better than seriously jeopardizing all, or at least a significant portion, of his investment resources.

The other alternative is to seek professional therapeutic help. This normally will work for all of the 90% of unsuccessful traders--even those who are able to do it on their own. We say normally because the key element here is the quality and ability of the therapist from whom the trader is seeking assistance. Unfortunately, therapists are much like auto mechanics, investment advisors or just about any other type of professional in that there are good ones, average ones and downright bad ones. While we have always believed very strongly that a person should seek professional therapeutic help when he is having difficulty resolving a problem on his own, we nonetheless would strongly urge the reader to attempt to "fix" his subconscious psychological issues on his own unless he is very certain of the competency of the therapist from whom he is seeking assistance.

Fortunately, friends, family, business associates, and the like often can provide the trader with the name of a top-notch therapist in his area. Seeing a therapist is no longer viewed with the disdain that it was a number of years ago. In many localities, if fact, seeing a therapist is as normal or as routine as paying a visit to a dentist.

Another way the reader may locate an excellent therapist is to contact Taurus Corporation, as we suggest in Appendix E at the back of this book. We at Taurus maintain a directory of top-flight therapists in virtually every locality of this country as well as in Canada, Mexico and many countries overseas. In fact, we know many of these therapists personally, and those whom we do not know personally we have had excellent reports about from people whose judgment we trust greatly. We thus feel comfortable referring any of our readers to any of the therapists on our "List of Recommended Therapists."

A very famous therapist, Fritz Perls, the founder of Gestalt Therapy, used to be fond of using analogies about the role of the therapist as a gardener who is merely watering the seed (the client), or as a mid-wife at the birth of a child who merely assists in the delivery and does not actually have the child. The point of mentioning this is to stress that the therapist does not "make" changes in the client or actually alter the client's unconscious sabotage pattern. Instead, the therapist helps the client discover, deal with and change his own self-defeating patterns of behavior.

Over the years, we have encountered many different types of therapeutic approaches and have found some value in almost every one of them. The very best approach available to the commodity trader or any other individual in our viewpoint, however, is "The Option Technique" of Barry Neil Kaufman of Massachusetts. Mr. Kaufman has a wonderful series of self-help cassette tapes on this therapeutic process as well as a number of excellent books. Based upon the price that Mr. Kaufman charges for these materials, it is quite obvious that he is not in the therapeutic "business" in order to make money, but rather is doing it out of a desire to help his fellow human beings. Complete information on Mr. Kaufman, his institute, his materials and on how to contact him is given in Appendix E of this book, and we urge every reader, unless he is totally satisfied with his life in all aspects, to at least investigate "The Option Technique."

* * * * *

In essence, what we have been trying to accomplish in this chapter is to point out to the reader that (unless he numbers among the 10% of consistently successful commodity traders year-in and year-out and he is satisfied, in general, with the other major aspects of his professional and personal life) his own unresolved psychological issues within his subconscious--for which he has not, until this time, been responsible since, in this case, "ignorance of the law is an excuse"--are responsible for whatever dissatisfaction or lack of success he experiences.

Now that the reader--if he falls into the 90% bracket of unsuccessful traders--is aware of the extremely high probability of the reasons for his lack of total success, he is now responsible for deciding whether to stay where he is at or whether to grow and move on. The options which we have outlined in this chapter seem to us to be the most viable approaches to dealing with self-defeating behavior.

CHAPTER 16

OPTIONS AND BIG MOVE TRADING

As we began preparing this chapter on Commodity Options, we realized exactly how little information currently is available to the commodity trader on how to use Options as part of his trading program. For our purposes in this book, we are going to examine the most advantageous way a trader can use Commodity Options as part of his Big Move trading program.

For traders who wish to concentrate exclusively on Options and totally disregard establishing Commodity Futures positions, there literally are a myriad of approaches and factors which must be taken into consideration. Trading Commodity Options exclusively, however, is beyond the scope of this volume.

But since we have found that there is such a dearth of specialized information on Commodity Option trading, we have decided to continue our research in the Commodity Option field. We hope within the next year to publish a book which is devoted entirely to the trading of Commodity Options and all of the many different approaches to this field. We plan to provide in this new book a number of new techniques as well as a far better approach to the entire field of Options than has ever been offered before.

As we write this volume, six commodities currently may be traded as Options: Sugar, the Deutsch Mark, Gold, T-Bonds, the

NYSE Index and the S & P Index. Shortly, Commodity Options will be available in Soy Beans, Cotton, Cattle, Wheat, Corn and Hogs. This will give us a good, representative number of commodities for which we can consider using Options instead of straight Futures contracts, insofar as we will have two Stock Indices, one Financial Instrument, one Precious Metal, one Food, three Grains, one Fiber and two Meats. This will mean that there still are approximately 18 to 20 commodities in which, as of now and in the near future, Option trading will not be permitted.

But nearly half of the major commodities may soon be traded as Options. Hence, whenever a trader is considering a Big Move position in any of these 12 commodities which may be traded as Options, it will behoove him to examine the feasibility and desirability of making his Big Move trade as an Option trade as opposed to a Futures contract trade. Since many complexes tend to move in unison, it is wise for the trader, when he is looking at a particular commodity that is not available as an Option candidate, to examine the members of the complex in question which are available for trading as Options in order to see if any of them also meet the criteria which we have established for our Big Move trades--i.e., historical price levels, the nine Confirmation Signals and Monetary Risk.

A trader may, for example, be examining a potential Big Move long position in Silver and--for reasons we will develop later in this chapter--prefer to have an Option instead of a Futures contract. Since the only other Precious Metal--as of this writing--which is available as an Option is Gold, then the Big Move trader--assuming that he definitely wishes an Option position as opposed to a Futures Contract--should examine all of the Big Move criteria for Gold in order to see if Gold is a viable alternative for him. If it is, then he may find that establishing a Call in Gold would be far preferable to establishing a long

Futures contract position in Silver. This also would be true of some of the Currencies, the Financial Instruments, Grains, and Meats.

Our approach to Options trading as part of our Big Move trading program is in line with our philosophy throughout this book: To keep our approach as simple as possible. Thus, instead of examining all of the sophisticated possibilities which exist for Options trading, we will look at Options only as a part of our Big Move Trading Program, when the Money Management aspects are more favorable for an Option position than they are for a Futures position.

This is best illustrated by the use of an example. On Wednesday, Oct. 3, 1984, the closing price of March, 1985 Sugar was 6-cents a pound:

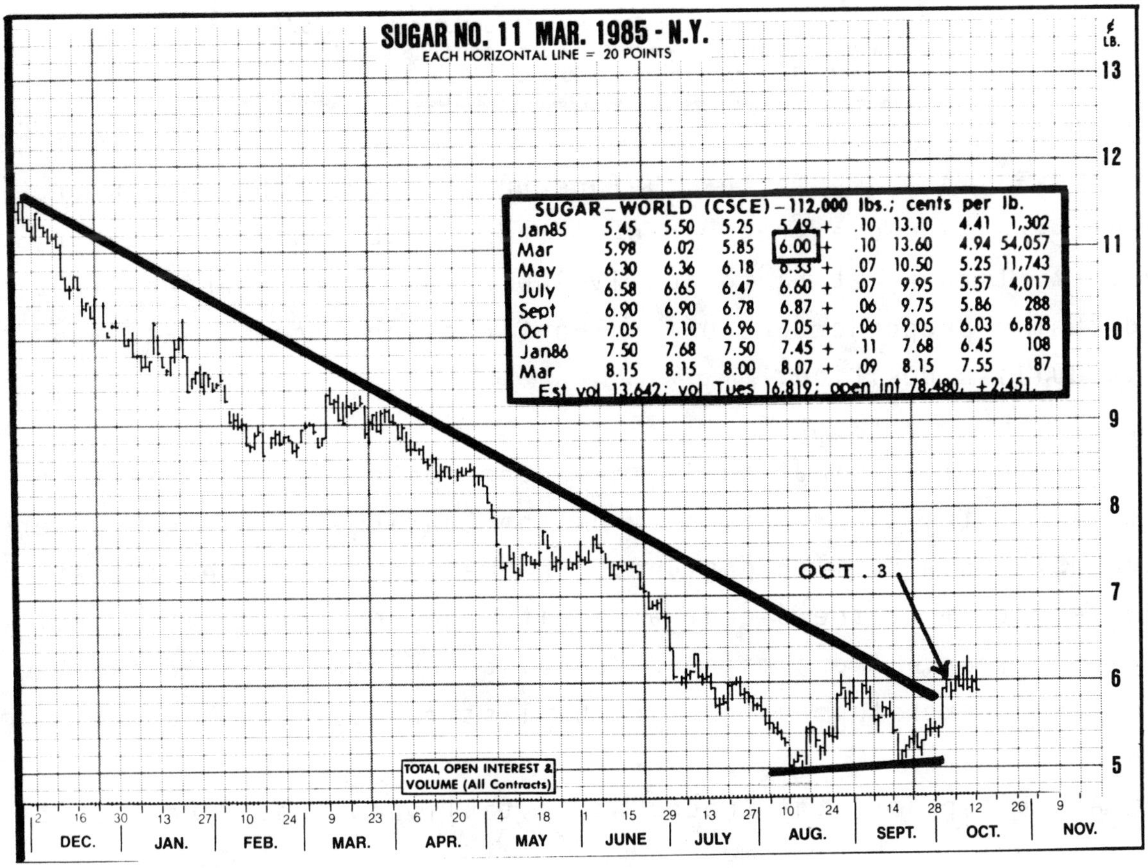

On the same date, the premium for a Call position of March, 1985 Sugar with a Strike Price of 6-cents (giving the trader the right to purchase a contract of March Sugar at 6-cents) was 0.61. Since each .01 premium equals $11.20, then the cost for this Call Option was $683.20.

The premium prices for Sugar Options of that date are shown in the following illustration:

SUGAR OPTIONS

COFFEE, SUGAR & COCOA EXCHANGE

Representative Sugar Option Prices 10/03/84 ¢/lb.

	Mar85 6.00		Jul85 6.60		Oct85 7.05		Mar86 8.07	
Strike	Settlement		Settlement		Settlement		Settlement	
Price	Call	Put	Call	Put	Call	Put	Call	Put
5.00	1.15	0.45	2.05	0.55	2.70	0.45		0.45
6.00	0.61	0.80	1.13	1.00	2.30	0.82	3.30	0.90
7.00	0.40	1.73	0.97	1.60	1.20	1.50	2.25	1.90
8.00	0.27	2.50	0.66	2.35	0.80	2.20	1.50	2.90
9.00	0.18	3.50	0.44		0.53	3.20	1.00	3.90

Est. Vol. 59 Call for free educ. brochures (212) 938-2966
Vol. 10/2/84 85 Open Int 10/2/84 calls 2,872 puts 245
Each .01 premium $11.20 e.g., 50 = $560

We will now assume that before he looked at the Option premiums, the Big Move trader had already established that Sugar was, in fact, trading at historically low price levels--which it was--and that a preponderance of the Confirmation Signals was favorable to a Bullish position.

A careful examination of the Sugar market at this point in time indicates that a majority of the Confirma-tion Signals were favorable to a Bullish posture. The market had formed a neat double-bottom at the 5-cent area with the lows of early August and mid-September. And a major descending resistance trendline had now been broken through during the last two days of trading.

At this point, the trader has established that March, 1985

Sugar appears to be an ideal Big Move trading candidate.

Now he must decide whether he wishes to trade a Futures Contract position or to purchase a Call Option on Sugar. His major consideration at this point is Money Management.

The reader can see on the preceding illustration that the appropriate point for an Initial Protective Stop would be just below the contract low or at approximately 4.90-cents. To buy at the open of the market the next day, which probably would be in the vicinity of 6-cents, and to place Initial Protective Stops at 4.90-cents, with each cent in Sugar being worth $1,120, entails an Initial Dollar Risk of $1,232, as opposed to the risk of only $683.20 for a Call Option.

With the purchase of the Call Option, there is no possibility for margin calls and no danger of being trapped in limit-down days, and the trader has firmly established his fixed risk.

In fact, the risk for a Call Option on March, 1985 Sugar with a strike price of 6-cents is only 55% as much risk as a Futures contract purchased at 6-cents with Initial Protective Stops at 4.90-cents. It is true, of course, that if the trader's analysis of the Sugar market is correct and prices do bring a major Bull move, at whatever point he exits the market, he will have lost, in effect, his $683.20.

For argument's sake, however, let us assume that the trader has determined from the weekly charts that a reasonable move upward would entail reaching at least a first Target Level of 10-cents. At 10-cents, his profits on a Futures position would be $4,480. On an Option Call position, they would be that much less the premium of $683.20 he paid for the Sugar Option. To us this seems a very reasonable amount to pay--whether it is referred to as a premium or as an insurance policy--to firmly establish the risk.

In addition, all of the worries of Trailing Protective Stops or having his Trailing Protective Stops violated due to a UFO of brief duration are eliminated for the trader.

Another way of looking at this situation is to examine the Risk/Reward Ratio.

In the case of the Call Option, the trader is risking $683.20 for an anticipated profit--when Sugar reaches 10-cents--of $3,805, or a Risk/Reward Ratio of 0.179. In the case of the Futures contract position on Sugar, he is risking $1,232 for an anticipated return of $4,480, a Risk/Reward Ratio of 0.275. From a Risk/Reward Ratio standpoint, the Call Option position is substantially more favorable.

Yet another approach for the trader to utilize would be to consider that the purchase of two March, 1985 Sugar Options would cost $1,366--only $134 more than one Futures position.

If Sugar did reach his Target Level of 10-cents, he would have netted $4,480 on the one Futures contract position for March, 1985 Sugar. But for only $134 more risk, he would have two Call Option positions which would be worth approximately $7,610.

Obviously, then, for approximately the same amount of money, a trader can almost double his potential returns without incurring any additional risk other than the slight amount of $134, in this case, in additional premium costs.

The weekly chart shown below for Sugar illustrates not only the initial Target, but also subsequent Target Levels which might be achieved:

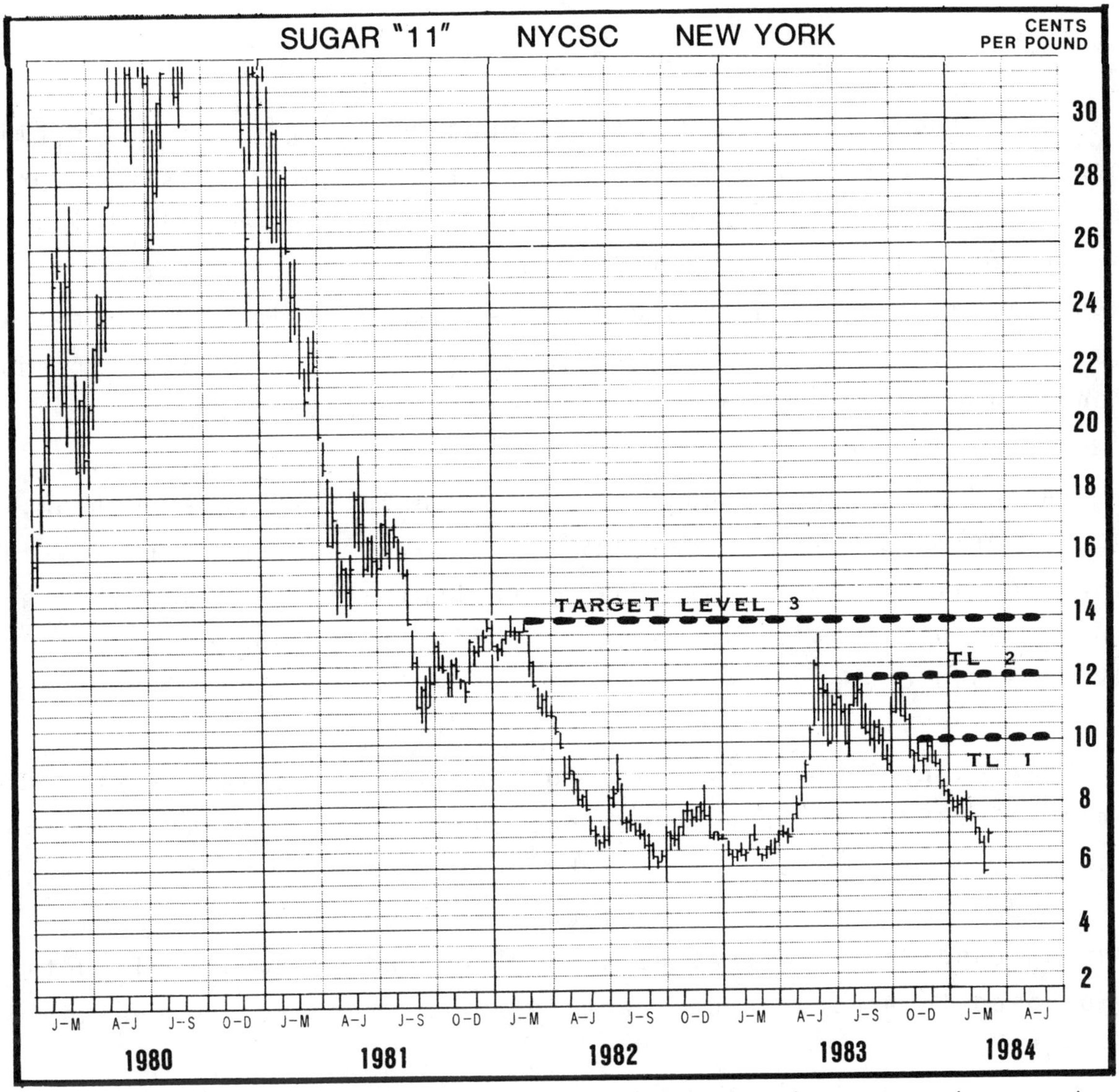

It can be seen that if Target Level 2 at 12-cents is reached, then the calculations change significantly. The percentage amount of the Call premium becomes relatively less and less as each additional Target Level is reached.

Even if his calculations about a Big Bull Move coming in Sugar were incorrect, the trader would lose no more--or only slightly more--by having a double position in a Sugar Option as opposed to a single position in a Sugar Futures contract.

While March is the nearby Option contract month for Sugar at that point in time, he could go to the July, 1985 Sugar Option.

Using the figures shown in the preceding Sugar Options premium chart with the Call premium for July, 1985 Sugar at a strike price of 6-cents at 1.13, he could figure that the cost of a Call Option would be $1,265--only $33 more than he would risk on a Futures contract in March Sugar at 6-cents with Initial Protective Stops at 4.90-cents. And he would be getting four months of additional time for the move in Sugar prices to develop.

When deciding which contract month to select for an Option, the trader must rely on previous price moves in the commodity in question--i.e., how rapidly they have typically developed in the direction the position is being established in--and on his own patience and conservatism--or lack thereof.

Looking at the weekly chart for Sugar for the late spring and summer of 1983, it can be seen that Sugar increased in price from about 7-cents to 13.5-cents in the period of three months. Hence, the trader--once he has determined that Sugar is a viable Big Move trading candidate and that he wishes to trade a Sugar Call Option as opposed to a Futures contract in Sugar--must decide whether it is better to:

1. Risk half the amount of Initial Risk on an Option position and buy one Call in March, 1985 Sugar as opposed to buying a single Futures contract, or:

2. Risk the same amount on the Options position--in this case, two call Options on March, 1985 Sugar--as he would on a single Futures contract, or:

3. Go to a more distant Option contract month--in this case, July, 1985 Sugar--risking the same amount for an additional four months of price movement as he would for a single

Futures contract position on March, 1985 Sugar.

There are, unfortunately, no hard-and-fast rules to follow in making this kind of analysis because Option premiums and the amount of Initial Dollar Risk on a Futures contract position will vary from commodity to commodity and vary from one point in time to another, depending upon the public's perception of that commodity's future potential to stage a price move.

We therefore urge the trader--once he has decided to go with an Options contract--to examine the premiums for the Options position based upon how much Initial Dollar Risk he is willing to take vis-a-vis the amount of risk he would have to take on a Futures contract position.

What we primarily intend to point out here is that, in many cases, the Option approach can yield much more in potential profits than a Futures contract position. Not all instances will be as favorable as the example for 1985 Sugar which we have selected, but we did select this example at random and it is fairly representative of what the Big Move trader will find as he starts examining potential Option positions for his Big Move trade.

As a result, we see no disadvantages to using Options in a Big Move trading program as long as the dollar figures come out favorably for the Option approach, as we have described in the preceding paragraphs.

With Options, the trader has a definite fixed risk limited to the cost he pays for the Option premium. He also can profit nearly as much from his Options position with a fraction of the risk as he can from a Futures contract position. Because time is factored into the Option premiums, Options in distant months will be easier to arrange than a Futures contract position in the same month, due to the thinness and illiquidity of distant Futures contract months. If a Big Move trade does continue for a number of months, the trader may have to roll over his position in a Futures contract several times, increasing his brokerage commission costs. And the trader definitely has more staying power with Options because no margin requirements means that he can stay in the position no matter how far the market moves against him, whereas in a Futures contract position, the market may move through his Initial Protective Stop--because of its placement, a UFO, or some other factor--and then reverse and go roaring off in the direction he originally wanted the market to go without offering him an Entry Point with a reasonable risk at which he could establish a new Futures contract position.

We would like to point out also that a trader can Pyramid with Option positions, just as he can with Futures Contract positions. The calculations for establishing when to enter the Pyramid, paper profits, and the like are all the same with one exception. That exception is that Pyramiding with Options positions does require the trader to put up more money for the premium price, insofar as he will not be able to use paper profits for the Pyramiding. Given the many advantages of using Options positions, however, this slight additional "up-front" money is but a minor disadvantage--one which we do not feel really detracts from using Options for Pyramiding positions in a Big Move trading program.

* * * * *

As we mentioned at the beginning of this chapter, there are a multitude of sophisticated approaches and variations to using Options in trading commodities. In addition to the Commodity Options book we are presently outlining, we are definitely considering the publication of an Options newsletter sometime in the near future. This will enable us not only to put all of these principles into practice by making actual Options recommendations, but also to provide a teaching tool for our readers. Basically, we are planning to introduce the material which will be included in our Option book in our Option newsletter so our newsletter subscribers will be able to gradually build upon their base of knowledge.

For those traders who are interested only in Big Move trading, however, we believe the very simplified approach we have outlined in this chapter is the ideal way to approach Commodity Options. A trader can very significantly increase his overall profits by intelligently and judiciously using Commodity Options as a part of his Big Move trading program.

CHAPTER 17

PUTTING IT ALL TOGETHER

When we began this book, we suggested that the reader might find reading this volume an adventuresome experience--much as we did as we wrote it. The experience of writing this book and putting it together has, in fact, been an adventure as well as a learning experience for us.

The production of this book has taught not only us, but also the members of our staff--not to mention many other people with whom we interface a great deal--not only about the markets themselves, but also about all of us as people. We went to great lengths to keep this book as simple as possible, yet make it as comprehensive and helpful as possible.

We had deadlines almost impossible to meet, scheduling mishaps, computer breakdowns and many other glitches appear along the way. Not the least of these was the fact that this book has been in preparation for an inordinate length of time. Its conclusion had been marred over the past year by many factors beyond our control--such as illness, personal tragedy and even death.

We have reiterated repeatedly throughout this volume that we have attempted to keep our approach to Big Move trading as elegantly simple as possible. We hope most readers have found this to have been the case, although some beginners may have found our explanations and illustrations a bit complicated.

We hope that none of our readers has been disappointed at the simplicity of our approach to Big Move trading. It would have been very simple for us to "jazz up" this book with a bunch of esoteric gobbledygook and thereby attempt to impress some readers with our mystical approach to the market place or with an exquisitely complicated technical methodology.

It has always been our experience that the simplest approach to any problem or project in life is very often the best, and we have found Big Move trading to be no exception to this philosophy. If the reader wishes to have an overly-complicated, overly-technical, overly-abstruse methodology, he can study any of a multitude of books and computer programs on the market place to fulfill that wish. We have, over the years, examined virtually every technical methodology which has been published--whether in a magazine, book or computer software program--and found all of them lacking in reliability over any extended period of time.

The reader may have guessed by now that some element of judgment or intuition is involved in selecting all trades--whether they be Big Move trades or not. This is true even if a trader is using a very mechanical methodology to enter the markets because it is very easy for him to talk himself out of some positions or double up on other positions when he, in fact, should not. This falls either in the realm of healthy, OK judgment or self-destructive, sabotaging psychological factors.

We believe Big Move trading represents no exception to the approach of a trader's using his own judgment and experience, at least to a certain degree. When we speak of having a majority--or at least close to a majority--of our Confirmation Signals pointing in the direction in which we are considering establishing our Big Move position, this leaves some room for judgment. After all, sometimes we find some potentially very profitable positions in which only two or three Confirmation Signals call for a move in our direction. Other times, seven or eight Confirmation Signals call for a Big Move in our direction, yet we will somehow intuitively sense that there is something not quite right with the position and decide to stay out of it. These are matters of judgment.

The reason we devoted an entire chapter in this book to the psychology of trading, emphasized that the trader be certain that he has no unresolved psychological issues which might sabotage his Big Move trading program, and included a book on "intuition" in the suggested reading list in Appendix D of this volume was to underline the importance we place on these factors.

The overview of how each individual precept in this book works and how they all interrelate and work together is fairly simple and relatively easy to grasp.

Basically, we are looking for a commodity whose price level is such that it has a high probability of a sustained and very profitable Big Move. Once we have isolated such a commodity, we subject it to a number of "tests"--our nine Confirmation Signals. Assuming that our commodity meets a sufficient number of these Confirmation Signal criteria favorably, then we look at the financial risks involved from a Money Management standpoint. If the reward is favorable compared to the risk--and this is, of course, partially determined by our Initial Entry Point, our Initial Protective Stop and our Target Levels--then we enter our trade as a resting buy or sell order. Once our position is filled--assuming that our Initial Protective Stops hold--then we proceed to trail our stops using one of several different techniques. We alter these techniques as our Target Levels are approached and passed until our position has stopped itself out.

We also have the option of increasing our potential profits on any given trade by Pyramiding, and/or buying Put or Call Options if an Option is available for that particualar commodity. If an Option contract is not offered for the commodity we wish to trade, we examine other commodities which are closely related to or are in the same complex as the commodity we with to trade. This tells us whether any of these other commodities for which Option trading is allowed, could be utilized for our Big Move position.

We also go to great lengths to find a broker who is amenable to our Big Move trading philosophy, who is content with our trading infrequently and our holding our trades for a significant length of time, who does not offer us unsolicited advice, and who does not encourage us to deviate from our Big Move trading program or to trade more frequently.

A large part of our Big Move trading program also is examining ourselves as honestly as possible to see if any psychological "garbage" which we are not aware of is sabotaging our investment program and/or other areas of our investment, professional and personal lives.

We originally had planned to use this chapter to go into great detail restating and repeating all of the principles we explored earlier in this book. Upon further consideration, however, we concluded that because we already have presented them in detail, chapter by chapter, in this book, the reader already should have a good feel for the material without our condensing and repeating it all over again.

As a special aid for the reader, however, we shall summarize our Big Move trading program philosophy. In checklist form, then, the steps of our Big Move trading program are:

1. We locate commodities which are trading at historic high, low or mid-range price levels, based upon approximately the last seven years of trading, using monthly price charts.

2. We examine these commodities which we have isolated to see how many of our nine Confirmation Signals are indicating that a commodity is going to turn in direction (in the case of historically high or low price commodities) or if a preponderance of the Confirmation Signals indicate an imminent move in one direction or the other (in the case of commodities trading at mid-range prices).

3. We use any one of several methods to determine our Initial Entry Point and Initial Protective Stop point, thereby clearly defining our Initial Dollar Risk.

4. Having determined the Initial Dollar Risk, we go back to our monthly charts and determine--based upon historical support and resistance levels--different potential Target Levels to be sure that the potential reward or profit is sufficiently great for us to assume the amount of risk we are taking.

5. Assuming that the Risk/Reward Ratio works out favorably, we go ahead an initiate our positions, Trail Stops as the position moves in our direction.

6. We let the market take us out of our positions by our use of Trailing Stops, varying our method of Trailing Stop

placement as different Target Levels are reached and/or surpassed.

7. Depending upon our own investment philosopy and personality, we do or do not elect to Pyramid our positions by using paper profits in order to increase our potential profits.

8. We examine--before we establish any position--whether an Option in the particular commodity we are considering is potentially more profitable to us. If Option contract trading is not permitted in the commodity under we are considering, we examine other similar commodities to see if we can establish an Option position in one of those in lieu of a regular Futures Contract position in whatever commodity we had selected.

That is basically it. Our methodology is not overly complicated but, as a very famous organization we are familiar with would put it: "It's simple, but it's not easy."

Big Move trading is not easy because it does require a lot of patience and it does require some work. It is not an easy method from the standpoint of buying or selling a position everytime the Bullish Consensus gets beyond a certain point, or everytime a certain type of Moving Average crosses another type, or anytime any one certain technical indicator changes. A Big Move trading program requires that a trader follow as many commodities as possible so that he is prepared to establish positions as prices move into historical high, low, or mid-range levels and can act rapidly as the Confirmation Signals come into line favoring the establishment of the positions.

We have found from our experience that between 29 and 32

commodities--including some thinly traded commodities which might be best left off the list--can be so analyzed and tracked in no more than two hours per day of chart marking and analysis--plus several additional hours each weekend. Obviously, if a trader has the time, he can execute a more careful and exacting analysis, especially of the Confirmation Signals, by spending more time than this during the week and on weekends. But this is not absolutely necessary in order to achieve a fair amount of success in a Big Move trading program.

Patience is perhaps the most necessary prerequisite for a trader to have when he is engaging in a Big Move trading program, as he often will find that he must wait for months on end for a particular commodity to top or to bottom out, or to have a sufficient number of Confirmation Signals registering favorably, or to have his Initial Entry Point even hit after he has established his resting buy or sell order.

Patience for him, however, does not end with the filling of his Big Move order because many moves frequently take months in their formation before they begin to accelerate and seriously move towards the trader's predetermined Target Levels. If a trader knows that he must have more excitement in his trading program (more "action"), then we suggest he not get into Big Move trading, because it obviously is not for him. We would urge him instead to ask himself seriously if he is genuinely interested in making money, or if he is primarily interested in excitement whether or not he makes money.

We are frequently asked about the use of advisory letters and services by potential and existing Big Move traders. Our views on this matter, of course, are somewhat biased since we publish two commodity advisory newsletters ourselves--<u>Taurus</u> (Short-Term trading recommendations) and <u>Mega-Trades</u> (Big Move trading recommendations). We have found over the years--as we have previously mentioned--that trading advisors and commodity newsletters have their good times and their bad times. Needless to say, the better advisory newsletters tend to have longer and more frequent good times than the inferior advisory newsletters.

We do, as a part of our own educational process, read virtually every other reputable commodity advisory newsletter that is published. We do this because we might otherwise miss or overlook some particular piece of fundamental or technical information that might prove beneficial. We can heartily recommend the newsletters listed in Appendix E at the back of this book for those Big Move traders who wish to help their own market analysis with additional input.

We would caution very strongly, however, that no Big Move trader let himself be swayed in any way by the conclusions of any of these newsletters--including our own--if he is making his own commodity selections. It is very, very easy for a trader to come to the conclusion that a certain commodity is on the verge of a Big Move, then read several respected commodity advisory newsletters with the opposite conclusion and "talk himself out of" entering the position he felt was right. Years ago, we ourselves lost many, many profitable positions by letting ourselves be swayed by other well-meaning and well-respected commodity advisors. We try to be scrupulously careful not to let what any advisor is saying sway our own analysis or judgment. Instead, we utilize these other advisors only to see if there is anything we have overlooked.

We will appreciate any feedback or comments that our readers may have which might help us improve subsequent editions of this book for future readers. We will incorporate such revisions into future editions wherever possible.

We urge our readers to examine the Appendices in the back of this book carefully and to use them, as a great deal of thought and preparation went into them with the hope and intent that they would be valuable tools for every Big Move trader.

We truly wish that there were a "Holy Grail" for commodity selection. If there were, we would either be using it ourselves, and/or selling such a "Perfect Method" for $50,000 a copy. Unfortunately there never has been, is not now, and never will be such an ultimate methodology.

We suggest that the reader remember this whenever he receives a mailing piece or sees an advertisement in a magazine offering a "Perfect Method." We have repeatedly over the years reviewed, examined and dissected such systems and methods, only to find that--even if they were well-intentioned--they ultimately were not profitable unless a trader applied his own judgment to them--something all propagators of such systems and methods claim is not necessary.

We hope, and believe, that we have given the reader of THE MEGA-TRADE METHOD the tools which will enable him to make his own Big Move trading decisions in a rational and intelligent way and give him an extremely high probability of success in the market place. Were we to feel that we had done otherwise, we would not have published this book. The techniques outlined in this book are, in our belief, the closest thing there is to the "best method" to approach any and all commodity markets. Our method, however, is not perfect. Our methodology is subject to different interpretations by different Big Move traders. But if the principles we have outlined herein are adhered to fairly rigorously, such differences in interpertation over individual potential Big Move trades should be relatively infrequent and insignificant.

* * * * *

We have completed one adventure by finishing this book. Now we are looking forward--and we hope our readers are, too--to continuing another--a Big Move trading program that always will be exciting, sometimes be frustrating, and inevitably be profitable.

APPENDIX A

SEASONAL PATTERN CHARTS

Shown in this Appendix are the Seasonal Pattern charts to which we have referred so frequently throughout this text. Also included as part of the charts is the percentage reliabilities data which was not included in our earlier work, THE TAURUS METHOD.

These charts are from ones constructed by Jake Bernstein of MBH Commodity Advisors, Inc., P.O. Box 353, Winnetka, IL. 60093. Jake is the leading expert on Seasonal Patterns--as well as on several other areas of commodity trading--in the entire country. We are most appreciative that he allowed us to reproduce these Seasonal Patterns in this text.

The data from which these charts were constructed covers, in most cases, a 20- to 50-year time span of cash prices. We strongly recommend that percentage reliabilies of 65% or greater be considered as reliable, and of course, the higher the percentage, the more the weight that should be put upon the particular Seasonal Pattern. Those few commodities for which there are no charts at all are commodities for which there are an insufficient number of years from which to accumulate valid data and/or the overall reliability for any seasonal moves in these particular commodities is so low as to render any Seasonal Patterns as meaningless.

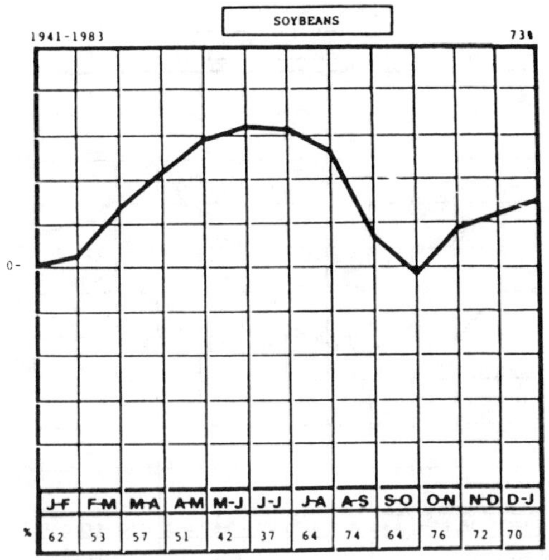
SOYBEANS
1941-1983
73%
0-
J-F F-M M-A A-M M-J J-J J-A A-S S-O O-N N-D D-J
% 62 53 57 51 42 37 64 74 64 76 72 70

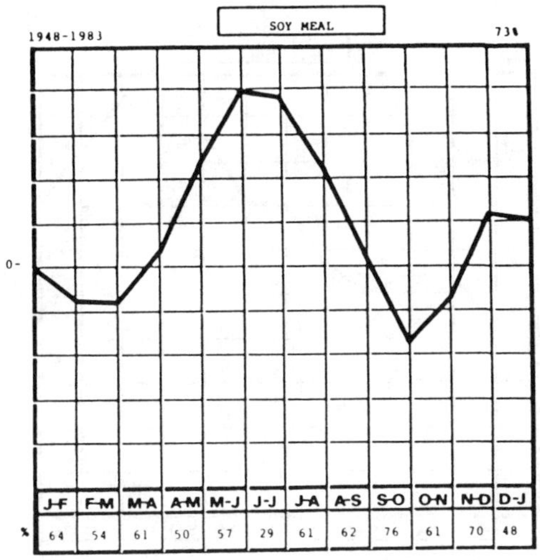
SOY MEAL
1948-1983
73%
0-
J-F F-M M-A A-M M-J J-J J-A A-S S-O O-N N-D D-J
% 64 54 61 50 57 29 61 62 76 61 70 48

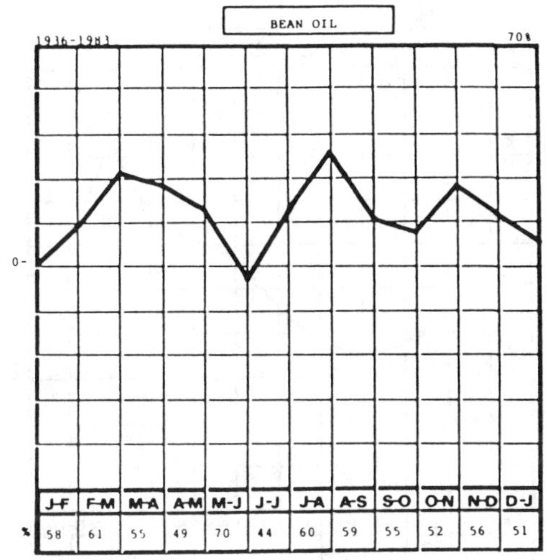
BEAN OIL
1936-1983
70%
0-
J-F F-M M-A A-M M-J J-J J-A A-S S-O O-N N-D D-J
% 58 61 55 49 70 44 60 59 55 52 56 51

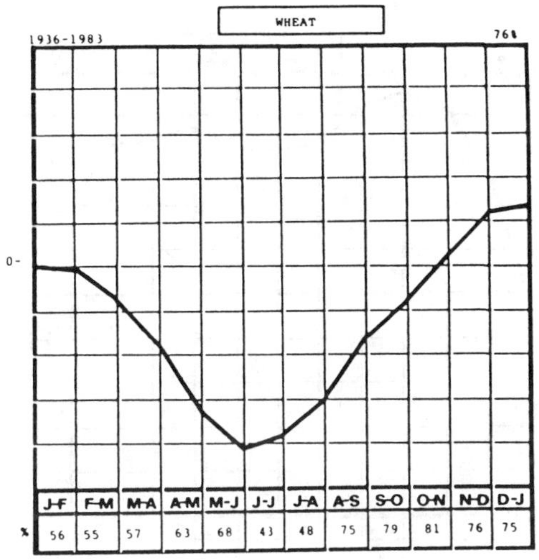
WHEAT
1936-1983
76%
0-
J-F F-M M-A A-M M-J J-J J-A A-S S-O O-N N-D D-J
% 56 55 57 63 68 43 48 75 79 81 76 75

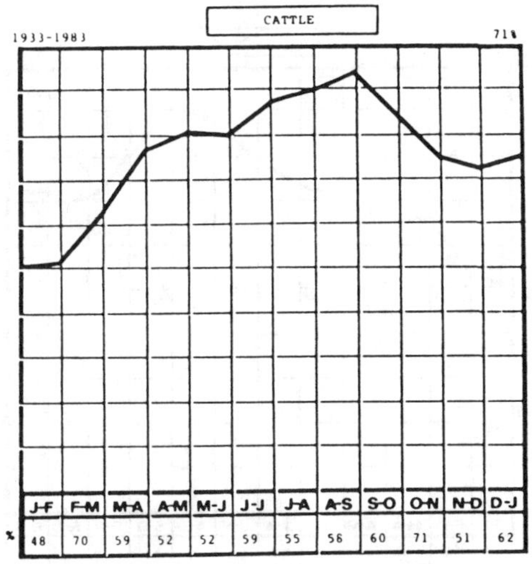
CATTLE
1933-1983
71%
J-F F-M M-A A-M M-J J-J J-A A-S S-O O-N N-D D-J
% 48 70 59 52 52 59 55 56 60 71 51 62

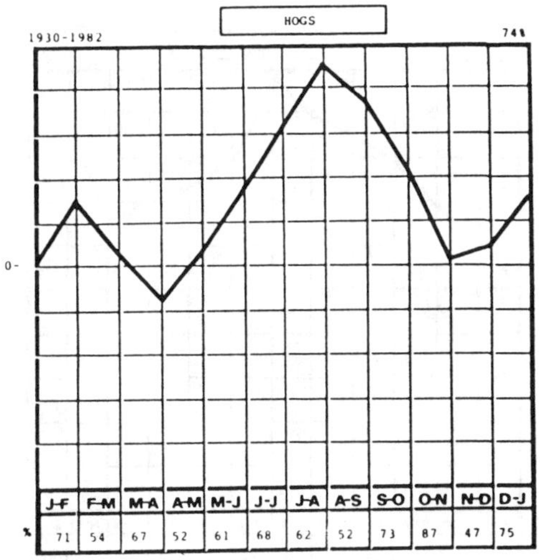
HOGS
1930-1982
74%
0-
J-F F-M M-A A-M M-J J-J J-A A-S S-O O-N N-D D-J
% 71 54 67 52 61 68 62 52 73 87 47 75

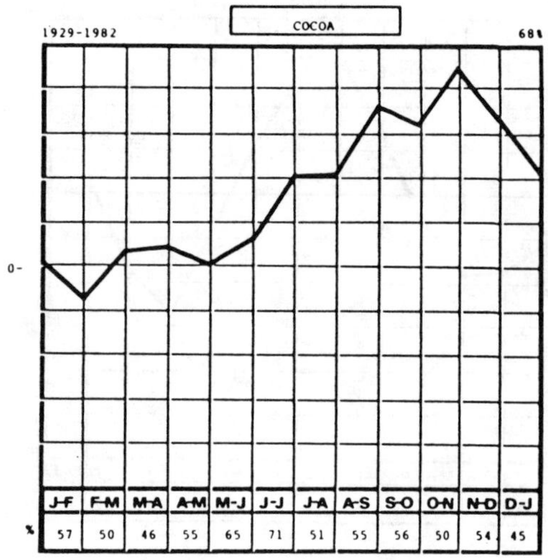
COCOA
1929-1982
68%
0-
J-F F-M M-A A-M M-J J-J J-A A-S S-O O-N N-D D-J
%
57 50 46 55 65 71 51 55 56 50 54 45

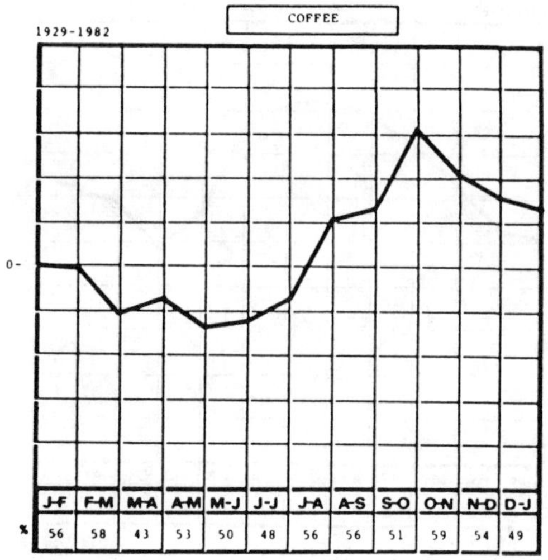
COFFEE
1929-1982
0-
J-F F-M M-A A-M M-J J-J J-A A-S S-O O-N N-D D-J
%
56 58 43 53 50 48 56 56 51 59 54 49

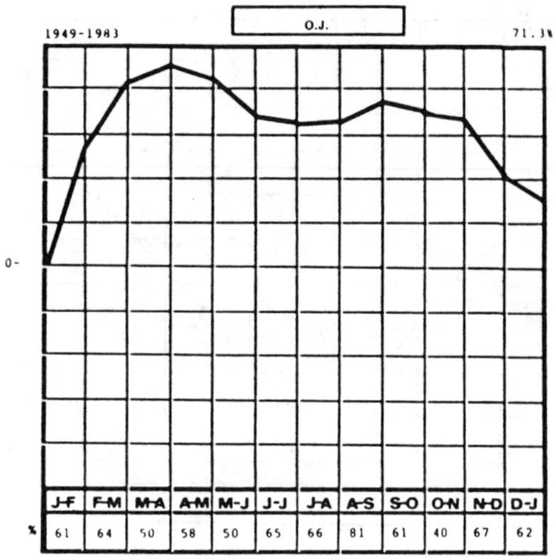
O.J.
1949-1983
71.3%
0-
J-F F-M M-A A-M M-J J-J J-A A-S S-O O-N N-D D-J
%
61 64 50 58 50 65 66 81 61 40 67 62

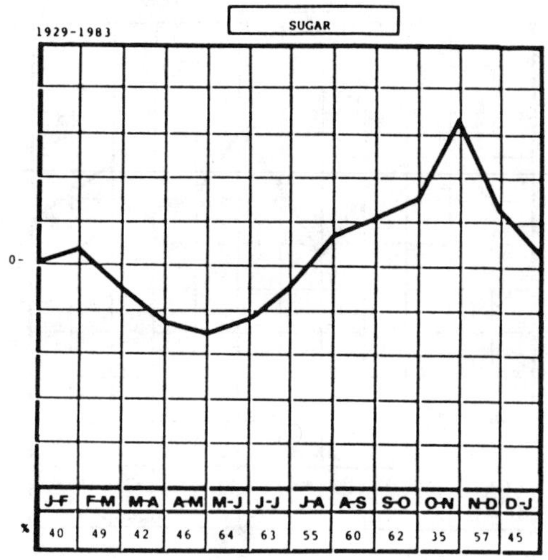
SUGAR
1929-1983
0-
J-F F-M M-A A-M M-J J-J J-A A-S S-O O-N N-D D-J
%
40 49 42 46 64 63 55 60 62 35 57 45

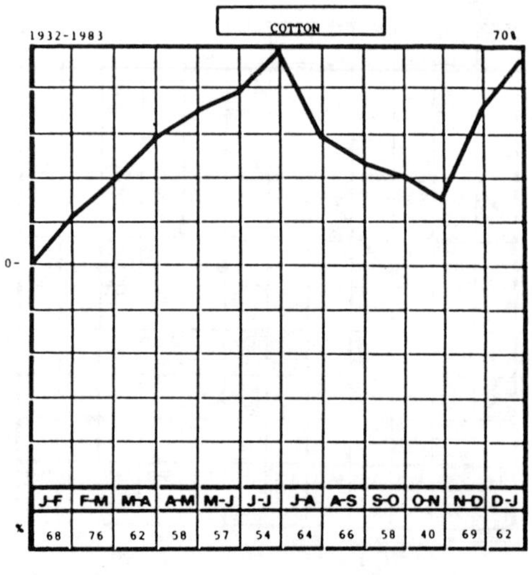
COTTON
1932-1983
70%
0-
J-F F-M M-A A-M M-J J-J J-A A-S S-O O-N N-D D-J
%
68 76 62 58 57 54 64 66 58 40 69 62

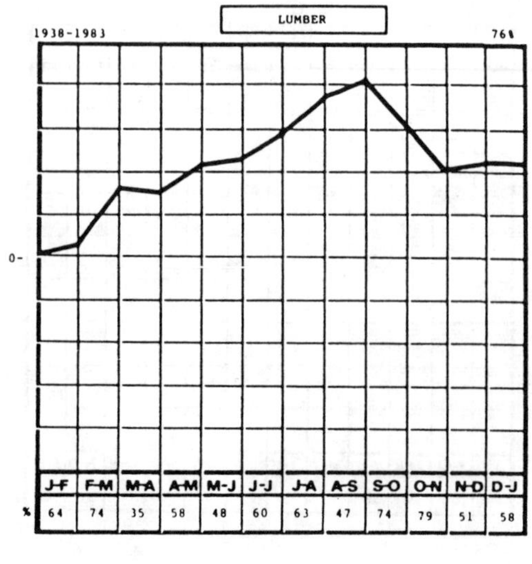
LUMBER
1938-1983
76%
0-
J-F F-M M-A A-M M-J J-J J-A A-S S-O O-N N-D D-J
%
64 74 35 58 48 60 63 47 74 79 51 58

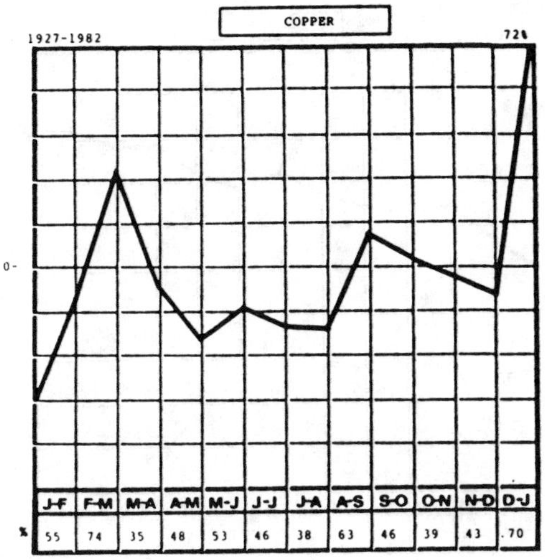
COPPER
1927-1982
72%
0-
J-F F-M M-A A-M M-J J-J J-A A-S S-O O-N N-D D-J
% 55 74 35 48 53 46 38 63 46 39 43 70

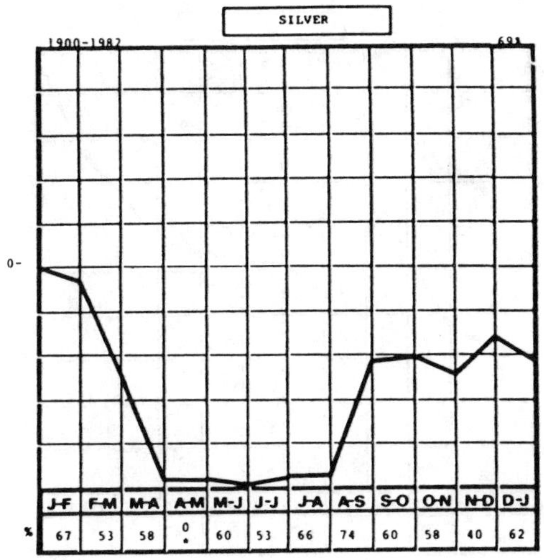
SILVER
1900-1982
69%
0-
J-F F-M M-A A-M M-J J-J J-A A-S S-O O-N N-D D-J
% 67 53 58 0 60 53 66 74 60 58 40 62

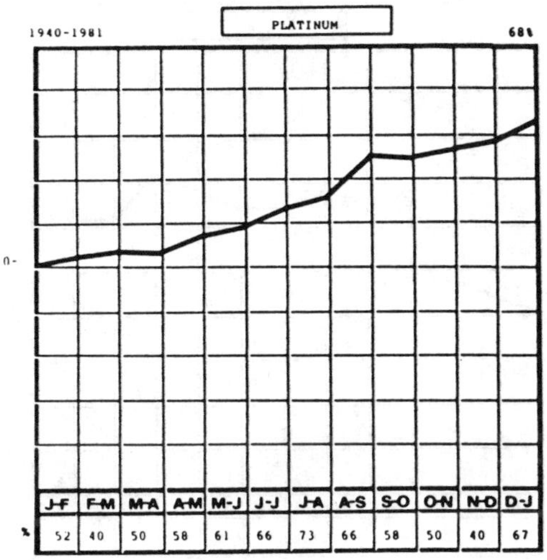
PLATINUM
1940-1981
68%
0-
J-F F-M M-A A-M M-J J-J J-A A-S S-O O-N N-D D-J
% 52 40 50 58 61 66 73 66 58 50 40 67

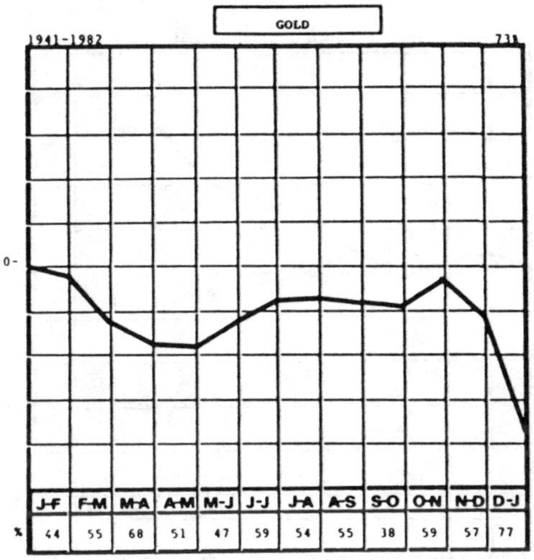
GOLD
1941-1982
73%
0-
J-F F-M M-A A-M M-J J-J J-A A-S S-O O-N N-D D-J
% 44 55 68 51 47 59 54 55 38 59 57 77

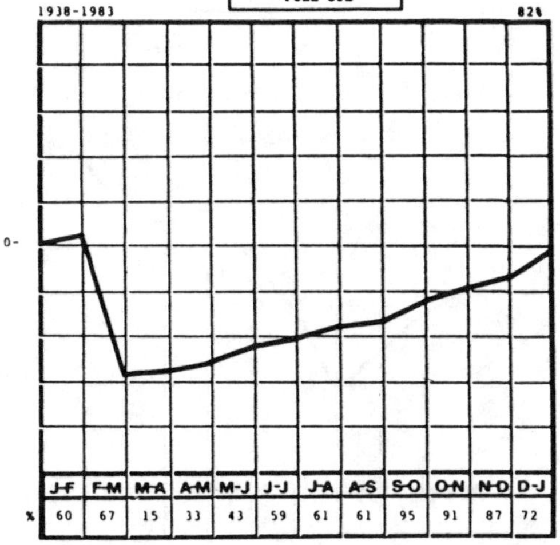
FUEL OIL
1938-1983
82%
0-
J-F F-M M-A A-M M-J J-J J-A A-S S-O O-N N-D D-J
% 60 67 15 33 43 59 61 61 95 91 87 72

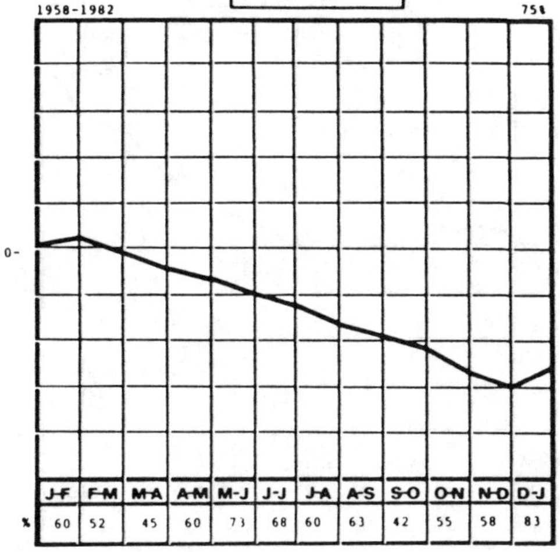
BR. PD.
1958-1982
75%
0-
J-F F-M M-A A-M M-J J-J J-A A-S S-O O-N N-D D-J
% 60 52 45 60 73 68 60 63 42 55 58 83

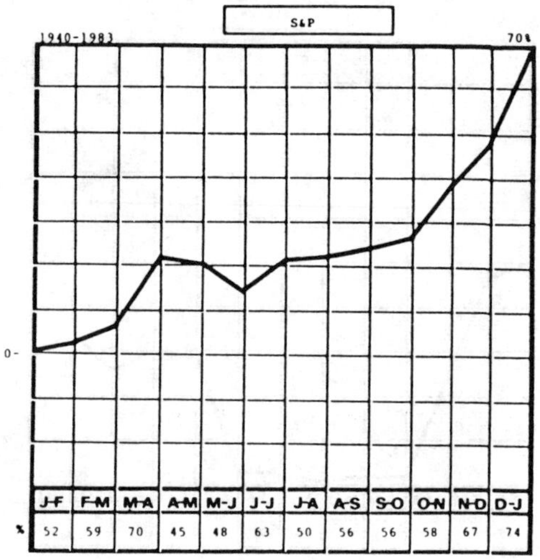
S&P
1940-1983
70%
0-
J-F F-M M-A A-M M-J J-J J-A A-S S-O O-N N-D D-J
% 52 59 70 45 48 63 50 56 56 58 67 74

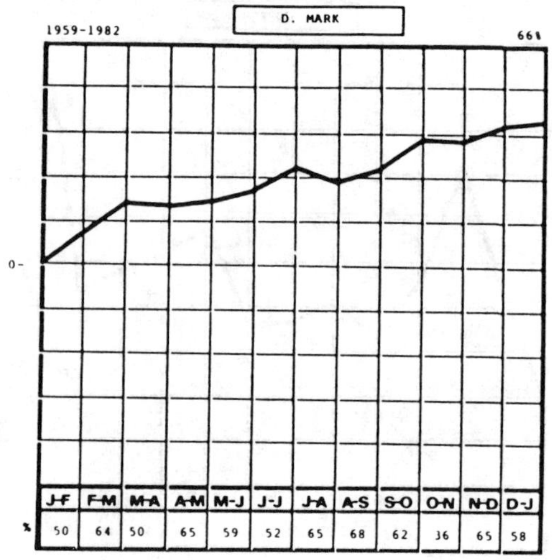
D. MARK
1959-1982
66%
0-
J-F F-M M-A A-M M-J J-J J-A A-S S-O O-N N-D D-J
% 50 64 50 65 59 52 65 68 62 36 65 58

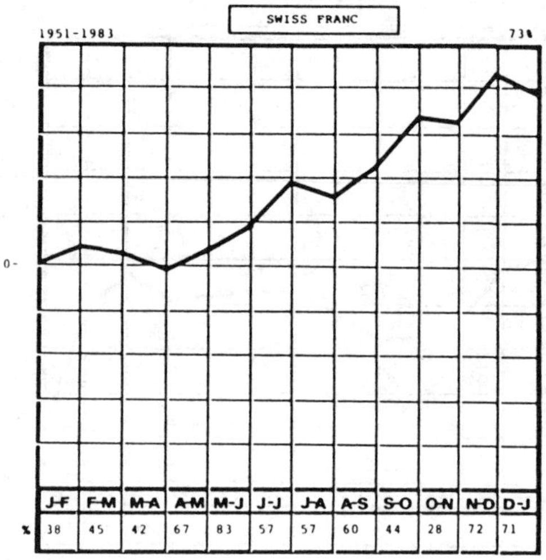
SWISS FRANC
1951-1983
73%
0-
J-F F-M M-A A-M M-J J-J J-A A-S S-O O-N N-D D-J
% 38 45 42 67 83 57 57 60 44 28 72 71

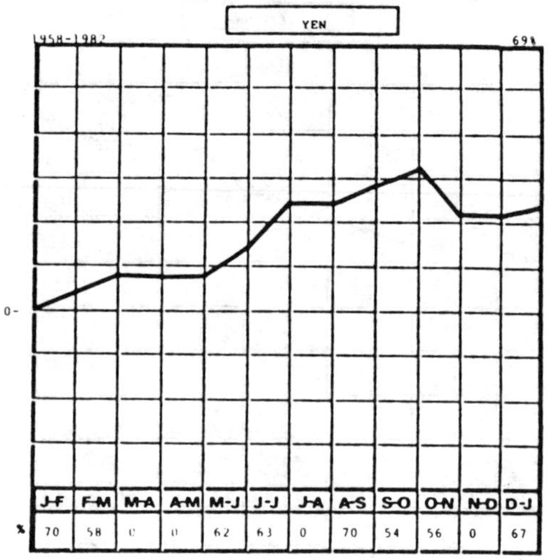
YEN
69%
0-
J-F F-M M-A A-M M-J J-J J-A A-S S-O O-N N-D D-J
% 70 58 0 0 62 63 0 70 54 56 0 67

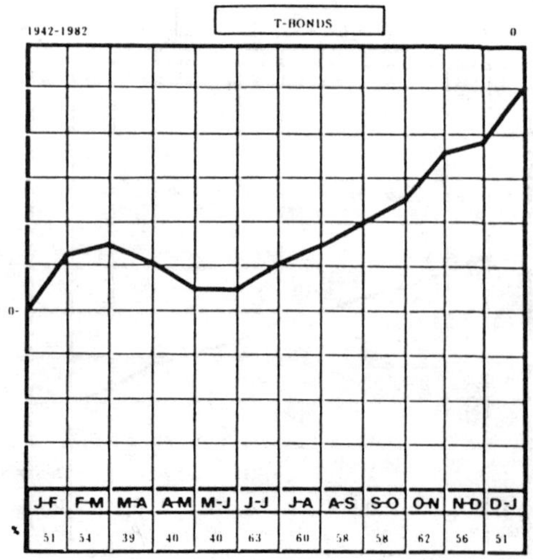
T-BONDS
1942-1982
0
0-
J-F F-M M-A A-M M-J J-J J-A A-S S-O O-N N-D D-J
% 51 54 39 40 40 63 60 58 58 62 56 51

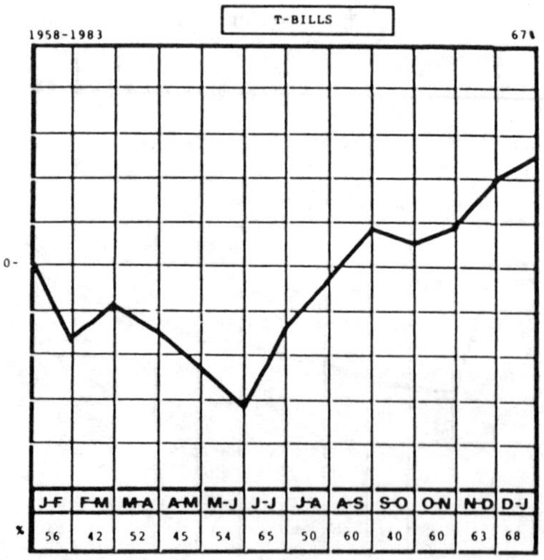
T-BILLS
1958-1983
67%
0-
J-F F-M M-A A-M M-J J-J J-A A-S S-O O-N N-D D-J
% 56 42 52 45 54 65 50 60 40 60 63 68

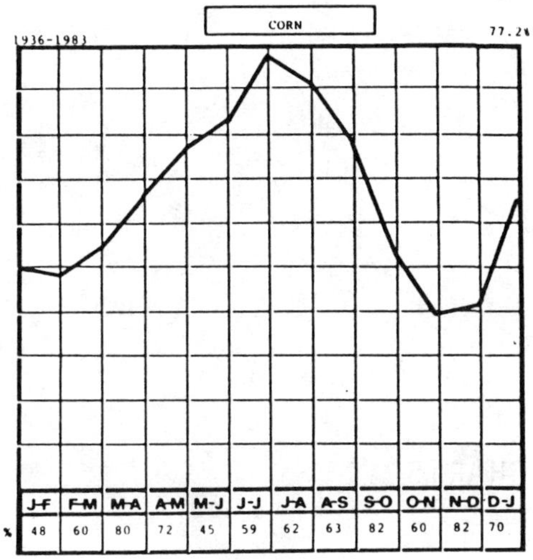
CORN
1936-1983
77.2%
J-F
F-M
M-A
A-M
M-J
J-J
J-A
A-S
S-O
O-N
N-D
D-J
%
48
60
80
72
45
59
62
63
82
60
82
70

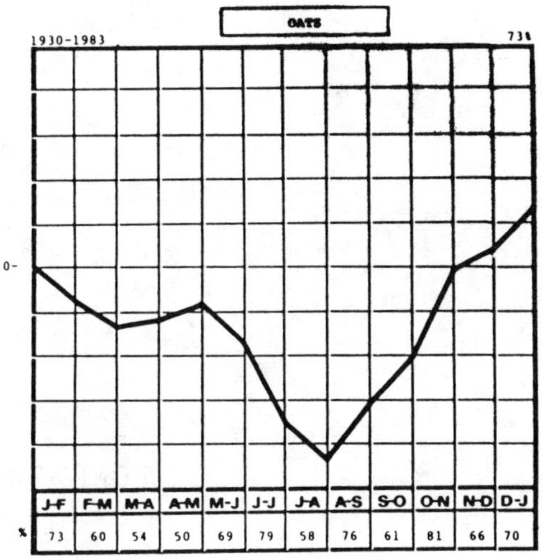
OATS
1930-1983
73%
0-
J-F
F-M
M-A
A-M
M-J
J-J
J-A
A-S
S-O
O-N
N-D
D-J
%
73
60
54
50
69
79
58
76
61
81
66
70

APPENDIX B

LONG-RANGE CYCLE CHARTS

While Long-Range Cycles are really more accurate and predictable than Shorter-Term Cycles, paradoxically, they are subject to larger time distortions when they are skewed or "of phase." Whereas a Short-Term Cycle of four weeks may be skewed by a week or two, a Long-Range Cycle may be skewed by a year or more.

Therefore, the trader must exercise a great deal of care to determine if a Long-Range Cycle has, in fact, bottomed or topped in order to be certain that he is trading with a Long-Range trend.

As evidence becomes available of exact topping or bottoming for any of these commodities' Long-Range Cycles, we will be modifying these graphs and publishing them in our Mega-Trades newsletter.

LONG-RANGE CYCLE: SOYBEANS

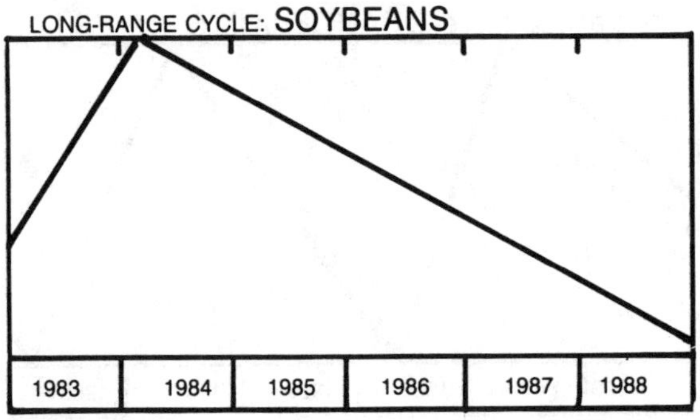

LONG-RANGE CYCLE: SOYBEAN MEAL

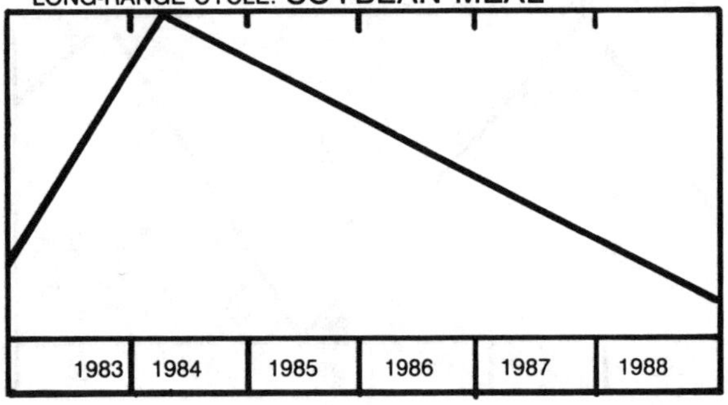

LONG-RANGE CYCLE: SOYBEAN OIL

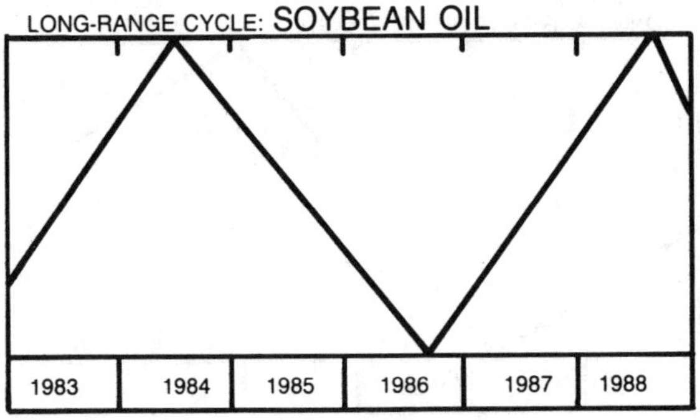

LONG-RANGE CYCLE: WHEAT

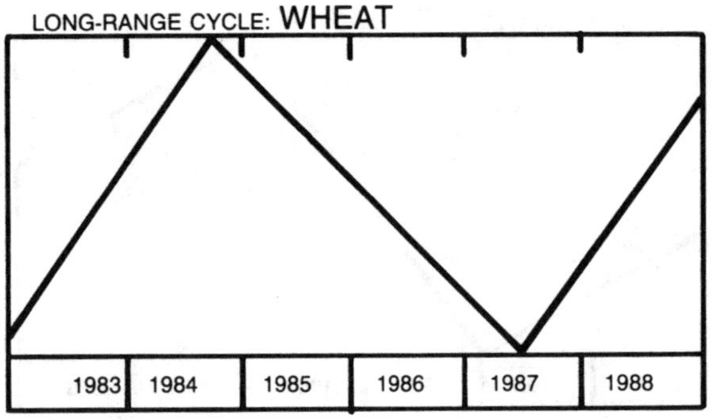

LONG-RANGE CYCLE: CATTLE

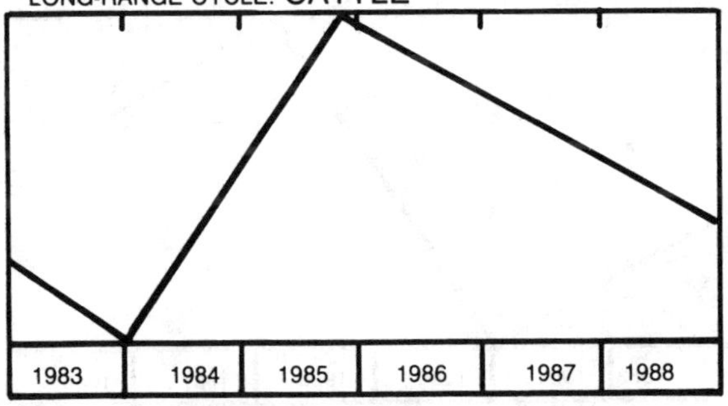

LONG-RANGE CYCLE: HOGS

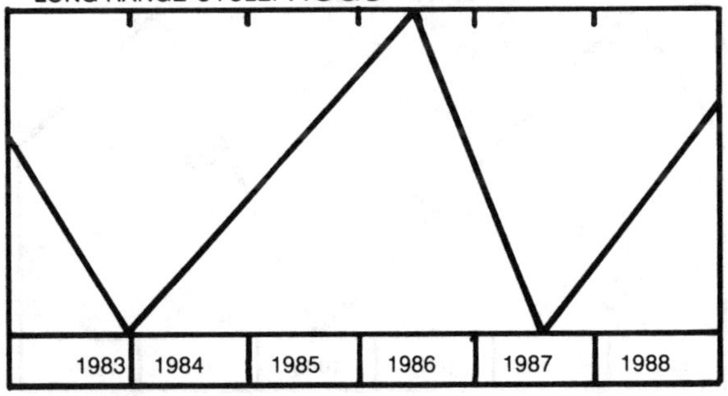

LONG-RANGE CYCLE: PORK BELLIES

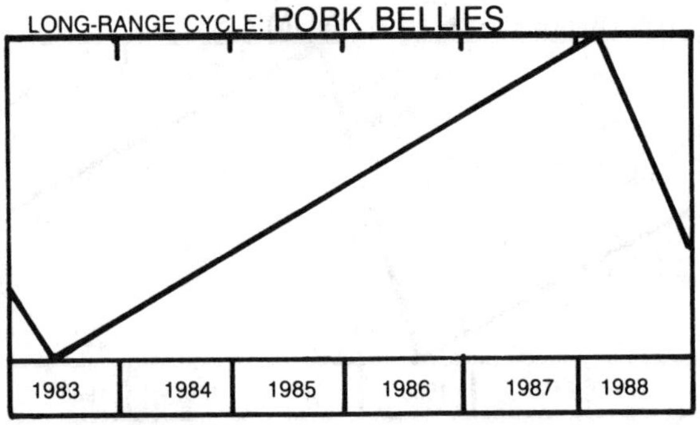

LONG-RANGE CYCLE: COFFEE

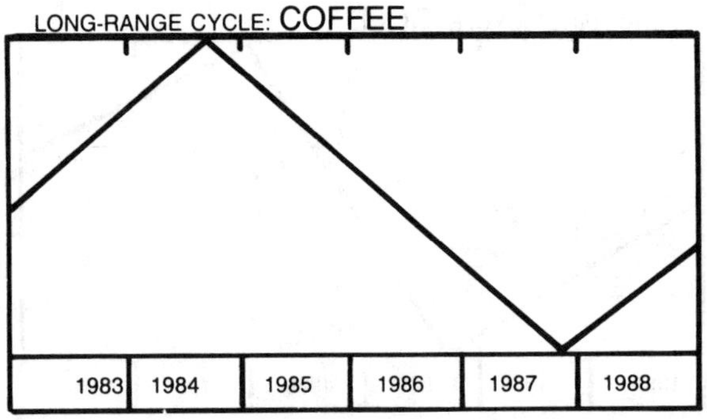

LONG-RANGE CYCLE: COCOA

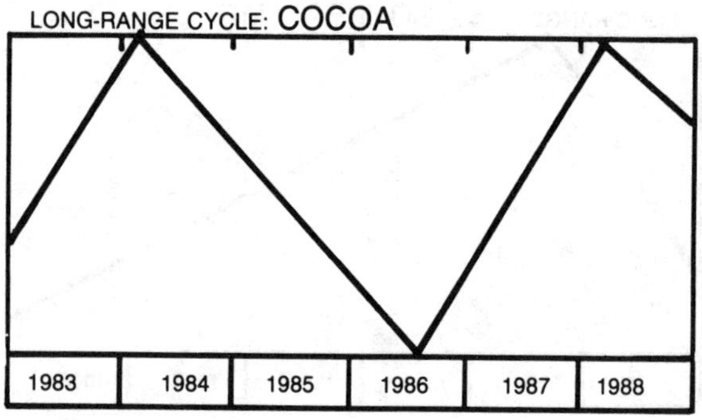

LONG-RANGE CYCLE: ORANGE JUICE

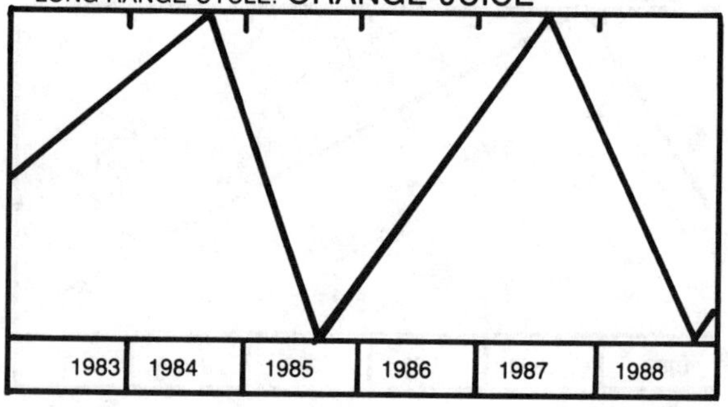

LONG-RANGE CYCLE: SUGAR

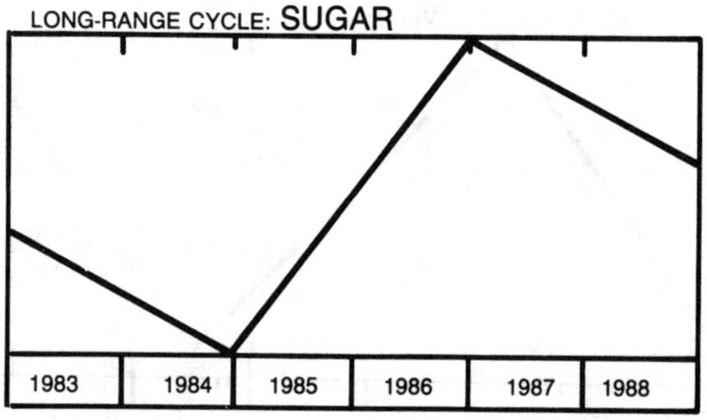

LONG-RANGE CYCLE: COTTON

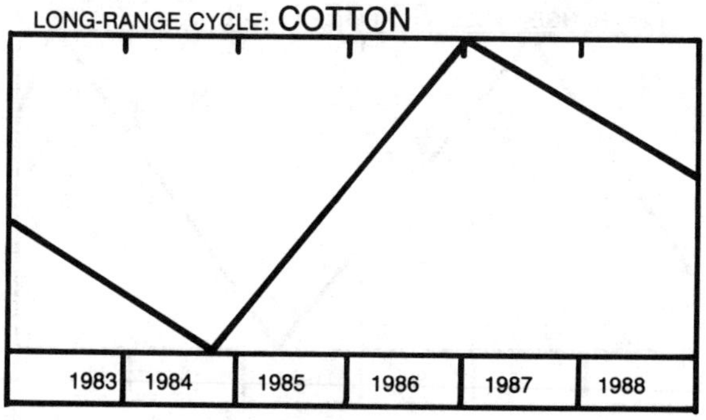

LONG-RANGE CYCLE: LUMBER

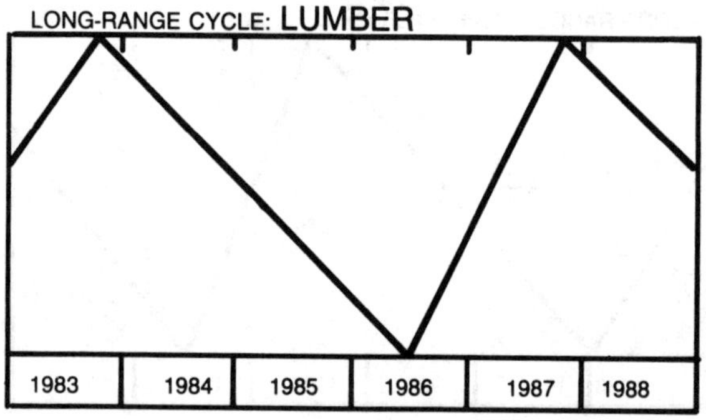

LONG-RANGE CYCLE: COPPER

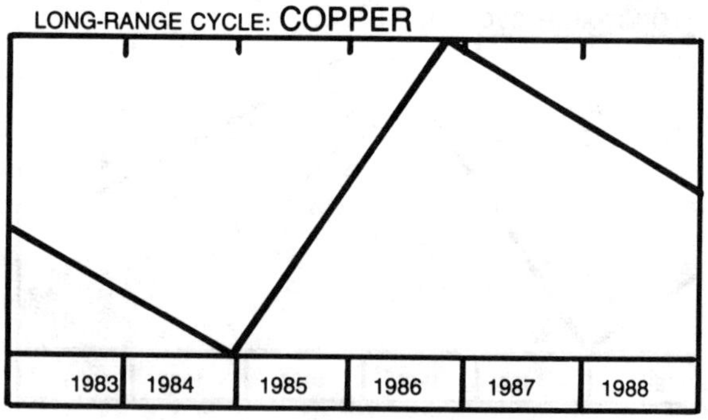

LONG-RANGE CYCLE: GOLD

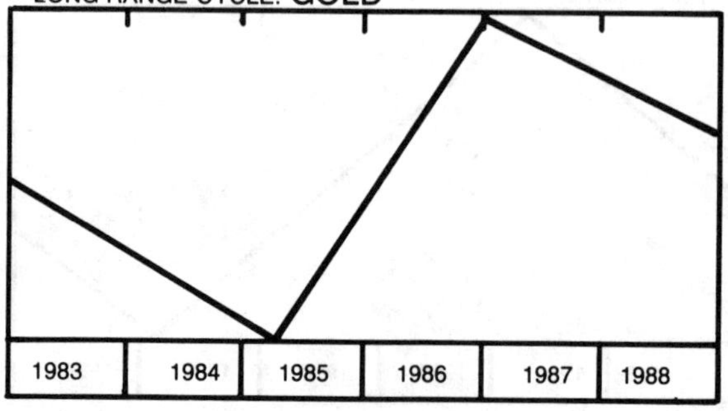

LONG-RANGE CYCLE: PLATINUM

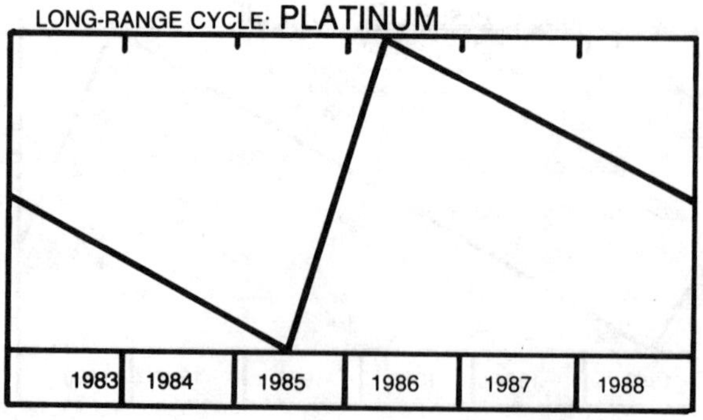

LONG-RANGE CYCLE: SILVER

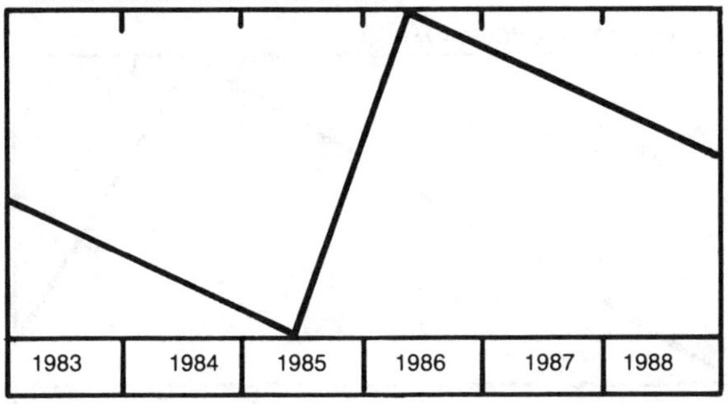

LONG-RANGE CYCLE: BRITISH POUND

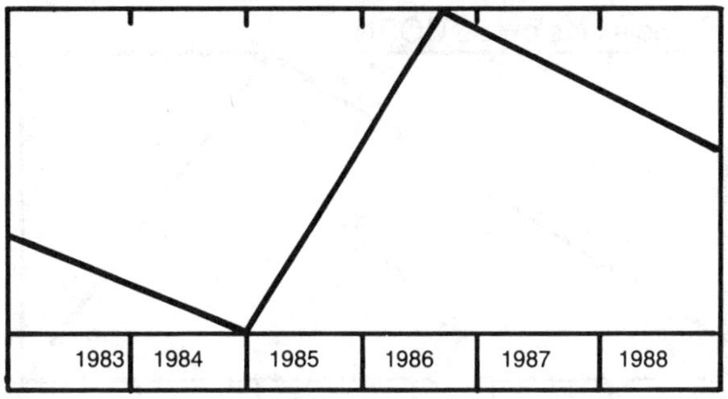

LONG-RANGE CYCLE: CANADIAN DOLLAR

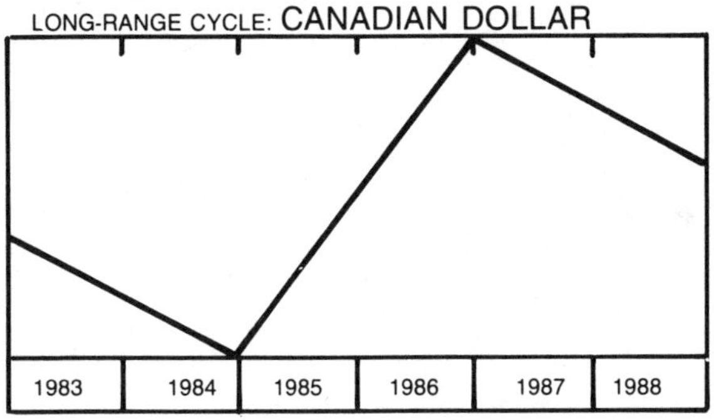

LONG-RANGE CYCLE: DEUTSCHE MARK

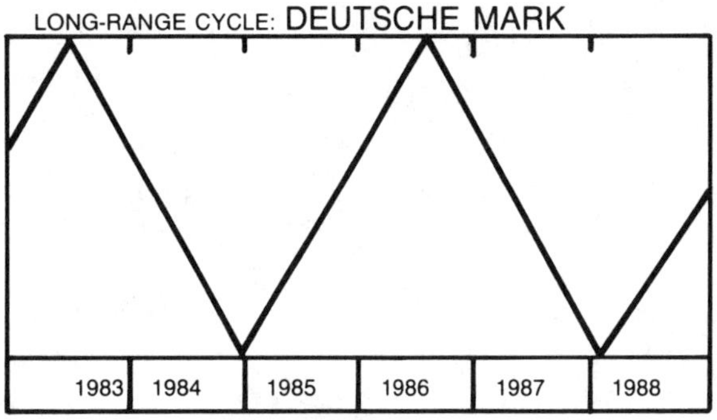

LONG-RANGE CYCLE: JAPANESE YEN

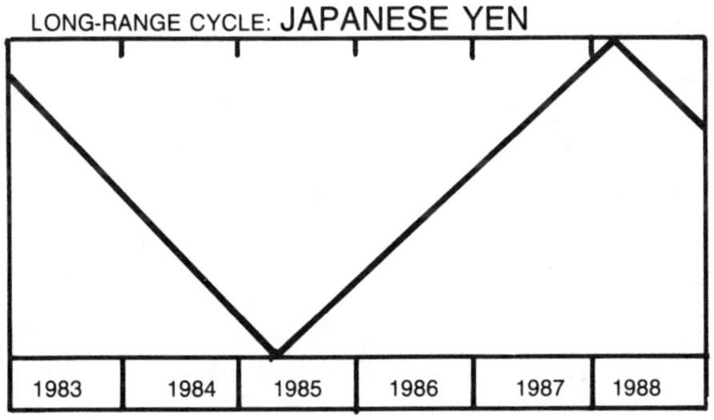

LONG-RANGE CYCLE: SWISS FRANC

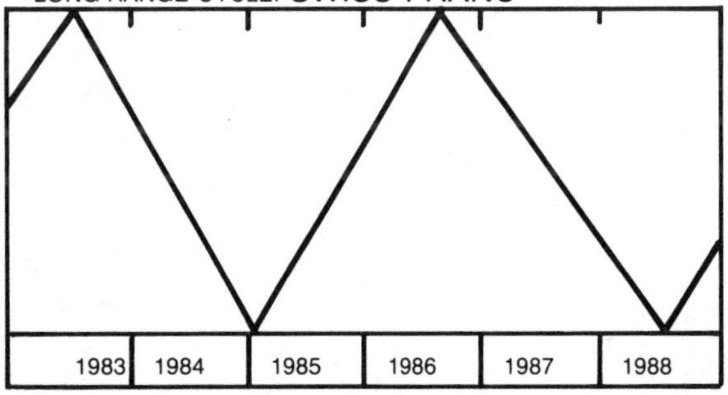

LONG-RANGE CYCLE: STOCK INDICES

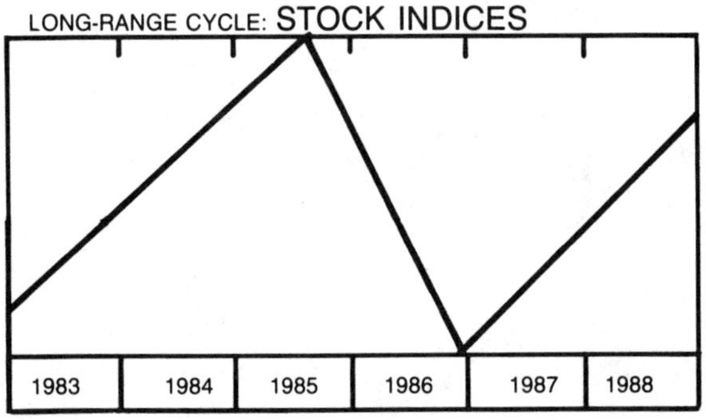

LONG-RANGE CYCLE: T-BILLS

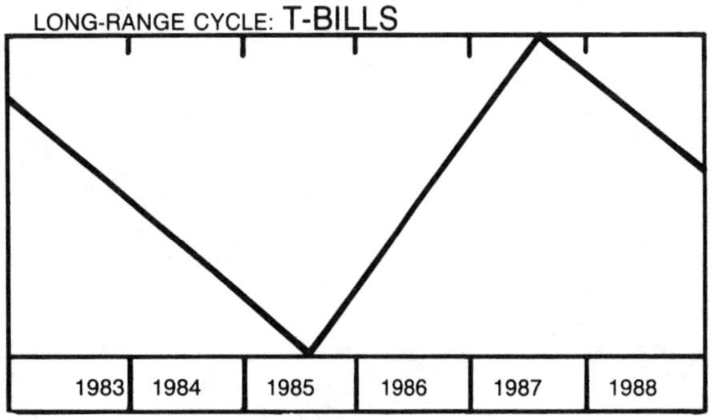

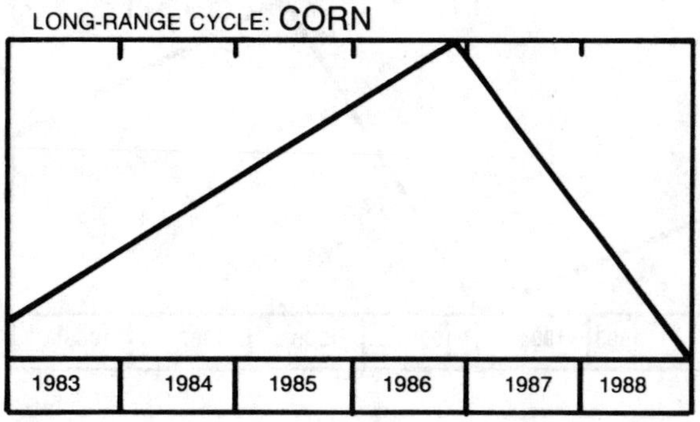
LONG-RANGE CYCLE: CORN
1983
1984
1985
1986
1987
1988

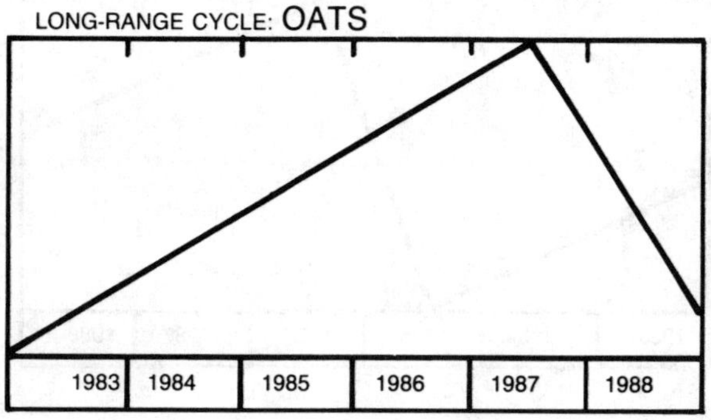
LONG-RANGE CYCLE: OATS
1983
1984
1985
1986
1987
1988

APPENDIX C

PROJECTED PRICE GRAPHS

PPG: **T-Bills**

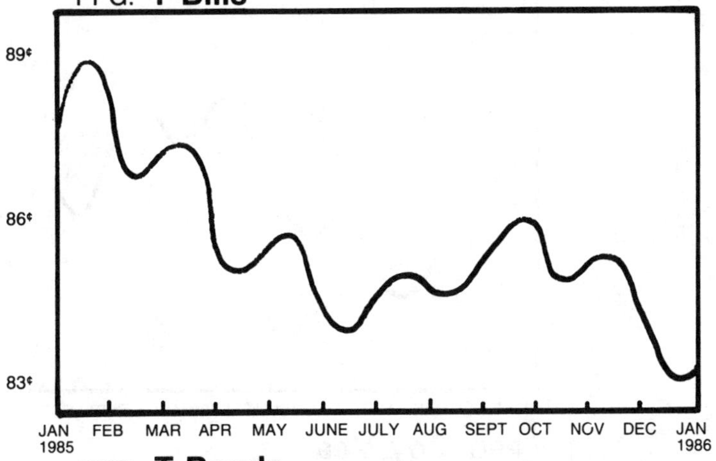

PPG: **T-Bonds**

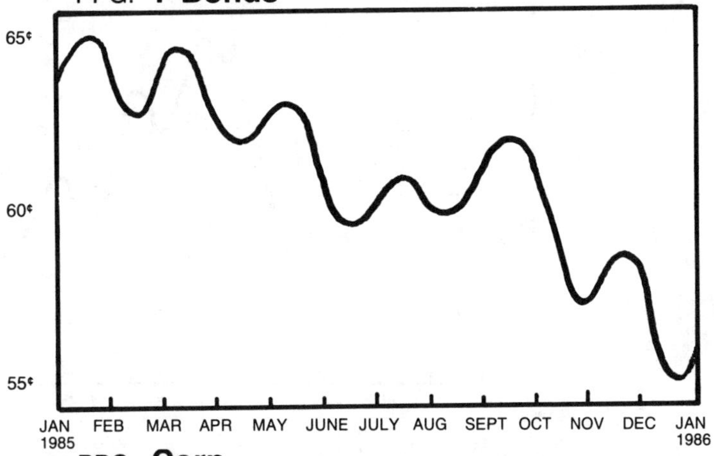

PPG: **Corn**

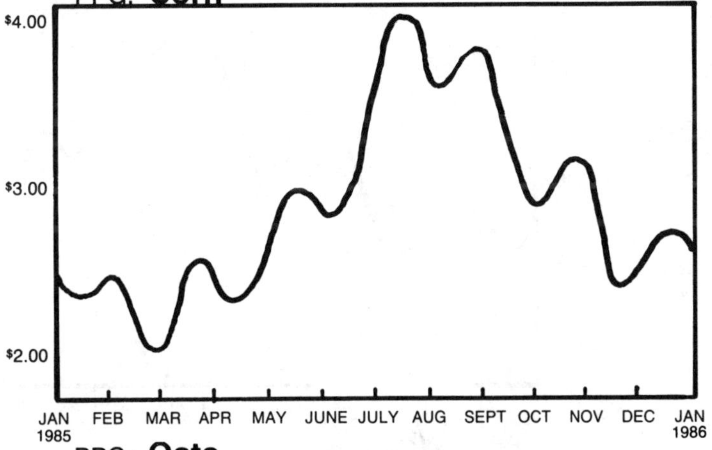

PPG: **Oats**

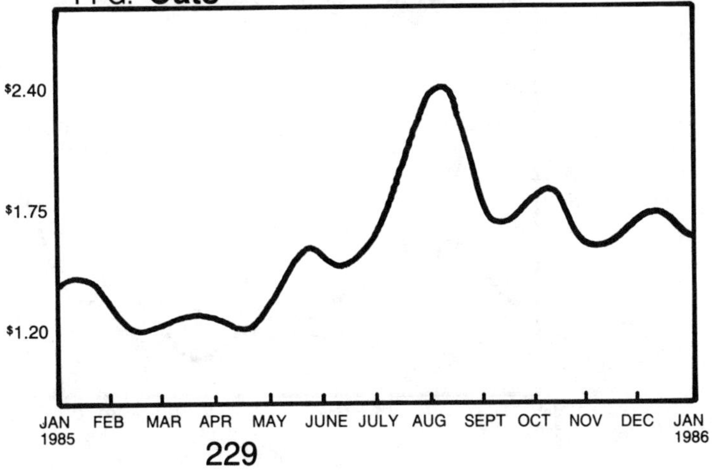

PPG: **Soybeans**

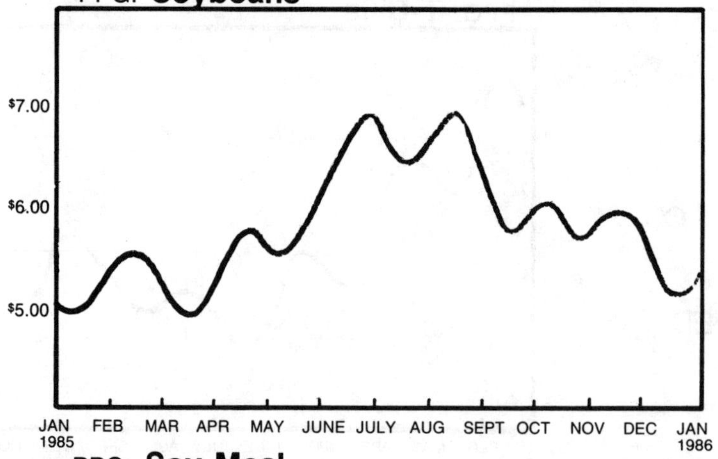

PPG: **Soy Meal**

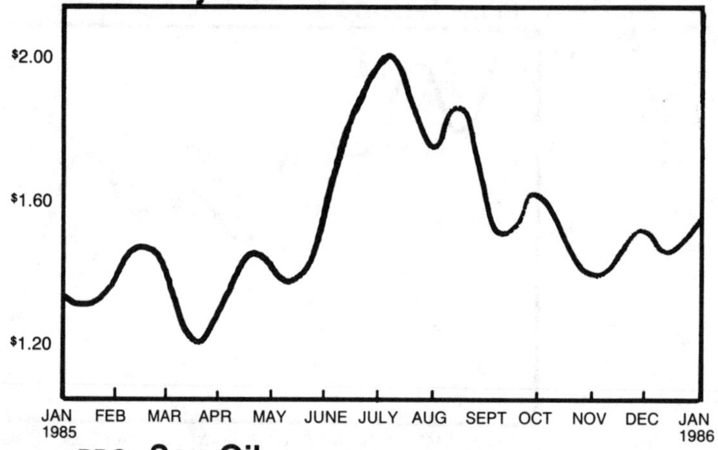

PPG: **Soy Oil**

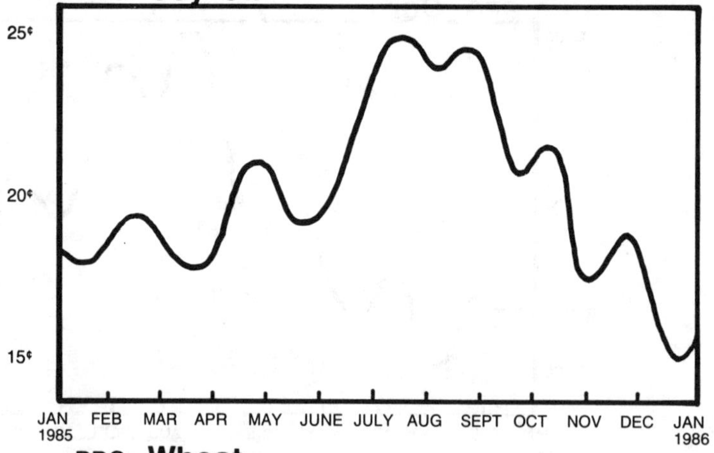

PPG: **Wheat**

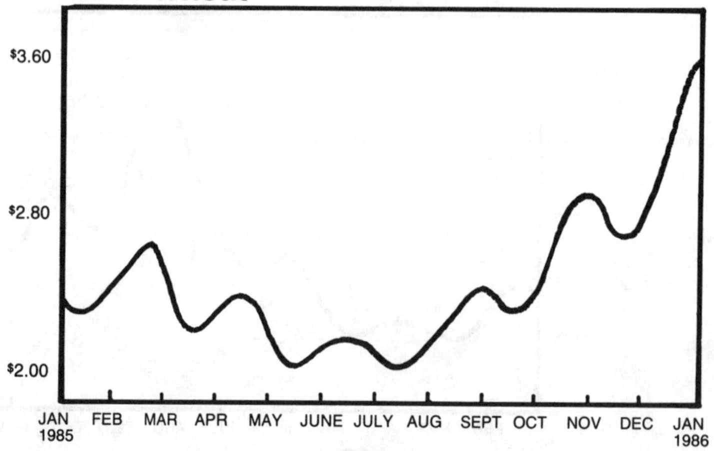

PPG: **Live Cattle**

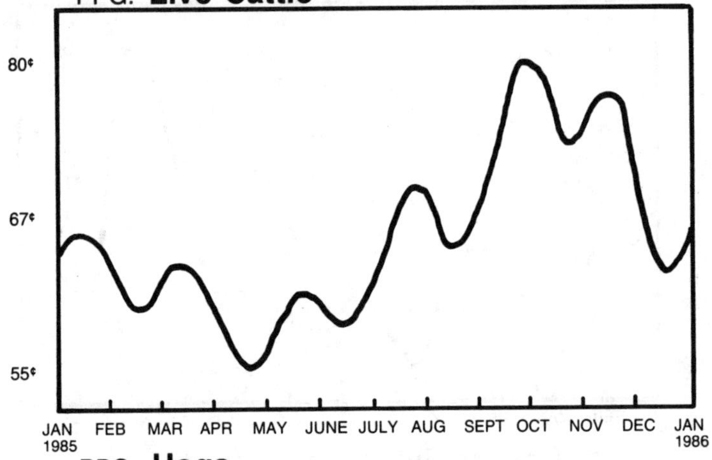

PPG: **Hogs**

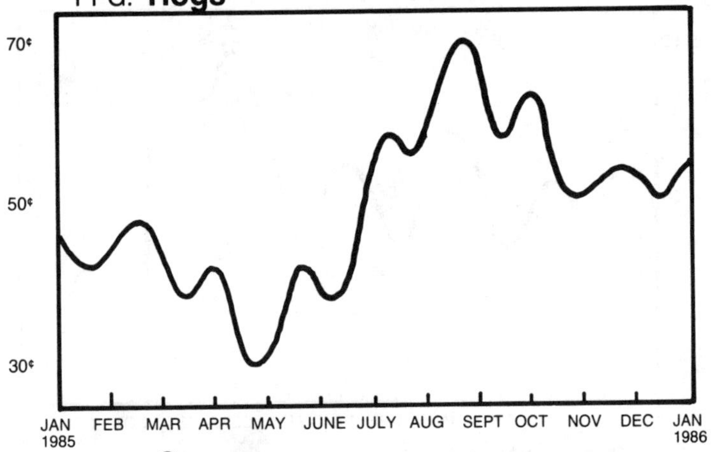

PPG: **Cocoa**

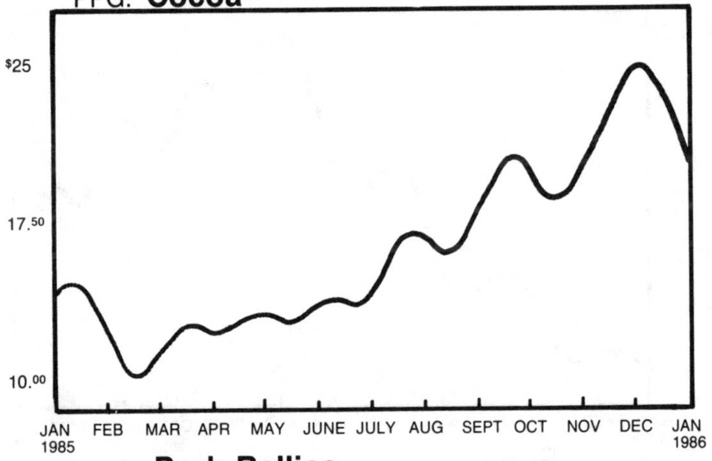

PPG: **Pork Bellies**

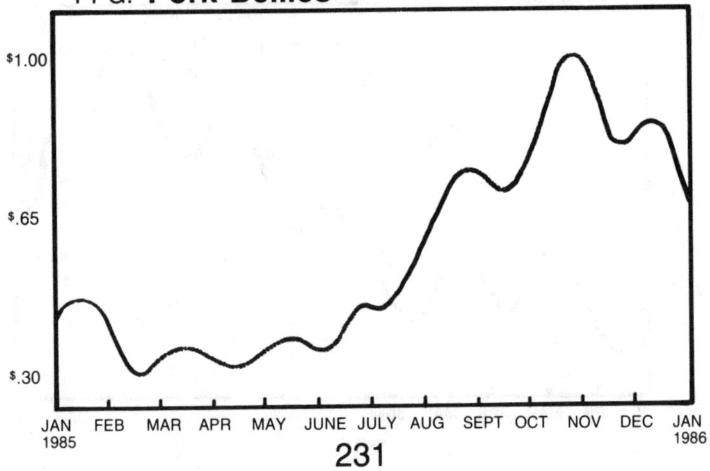

PPG: **Coffee**

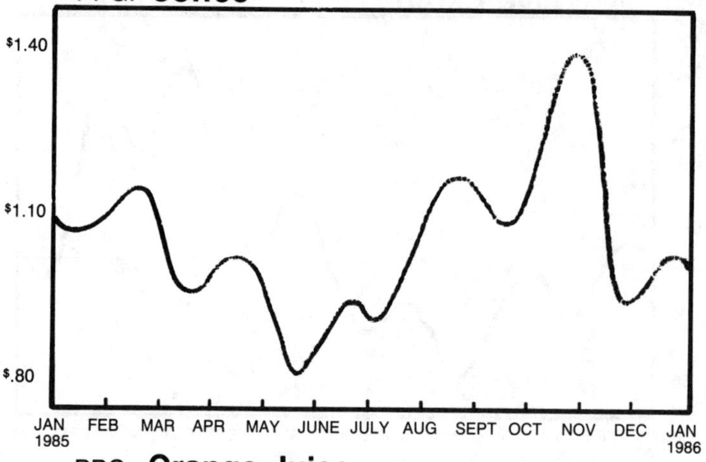

PPG: **Orange Juice**

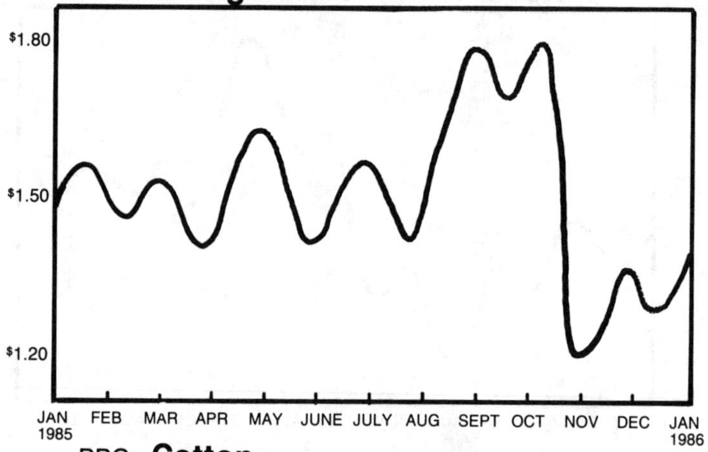

PPG: **Cotton**

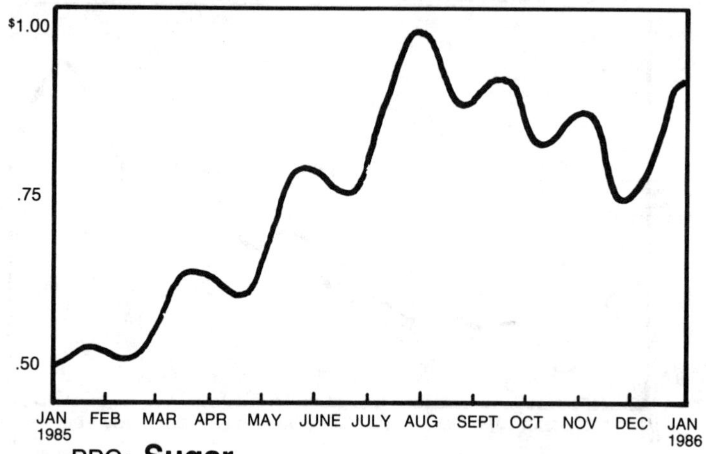

PPG: **Sugar**

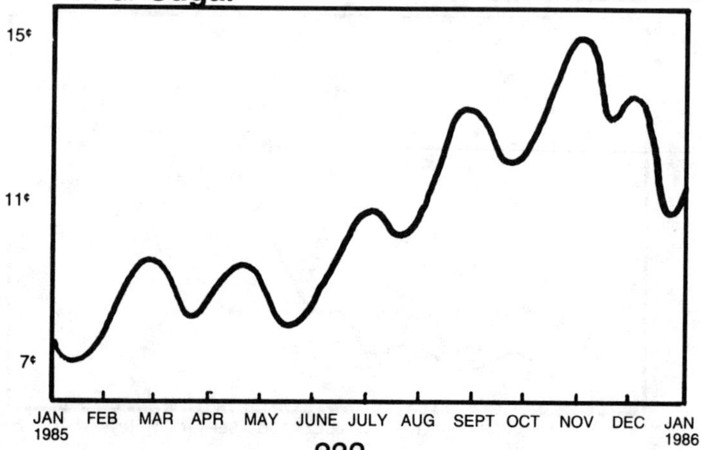

PPG: **Lumber**

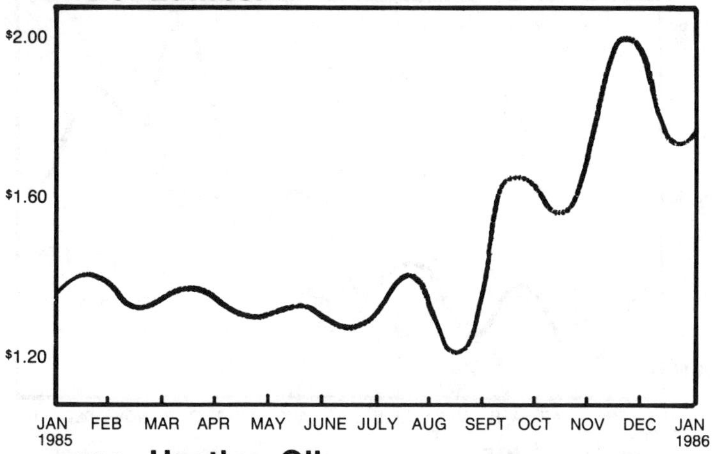

PPG: **Heating Oil**

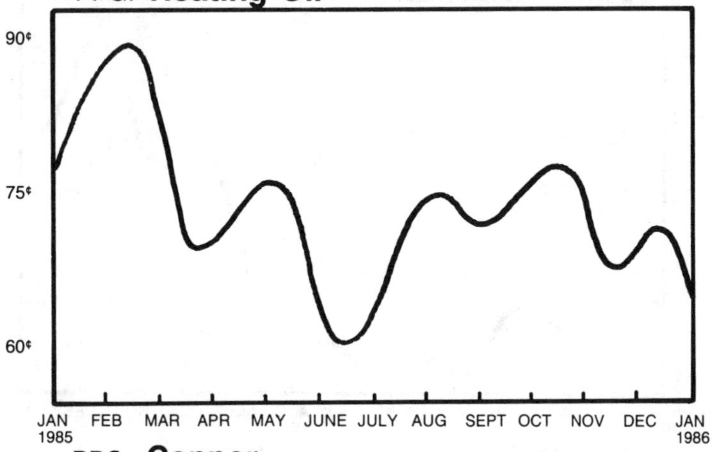

PPG: **Copper**

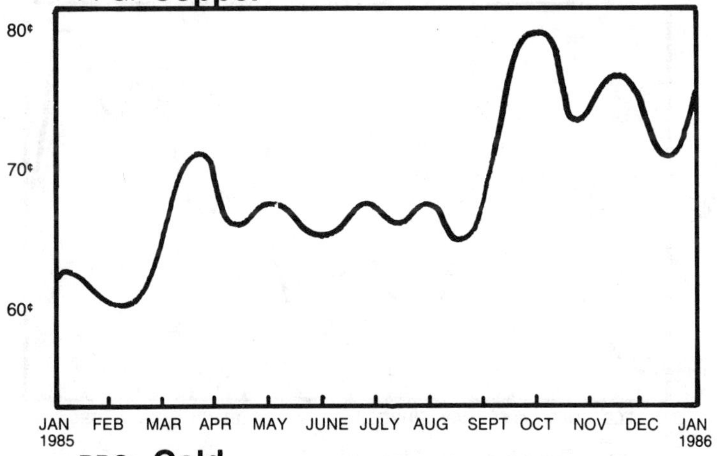

PPG: **Gold**

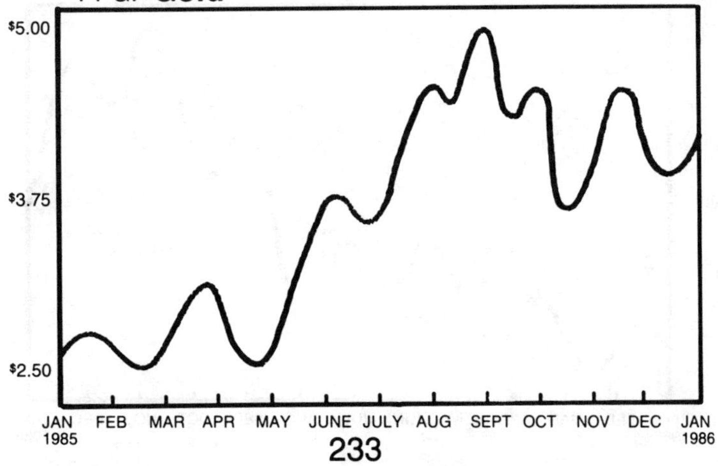

PPG: **Platinum**

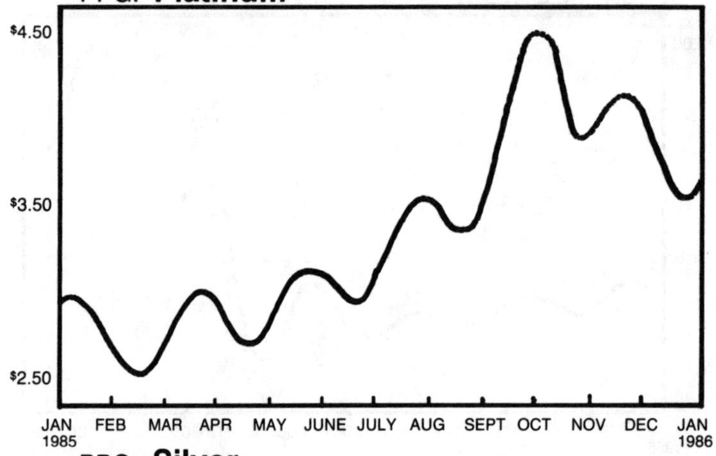

PPG: **Silver**

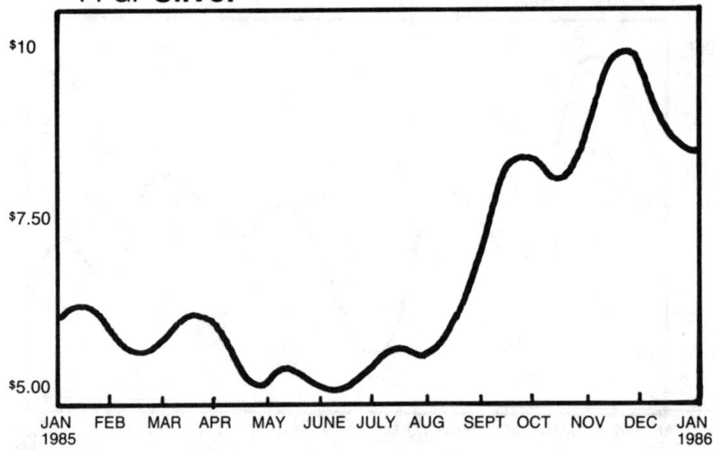

PPG: **British Pound**

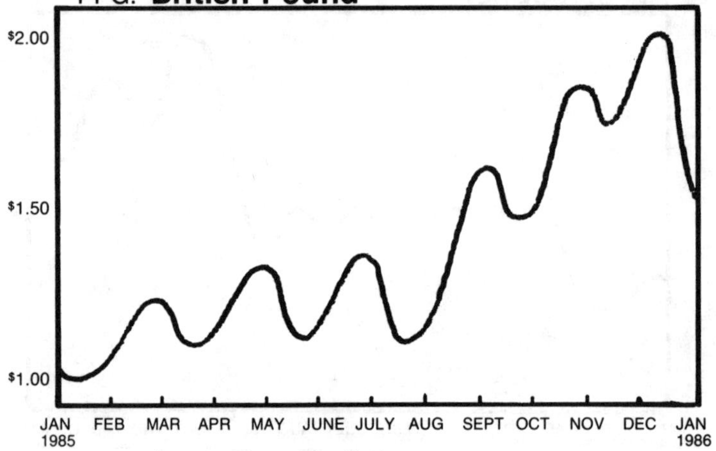

PPG: **Canadian Dollar**

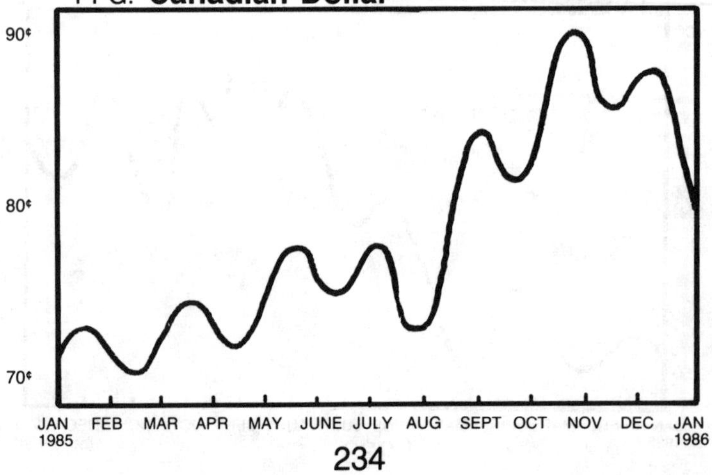

PPG: **Deutsche Mark**

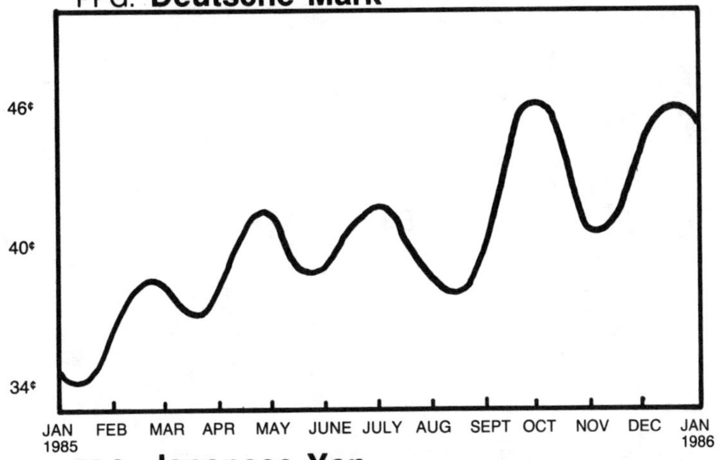

PPG: **Japanese Yen**

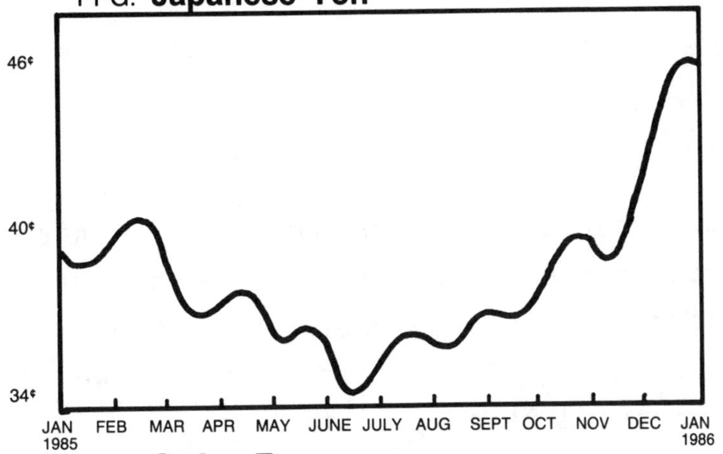

PPG: **Swiss Franc**

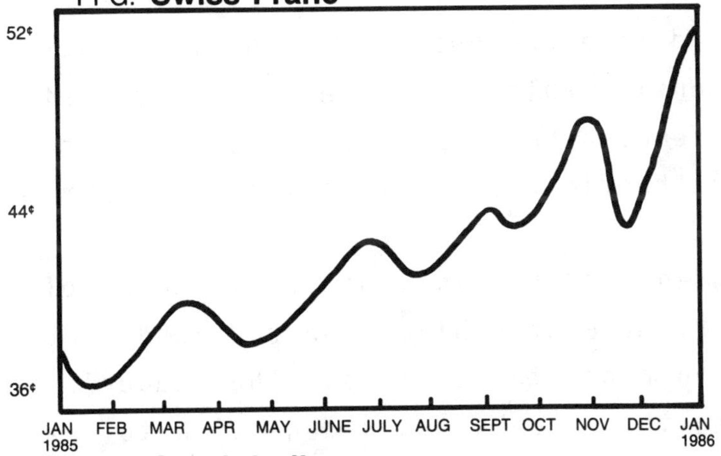

PPG: **Stock Indices**

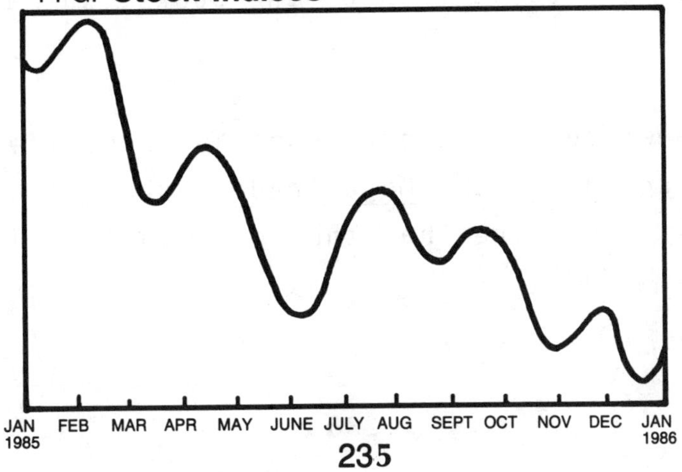

APPENDIX D

SUGGESTED READING LIST

We hope we have included enough material in this volume to satisfy most reader's needs, but we realize that many of our readers will want to pursue some areas of commodity analysis or psychology in greater detail. For this reason, we are including the following "Suggested Reading List."

While we could have expanded this list to include many, many more titles of considerable merit, we feel this list, as it stands, contains enough key books for anyone to become somewhat expert in either the field of commodity analysis or psychology.

We are providing as much information in terms of title, author, publisher, date of publication and ISBN number as is available to us in order to facilitate the reader's locating and/or purchasing these books, should he wish to. We also have included a brief text about each of the books, summarizing its contents.

As other, newer books are published in these fields, we will review them in our Taurus and Mega-Trades publications, but it is difficult for us to believe that the books in this list can be improved upon much.

SUGGESTED READING LIST

Charting Commodity Market Price Behavior, L. Dee Belveal, Commodities Press Division of Belveal & Co., Inc., Wilmette, IL. 60091, 1969. Library of Congress No. 71-88866.

This is an excellent book on technical analysis and chart interpretation featuring both explanations and demonstrations of the principles involved in chart-trading. Written simply and illustrated graphically, the book stresses the use of four major market-indicators in combinations to "measure" technical strengths and weaknesses. Those indicators are Price, Trade Volume, Open-Interest, and Open-Interest "Mix" information. This book is invaluable to both the novice market speculator as well as to the most experienced market practitioner.

The Commodity Futures Market Guide, Stanley Kroll and Irwin Shishko, Harper & Rowe, 1973. ISBN No. 06-033397-9.

This book gives an entirely positive, systematic analysis of the diverse facets of commodity trading as well as a practical approach to participating with profit in the commodity futures market. It reviews technical and fundamental methods of price and analysis, the logic and rationale of changing price differences as they affect both speculators and hedgers, government regulation of both domestic and international commodity markets, futures' versatility as both a pricing and a marketing medium, the varied uses of commodity put and call options, and trade use of futures, including a complete section of actual trade hedging examples.

The Commodity Futures Trading Guide, Richard J. Teweles, Charles V. Harlow and Herbert L. Stone, McGraw-Hill, Inc., 1969.

A complete guide to trading commodity futures, this book stands the test of time in that it is as valuable today as it was when it was written 15 years ago. The authors detail the role of the speculator in the commodity markets as compared with other types of speculation, the operation of the exchanges, the placement of orders and the opening of accounts, and how to formulate a trading plan and tackle the "random walk" theory.

Commodity Trading Systems and Methods, P. J. Kaufman, John Wiley & Sons., Inc., 1978. ISBN No. 0-471-03569-6

This book details the technical approaches to commodity trading which have proven to be reliable over the years. The book describes the major systems, evaluating each for purpose, use, and results--all from the investor's point of view. Geared more for the practiced commodity trader than for the neophyte, the specialized information in this mathematically-oriented book provides the tools for formulating technical analysis for accurate long-and short-term price forecasting.

Contrary Opinion, R. Earl Hadady, Hadady Publications, Inc., Pasadena, CA. 91101, 1983. ISBN No. 0-9611390-0-5.

Author Haday calls Contrary Opinion "the essence of the commodity futures game," and in this book, he brings this once vague factor into clear focus, presenting it in easy-to-understand quantitative terms to enable readers to use "the most powerful of all market tools."

Economics of Futures Trading, Thomas A. Hieronymus, Commodity Research Bureau, Inc., 1971. Library of Congress No. 75-181523.

This is a college level textbook for a course in commodity futures markets and trading. It's not only a "what it's all about," but a "how it's done" and "how to do it" book stressing the importance of understanding the economics behind the trading.

Elliott Wave Principle, Robert R. Prechter, Jr. and A. J. Frost, New Classics Library, 1981. ISBN No. 0-932750-02-8.

This book details how to use the Elliott Wave Principle successfully in the reader's own trading program. Other topics covered include how to use ratio analysis to forecast highs between bull markets and bear markets.

Games Investors Play, Michael P. Chisholm, Butterfly & Buttercups Press, 1981. Library of Congress no. 82-70369.

Written by the author of _The Mega-Trade Method_, this book is bases on the premise that investors' psychological problems, generally of a subconcious nature, sabotage their trading decisions and prevent them from succeeding in any type of investing. Basically a do-it-yourself workbook and text, it enables the reader to identify for himself what his problems are and offers him practical and concrete advice and techniques to use to overcome these problems. Mr. Chisholm is a practicing psychologist as well as a commodity advisor and analyst.

Getting Started in Commodity Futures Trading, Mark J. Powers, Investor Publications, inc., Cedar Falls, IA. 50613, 1982. ISBN No. 0-914230-01-8.

This basic beginners' handbook makes worthwhile reading for veteran investors. The book covers the pros and cons of commodity trading versus stock investing and delves into how to choose a broker as well as some aspects of technical analysis.

The Handbook of Commodity Cycles: A Window on Time, Jacob Bernstein, John Wiley & Sons, 1982. ISBN No. 0-471-08197-3.

This work tells how to use the fundamental but often overlooked principles of cyclical analysis for profitable short- and long-term trading. This reference and daily working guide is the first in-depth examination of the proven repetitive price patters which can actually help traders lower their investment risks. More than 130 charts and illustrations show the current status of market cycles, their history, and their probable course in years to come. The work also teaches how to recognize cycles of varying lengths; how to read timing signals to determine when a cycle is beginning, peaking or bottoming out; and how to apply cyclic price analysis in trading and money-managing.

How to Profit from Seasonal Commodity Spreads: A Complete Guide, Jacob Bernstein, John Wiley & Sons, Inc., 1983. ISBN No. 0-471-86432-3.

With the aid of computer analysis, author Bernstein researched thousands of commodity prices and evaluated hundreds of spread combinations, analyzing daily price data for up to 14 years and 21 different commodities. From these data, he isolated those time frames having the best profit reliability so that he could include only the most promising spreads--those with the great profit potential--here. What he came up with is the most complete, reliable compendium of seasonal spreads and spread combinations ever published. He also presents two new trading concepts--"seasonal run" and "percentage reliablity"--to help in the selection of the best entry and exit times.

Intuition, Milton Fisher, E. P. Dutton, Inc., New York, 1981. ISBN No. 0-525-93209-7.

This presents a step-by-step program designed to help the reader develop his intuition, recognize its signals, and put it to use in every facet of his life--in relationships, career, finances, sex, love and even in his sense of personal flair and style. Through techniques of relaxation, biofeedback, dream analysis, an Intuitive Diary and consciousness-raising sessions, the book guides the reader to learn to consult his own well-spring of inner wisdom and develop his intuitive potential.

The Investor's Almanac, 1984-85, edited by D. M. Wilkinson, W&W Publications, 1984.

This volume is crammed with an enormous amount of information and reference data that is useful to any investor in the commodities markets. Among the major sections of the fact-jammed work, which will be published annually, are: Financial News, U.S. Government Receipts and Outlays, the Federal Reserve, Banking, Precious Metals and Collectables, Coins, Commodities, Mutual Funds, the Securities and Exchange Commission, Stock Exchanges, Investment Portfolios, Investment Newsletters and Market Projections, Markets in Review, Economic Data, Taxation Data, the

Congress and an excellent reference glossary.

<u>The Kondratieff Wave</u>, James B. Shuman and David Rosenau, World Publishing Co., New York, 1972. ISBN No. 0-529-04561.

Shortly after World War 1, an obscure Russian economist, Nikolai Kondratieff, observed and analyzed the recurrence of an "economic wave" lasting about 52 years and operating throughout American history. He used the wave concept to predict with uncanny precision every period of growth and inflation, recession and social turmoil, war and depression that America would see, long after his own death and right up to the present day. In this fascinating book, authors Shuman and Rosenau outline the theory and then use it to make some important and startling predictions about our future and the changes it will bring.

<u>The Long Wave Cycle</u>, Nikolai Kondratieff, translated by Guy Daniels with introduction by Julian M. Snyder, Richardson & Snyder, New York, NY. 10004, 1984. ISBN No. 0-943940-07-9.

This is the classic work by Nikolai Kondratieff, the Russian father of the long wave economic cycle whose major work was published in 1925, in a new translation by Guy Daniels with an introduction by Julian M. Snyder. Kondratieff suggested that during a period of fifty years there would be (1) a decade of depression, (2) thirty years of technical innovation, and (3) ten years of economic uncertainty, as growth forces of the past subside. His charts have been redrawn in this volume to conform to the originals of the Russian edition, and his statistical tables are included in their entirety. This is the first translation from the original Russian to appear in the world.

Modern Commodity Futures Trading, Gerald Gold, Commodity Research Bureau, Inc., 1975. ISBN No. 0-910418-01-2.

This is a practical book devoted primarily to an explanation of the techniques and methods for successful commodity market trading. It also presents the mechanics and background of the commodity markets for thse who are new to them.

Opening Price Statistical Data on the Futures Markets, R. Earl Hadady, Hadady Corporation, Pasadena, CA. 91101, 1984. ISBN No. 0-9611390-1-3.

The data in this book shows that commodity prices tend to open at either the high or the low of the daily price range. The statistical studies in this book clearly identify which commodities have the greatest probability of opening at the extremes of their trading ranges. This knowledge can help the trader enter and exit the market with greater precision. The data also shows that opening prices tend to act as support or resistance depending upon where the market is relative to the opening and that using the opening to enter the market allows the trader to minimize his risks.

Point and Figure Commodity Trading Techniques, Kermit C. Zieg, Jr. and Perry J. Kaufman, Investors Intelligence, Inc., Larchmont NY. 1975. Library of Congress No. 75-18199.

Active commodity traders themselves, the authors have written a text directed to others who trade commodities, drawing on their experience in both the academic and practical fields to explain in detail the application of Point-and-Figure charting and analysis to commodities. Then they show how this technique can be applied also to options, bonds, international currencies and market indicators. The work is a "must" for the commodity trader and an advanced tool for the professional as well. It features more than 100 charts as it presents extensive profitablility and reliability statistics and research.

<u>Profits Through Seasonal Trading</u>, Jack Grushcow and Courtney Smith, John Wiley & Sons, Inc., 1980. ISBN No. 0-471-06158-1.

An invaluable source, this book presents a complete and thorough study of the seasonal cycles of commodity prices, investigating in detail 24 of the most actively traded commodities. Not only are the cash prices analyzed, but also the nearest futures contract and the seasonal tendencies of each of the individual contract months.

<u>Seasonality in Agricultural Futures Markets</u>, ContiCommodity Services Research Department, ContiCommodity Services, Inc., Chicago, IL. 60604, 1983. ISBN No. 0-9610098-0-2.

This book is the product of research to analyze the seasonality of outrights and spreads. The purpose of which was to segregate the reliable, profitable trades from the more risky, less reliable trades. It is an excellent reference guide and aid to traders who feel that seasonality, price history, and fundamental influences are important. For each commodity outright or spread, the work presents a trade headline, a fundamental and historical analysis, a seasonality chart, a seasonal factors and DRV table, a trading record table, a highs and lows table and a comparative price action chart.

The Taurus Method, Michael P. Chisholm, Taurus Corporation, Winchester, VA. 22601, 1983.

Those readers who studied this book were among the first in line to urge author Chisholm to complete The Mega-Trade Method. Considered by many experts to be the best single work to date on commodity trading, this book covers such subjects as: chart reading, fundamentals, cyclical and seasonal analysis, volume and open interest, stop placement, top and bottom picking, pyramiding, long-range trading, order placement, the trader-broker relationship, money management and the psychology of successful investing. It's a must for every trader's desk.

Technical Analysis in Commodities, edited by P. J. Kaufman, John Wiley & Sons, Inc., 1980. ISBN No. 0-471-05627-8.

For readers interested in technical analysis in futures markets, this book is a must. The book offers a collection of articles representing the state-of-the-art in technical analysis. The contributions range from the non-mathematical to the highly mathematical, from historical background to the most advanced developments in price analysis and modeling. Complex though it may be, the work does offer some interesting insights into price distortions, moving averages, computer testing and the like.

Techniques of a Professional Chart Analyst, Arthur Sklarew, Commodity Research Bureau, Inc., New York, NY. 10006. ISBN No. 0-910418-10-1.

This practical book is about using commodity price charts and other simple technical indicators to time trades better, spot price trends, estimate the distance a new price thrust will travel, locate logical points to place "buy" and "sell" stops and identify potential trend reversal points. The trading strategy and tactics presented are deceptively simple, but require no special equipment or methematical skill. Plenty of graphic illustrations help the reader understand the more salient points. We highly recommend this book to anyone who wants to learn more about charting techniques and interpretation.

<u>To Love Is To Be Happy With</u>, Barry Neil Kaufman, Coward, McCann & Geoghegan, Inc., New York, NY., 1977. ISBN No. 698-10779-9.

The cornerstone of what author Kaufman calls the Option Process is a very simple, beautiful, accepting and non-judgemental attitude: "To love is to be happy with...." Through the facinating and intimate stories of Kaufman and those he shares his philosophy with, the reader becomes part of an awe-inspiring discovery of himself. The reader will find himself not once, but many times in this book, and he will come to hold himself differently. The book is in many respects a love story in which the reader will find himself feeling very good about a very special person: himself.

<u>Trading Strategies</u>, "A Compilation of Technical Tools and Guidelines Used by Futures Professionals", Futures Symposium International, 1984.

This work captures in book form a sampling of the market research and trading information presented at the First Annual Futures Symposium in Chicago in October, 1983. Throughout the articles the reader will find both specific technical information and market-tested and proven rules and guidelines that he can integrate into his own trading methods and experience. One of the articles, "Trading the Big Moves in Foreign Currencies, 1984-88," was prepared by The Mega-Trade Method author Michael P. Chisholm.

APPENDIX E

SERVICES FOR BIG MOVE TRADERS

In this Appendix we will list the different services referred to throughout the course of this book. We have categorized these according to subject area and then listed the sources for the services. At the end of this section we are listing the complete addresses alphabetically and, where available, the telephone numbers of all of these services.

While we realize that in all of these categories, many, many other sources are available to the commodity trader, it has been our experience that the sources we have listed are the most reliable and useful for our purposes. We do not mean to disparage or be critical of any service which does not appear on this list. It is quite possible that we may have overlooked some valuable services which could be utilized by Big Move traders.

We will update and revise this list in subsequent editions of this book, and any changes in any of the sources in the meantime will appear in the Mega-Trades newsletter. We welcome feedback and suggestions from our readers as to services not listed in this Appendix that they feel should be listed. We would greatly appreciate our readers' telling us why they feel this way and--in case we are unaware of the particular source they are referring to--sending us their suggested services' addresses so that we may contact them and consider listing them in the Mega-Trades newsletter and in subsequent editions of this book. By the same token, if any of our readers has had bad experiences with any of the sources we have listed, we would also appreciate their letting us know about that. We will most definitely consider dropping from future lists of these services any source now listed about which we receive sufficient negative feedback.

ATTORNEYS

Taurus Corporation (Taurus maintains a list of extremely competent and reputable attorneys specializing in commodity law throughout the entire United States).

BROKERS

Taurus Corporation (Taurus maintains a list of brokers who are familiar with Big Move trading and who subscribe to the Mega-Trades newsletter throughout the country).

BULLISH CONSENSUS

Consensus
GRAPHIX
MarketVane

CHART SERVICES

Commodity Perspective
Commodity Research Bureau
Commodity Trend Service
GRAPHIX
Quotron

COMMITMENTS of TRADERS

Commodity Research Bureau

CYCLES

HAL Market Cycles
MBH Weekly Commodity Letter
Sanders Commodity Advisor

CYCLICAL TOOLS and INSTRUMENTS

Erlich Cycle Finder

ECONOMIC ANALYSIS

International Moneyline
Money Forecasts
Money & Markets
The Reaper

FUNDAMENTAL INFORMATION

Consensus
FUTURES Magazine
Wall Street Journal

MOVING AVERAGES

All of the chart services previously referenced.

NEWSLETTERS

The Dickson Letter
The Elliott Wave Theorist
HAL Market Cycles
International Moneyline
MarketVane
MBH Weekly Commodity Letter
Mega-Trades
Merriman Market Analysis
Money Forecasts
Money & Markets
Money Market Strategies
Newsletter Digest
The Reaper
Rocky Mountain Financial Forecasting
Taurus

OPTIONS

Mega-Trades

PERSONAL CONSULTATIONS & MEETINGS

Taurus Corporation arranges personal telephone and in-person meetings with the author of this book and publisher of Taurus and Mega-Trades, Mr. Michael P. Chisholm.

SEASONAL DATA

Appendix A
MBH Weekly Commodity Letter
Mega-Trades

SPREADS

Tiger on Spreads

THERAPISTS

Taurus Corporation (we maintian a directory of excellent and reputable therapists in virtually every locality in the United States, Canada, Mexico, and many other foreign countries).

VOLUME and OPEN INTEREST

All of the chart services previously referenced in that section.

ALPHABETICAL LISTING OF NAMES AND ADDRESSES OF SERVICES:

COMMODITY PERSPECTIVE
30 S. Wacker Dr., Suite 1220
Chicago, IL. 60606
312-750-8810

COMMODITY RESEARCH BUREAU
75 Montgomery St.
Jersey City, NJ. 07302

COMMODITY TREND SERVICE
1224 U.S. Highway 1
N. Palm Beach, FL. 33408
305-694-0961

CONSENSUS
P.O. Box 19086
Kansas City, MO. 64141
816-471-3862

THE DICKSON LETTER
P.O. Box 8491
Incline Village, NV. 89450
702-831-5843

ELLIOTT WAVE THEORIST
New Classics Library
P.O. Box 1618
Gainesville, GA. 30503
404-536-0309

ERLICH CYCLE FINDER
Chicago Board of Trade
Suite 1800
141 N. Jackson Blvd.
Chicago, IL. 60604
800-621-3098

FUTURES MAGAZINE
219 Parkade
Cedar Falls, IA. 50613
319-277-6341

GRAPHIX
30 W. Washington St.
Suite 1432
Chicago, IL. 60602
800-663-8364

HAL MARKET CYCLES
2020 E. Prince Rd.
Tucson, AZ. 85719
602-795-3061

INTERNATIONAL MONEYLINE
25 Broad St.
New York, NY. 10004
Information: 212-334-1200
Subscriptions: 212-334-1223

MARKETVANE
Hadady Corporation
61 S. Lake Ave. #309
Pasadena, CA. 91101
818-795-1957

MBH WEEKLY COMMODITY LETTER
MBH Commodity Advisors, Inc.
Box 353
Winnetka, IL. 60093
312-446-9210

MEGA-TRADES
P.O. Box 767
Winchester, VA. 22601
703-667-4827

MERRIMAN MARKET ANALYSIS
15823 Kirkshire
Birmingham, MI. 48009
313-642-9262

MONEY FORECASTS
Martin D. Weiss Research, Inc.
Box 2923
West Palm Beach, FL. 33402

MONEY MARKET STRATEGIES
MBH Commodity Advisors, Inc.
Box 353
Winnetka, IL. 60093
312-446-9210

MONEY & MARKETS
Martin D. Weiss Research, Inc.
Box 2923
West Palm Beach, FL. 33402

NEWSLETTER DIGEST
2335 Pansy Street
Huntsville, AL. 35801-3899

QUOTRON FUTURES CHARTS
Market Advisory
P.O. Box 1424
Racine, WI. 53401
441-634-3373

THE REAPER
P.O. Box 39026
Phoenix, AZ. 85069
800-528-0559

ROCKY MOUNTAIN FINANCIAL FORECASTING
5601 Sacajawea Way
Loveland, CO. 80537
303-663-4688

SANDERS COMMODITY ADVISOR
P.O. Box 3961
Davenport, IA. 52808
319-386-0338

TAURUS
P.O. Box 767
Winchester, VA. 22601
703-667-4827

TIGER ON SPREADS
P.O. Box 1414
McLean, VA. 22101
202-463-8608

WALL STREET JOURNAL
200 Burnett Rd.
Chicopee, MA. 01021